STATE PHOBIA AND CIVIL SOCIETY

STATE PHOBIA
AND CIVIL SOCIETY

THE
POLITICAL
LEGACY
OF
MICHEL
FOUCAULT

MITCHELL DEAN AND KASPAR VILLADSEN

STANFORD UNIVERSITY PRESS
STANFORD, CALIFORNIA

Stanford University Press
Stanford, California

Printed in the United States of America on acid-free, archival-quality paper

Library of Congress Cataloging-in-Publication Data

Dean, Mitchell, 1955- author.
  State phobia and civil society : the political legacy of Michel Foucault / Mitchell Dean and Kaspar Villadsen.
      pages cm
  Includes bibliographical references and index.
  ISBN 978-0-8047-8949-3 (cloth : alk. paper)--ISBN 978-0-8047-9697-2 (pbk. : alk. paper)--ISBN 978-0-8047-9699-6 (ebook)
  1. Foucault, Michel, 1926-1984--Political and social views. 2. State, The. 3. Civil society.
4. Political science--Philosophy. I. Villadsen, Kaspar, author. II. Title.
  JC261.F68D43 2015
  320.092--dc23
                                        2015031109

Typeset by Bruce Lundquist in 10/14 Minion Pro

CONTENTS

ACKNOWLEDGMENTS

We warmly thank Emily-Jane Cohen and Friederike Sundaram for their kind and patient editorial support during this project, and Jeffrey Bussolini and Sandy Schram for their detailed and constructive readings and comments on the draft of this text. We also thank our colleagues in the Department of Management, Politics and Philosophy at Copenhagen Business School for their intellectual input and moral support, especially Marius Gudmand-Høyer and Sverre Raffnsøe, who commented directly on this material, and the Politics Group for being a nurturing and stimulating intellectual environment. Many others contributed to the book's themes in discussions with us in various PhD courses and seminars, including Thomas Dumm, Michael Behrent, Paul du Gay, Torben Bech Dyrberg, and Mads Peter Karlsen. Mitchell would like to thank his partner, Jeni, for her continued love, care, and almost infinite patience while yet another book project was being finished. Kaspar would like to thank his family and friends for displaying that same care and patience.

The first three chapters of this book were developed on the basis of an article by Kaspar Villadsen and Mitchell Dean (2012), "State Phobia, Civil Society, and a Certain Vitalism," published in *Constellations: An International Journal of Critical and Democratic Theory* 19 (3): 401–20. These chapters are significantly modified and expanded in relation to the original article.

Parts of Chapter 4 draw on an article by Kaspar Villadsen (2015), "Michel Foucault and the Forces of Civil Society," published in *Theory, Culture and Society* (early online April 2015).

Portions of Chapter 10 draw on an article by Mitchell Dean (2014), "Michel Foucault's 'Apology' for Neoliberalism: Lecture Delivered at the British Library on the 30th Anniversary of the Death of Michel Foucault, June 25, 2014," published in the *Journal of Political Power* 7 (3): 433–42.

ABBREVIATIONS

We have tried, where possible, to cite interviews, essays, and other minor works as they appear in the *Essential Works of Foucault* (*EFW*), 3 vols. (New York: New Press, 1997–2000). These volumes can now be taken as the standard English translation for most of these works and are the most readily available. So that the reader will be able to follow which particular work is referenced from these volumes, we have used the following abbreviations in the in-text citations:

DI   "About the Concept of the 'Dangerous Individual' in Nineteenth-Century Legal Psychiatry," *EFW* 3:176–200.

ECS   "The Ethics of the Concern for the Self as a Practice of Freedom," *EFW* 1:281–301.

IT   "So Is It Important to Think?" *EFW* 3:454–58.

LIM   "Lives of Infamous Men," *EFW* 3:157–75.

MSP   "The Moral and Social Experience of the Poles Can No Longer Be Obliterated," *EFW* 3:465–73.

NGH   "Nietzsche, Genealogy, History," *EFW* 2:369–91.

OS   "'*Omnes et singulatim*': Toward a Critique of Political Reason," *EFW* 3:298–325.

PTI   "The Political Technology of Individuals," *EFW* 3:403–17.

QM   "Questions of Method," *EFW* 3:201–38.

SP   "The Subject and Power," *EFW* 3:326–48.

TJF   "Truth and Juridical Forms," *EFW* 3:1–89.

TP   "Truth and Power," *EFW* 3:111–33.

TPH   "Theatrum philosophicum," *EFW* 2:343–68.

WE   "What Is Enlightenment?" *EFW* 1:303–19.

STATE PHOBIA AND CIVIL SOCIETY

INTRODUCTION

"Whoever that woman in my dream is, it is not my mother," said Slavoj Žižek, when he humorously characterized the academic Left's relationship to the state, social class, and conventional political questions (2008, 338). Imagine, if you will, the modern poststructuralist prostrate on the psychoanalyst's couch, avoiding at all costs confrontation with particularly traumatic issues: state, class, politics, fundamental social conflicts . . .

This book is inspired by a similar experience, which its authors found they shared. In recent years the state has become a kind of "no-go" zone for those who work within a Foucauldian or wider poststructuralist perspective. According to its protagonists, the state is decentered, deconstructed, and displaced, both as an oppressive order and as a misleading concept. It is somewhat surprising, then, to discover that in his recently published lectures Foucault himself used the concept "state phobia" to criticize and warn against political ideologies that exaggerate the state's negative role in society and in human history. We take seriously his rejection of normative "state phobia." It is in part a response to ultra-leftism and in part a critique of tendencies in his own thought. Paradoxically, it is often precisely this state-phobic imagery that Foucault uses to delineate his own theoretical and analytical position. He rejects the Manichean image of the state as "the coldest of all cold monsters" (*monstre froid*), an impressionistic nineteenth-century image he found in Nietzsche. He presents what he calls the "juridical-political theory of sovereignty," and its key terms *State*, *Sovereign* and *Law* (often capitalized), as a foil for his analytics of power, first taking the form of a microphysics of power and later an analysis of what he called "governmentality." In rejecting this juridical-political theory, he rejects the key vocabulary for the analysis of the state, including that of legitimacy and authority and questions of law and legality. His rejection of this vocabulary also deprives Foucault of an extended analysis of democracy. Moreover, his very definition of *sovereignty* as a "right of death" suggests an omnipotent state that in itself is fundamentally dangerous. It is hard to read his repeated injunction to "cut off the king's head in political theory" as anything but fundamentally antistatist, at least theoretically and analytically.

The challenge to state phobia is issued in Foucault's "governmentality" lectures of 1978 and 1979, which would not be published, however, for another quarter of a century. Nevertheless, in the 1990s certain authors would base their studies on little more than fragments of this work and offer diagnoses of "neoliberal" or "advanced liberal government" and concomitant transformations of the welfare state and the emergence of new technologies of government (Burchell, Gordon, and Miller 1991; Rose and Miller 1992; Barry, Osborne, and Rose 1996; Dean and Hindess 1998; Dean 1999; Rose 1999). As Foucault did in the 1970s, these "governmentality writers" in the United Kingdom and Australia refused to consider the state as the center of control by political agents or classes and the exercise of power, legitimate or otherwise. Instead, they focused on the programs and rationalities of government that work across multiple alliances between different actors—including those of the public sector, communities and community organizations, businesses and firms, and citizens themselves—and that enjoin these agents to take on certain forms of self-government and responsibility. Their analyses undoubtedly provided different critical perspectives on the exercise of political power at the end of the twentieth century. They avoided the contemporary knee-jerk denunciation of public policies and their implementation as either "neoliberal" or as functional to capitalism. But the question remains whether they—and indeed we, the current authors—went too far in the evacuation of the form of the state in political analyses and displacement of sovereignty.

Much of this literature undertook a "diagnostics of the present" that explicitly rejected normative theory or explicit value positions. However, when post-Foucauldians were inevitably forced to move beyond this merely diagnostic and analytical position and offer a more normative idea of the potential in the present, they often appeared to favor some form of "identity politics." This politics is defined by a series of demands for respect for cultural, sexual, and lifestyle minorities and the desire to create room for individuals and collectives to generate their own identity by devising differentiated cultural, social, and legal policies. Common to Foucault's various followers and successors is a value-orientation toward nonstate movements, as well as grassroots and unconventional forms of political activism and resistance and a devaluation of more conventional party and trade-union forms of political organization. It is ironic, perhaps, that Foucault's inheritors should end up favoring a type of civil-society politics over a state-based one—not least because, as we suggest here, Foucault himself was often suspicious of political action based on civil society.

In this book we take Foucault's lecture series delivered in the academic years 1975–76, 1977–78, and 1978–79, as a key to his political perspective and its development. It is noteworthy but little remarked upon that in final lectures of each of these years Foucault takes considerable time to address images of civil society as a body comprising vital forces and virtuous ethics and serving as a site of truth production. In each of these lectures he directs critical comments to those who dream that one day the state will dissolve and merge with civil society. It is a dream that can be found in certain forms of thought associated with the French and American Revolutions and in the Marxist-Leninist precept of the "withering away of the state." It reappears in the wake of the collapse of Soviet socialism in Eastern Europe. In the current decade we find it in the Tea Party faction of the Republican Party in the United States. It is a dream that occurs across the political spectrum from radical Maoists after May '68, feminist critiques of patriarchy, democratic rejections of bureaucracy, to today's libertarians and those whom we will call, consonant with Foucault, "neoliberals." It is a dream that appears in proponents of globalization and advocates of cosmopolitanism.

We want to emphasize that Foucault, to his enduring credit, did not succumb to the seduction of this Siren song of civil society. He sought to problematize political ideologies that operate with the idea of a "people," "a mass of vital forces," or "omnipresent market forces" that will become society's primary driving force and obviate the need for the "steering" functions of the state. These are ideologies that dream of the dissolution of the state in terms of its ethical, vital, or economic externality or that reduce it to a series of techniques or mechanisms. We are concerned, however, that Foucault's own analysis and theoretical perspectives have not proved secure enough to prevent contemporary social and political thought inspired by him from humming these Sirens' melodies. In this respect we should be prepared to consider that Foucault's theoretical and analytical antistatism might have contributed to contemporary critical thought and political practice losing its way.

The theme of civil society has long been associated with that of theology and religion, as Dominique Colas (1997) has shown. So is the case with Foucault. From his journalistic pieces on the Iranian Revolution to his analysis of the role of the Christian pastorate in the history of governmentality, Foucault enters the terrain of political theology and secularization, which had been strongly debated in Germany in the 1960s (Löwith 1949; Blumenberg 1985; Schmitt 2008). He is keen to emphasize both the secular rationalization involved in modern or liberal government and the dangers that that same governmental rationality poses in terms of its retheologization. One example of this is the kind of "counterconducts" he finds can be made on the basis of the notion of civil society. For Foucault, governing through civil society has certain "eschatological" features, portending an end *of* and an end *to* history. They imply a linear, teleological understanding of history in which history progresses toward the final fulfillment of divine intentions and goals. Christian eschatology foresees the triumphant Second Coming of Christ often after an age when the Spirit comes to dwell in the hearts of all humans or, at least, of the faithful. Similarly, the notion of civil society as a sphere of virtue and instructive solutions to human problems seems often to replicate the age of the Holy Spirit that promises a final victory of good over evil and an end to suffering, conflict, and death. We ask here whether the forms of power and governance Foucault himself viewed as characteristic of the present, in which power comes to be immanent to the self-governing capacities of individuals, do not evince a similar theological character.

One peril of political eschatologies is that they promise that domination and illegitimate social differences will cease when society learns to be at one with itself—when, for example, "the people" finally unite to take state power, "the nation" rules itself, or the "market" is finally allowed to work freely and unhindered. Moreover, while notions of "global civil society" often appear as the harbingers of a universal peace and cosmopolitan society, they rarely escape the political in the strong sense of the friend-enemy relationship. They cannot, or appear not to be able to, escape the identification of a group, of a force, or an institution, as the enemy, an alien body, which is held responsible for the deformed and incomplete nature of society. They see, to continue the eschatological imagery, an Antichrist appearing to mislead the faithful in the Final Days. Any philosophy or politics that champions the idea of the final coming of a universal civil society can, therefore, easily descend into a kind of confessional conflict, or just war, against those forces deemed to be standing in the way of this inevitability. Today, unfortunately, those forces are often identified with either the state or its enemies.

On the one hand, then, Foucault's perspective mixes a theoretical and analytical antistatism with a critique of state phobia. On the other hand, poststructuralist political thought returns to an idea of civil society found in its multiple proxies—the multitude, molecular and minor politics, grassroots movements, or vital politics and "ethopolitics." It is the feedback loop between the two that we explore in this book. This loop is linked to a skeptical attitude toward the state found in what has been long identified as a kind of critical, independent, or even "Second Left" position and in "Third Way" social democratic politics. A legacy of those movements arose in the great cultural and political watershed of the 1960s and their long-term trajectory. It is contrary to a more conventional Left position that endorses social rights, welfare, public education, and health care and to the fundamental task of establishing and securing a political order essential for a civilized society, which had been a key concern for liberal and conservative thought. How did the "young Foucauldians" come to adopt such "state-phobic" positions, which involved their going to great lengths to avoid dealing with the state's role, analytically as well as normatively? Down which long and winding theoretical roads did they meander to reach an explicit or implicit negative position on the state, and what are the political consequences of this today? What authority did they claim from Foucault's work to do so? For our own part, given our long commitment to a broadly Foucauldian style of analysis and diagnostic of the present, we think it is time to confront the problem of the actual and potential political effects of this critique in the current situation.

The post-Foucauldian tendency toward state phobia coincides with two other discernible trends in contemporary society. First, in recent decades the governments of many liberal-democratic and welfare states have sought to limit the state's role in the provision of what were previously considered public services. These governments wish to stimulate actors, movements, energies, and subcultures outside of the state, but, at the same time, they fear that their political strategies and programs risk stifling those very energies. This governmental anxiety is visible in the embrace of local communities, nongovernmental organizations, private contractors, and civil society itself, permeating not only social policy but also public policy more broadly. Regardless of whether civil society and its agents act as "partners," "unfulfilled potential," and "zones or sources of inspiration" in state policy or as private agencies delivering services, these policies are nurtured by the hope that civil society contains the solutions, innovations, and ethics, as well as the entrepreneurship and efficiency, to deliver flexible, customer-centered public services. This applies not simply to the old problems of the burgeoning demands presented by the welfare state but also to what were previously considered the core functions of sovereignty in the military and security sectors. The emergence of this political-administrative rationality gives a renewed relevance to the genealogy of "state phobia."

Second, during the same period the social and political sciences adopted a skeptical approach to the state. Various theorists assert that national welfare states are waning as the loci of political attention and control relative to diverse, nonstate, and often transnational organizations and networks. They claim that the nation-state has been "hollowed out" and that systems of mobile governing networks have emerged, which are eclipsing the nation-state's increasingly superfluous institutions and structures. They write of "governance without government" and "the stateless state." They argue that the state, under pressure from both internal and external forces, is losing its legal and political sovereignty and therefore its capacity to effectively regulate that which used to be referred to as the national economy.

Such currents of thought often direct attention toward the newly discovered diversity that exists outside of both the individual state and the system of nation-states. This extrastate domain is epitomized by creativity, value-based discussion, and new forms of political activity located in either domestic or transnational civil society. As a result of this dual process, civil society, which was originally one of critical social theory's key concepts, has in recent years been increasingly rediscovered and instrumentalized in politics and governmental programs. This process poses serious challenges to any form of analytics that wishes to raise the future of the welfare state, political regulation, social integration, and even the relationship between the state and civil society.

All of this is at some distance from Foucault himself and the ever-expanding vectors and circles of impact and influence of his work. It is an understatement to say that Foucault has in recent years become increasingly well cited, even by those positions on governance or in management theory and organizational studies that were first opposed to his thought or believed themselves its very target. Yet our focus in this book is on neither these broad academic diagnoses nor the emergence of new political-administrative programs for the mobilization of civil society. Rather, we address certain prominent intellectual positions that have sought to question and straddle the state/civil society binary. These successors of Foucault claim to have overcome this duality, which they consider an analytical dead end because it does not allow us to understand the complex ways in which governing is practiced in contemporary societies, locally and globally.

We therefore start with two influential approaches, both of which draw on Foucault: Michael Hardt and Antonio Negri's rather grand diagnosis of contemporary society in terms of Empire and the multitude, and the self-styled "humble" analytics represented by Nikolas Rose and his collaborators. We will focus closely on how each position dissolves the state as a central analytical object—which they do, first and foremost, by claiming to overcome the opposition between state and civil society. We show common elements of the metaphysics of vitalism in both of these positions. This is covered in Chapters 1 through 3.

We then examine Foucault's own comments on the themes of state and civil society. Here we follow the trajectory of Foucault's political thought in the 1970s. We suppose that, while his thought rejects the construction of a theoretical system, it possesses an intelligibility that is revealed only through its unfolding. In Chapter 4 we investigate the case for an understanding of Foucault as a "saint," that is, as an advocate of diverse political movements of civil society outside the state. In an excursus we draw out nevertheless anti–civil society themes in Foucault's work in the early 1970s. In Chapter 5 we follow the route by which Foucault would deny the universality of the state, which is a key to political liberalism and the idea of a law-governed constitutional order, by recourse to a model of battle and war. While Foucault would decide to reject the model of war, his decentering of the state would continue in the work and lectures that followed. Thus, in Chapter 6 we reconstruct his analysis of technologies or *dispositifs* and find a kind of immanent and administrative-technical decentering of the state. Of particular note is Gilles Deleuze's reading of this becoming immanent of power and state in terms of "diagrams" and "virtuality." The latter is the focus of Chapter 7. In Chapter 8 we examine Foucault's more skeptical relation to civil society and his understanding of its relation to political eschatology in thought and practice. Chapter 9 profiles his genealogy of governmentality and the pastorate against the discussion on secularization and political theology, and more broadly, economic theology, and discovers a "point of indistinction" of his own narrative to the latter. Finally, in Chapter 10 we turn to the question of Foucault's relationship—and that of his most loyal assistant, François Ewald—to neoliberalism as a way of contextualizing our analysis much more deeply in concrete political positions. We are interested in the interpretation of Foucault by those closest to him and the intellectual trajectory they undergo. Both his assistants and supervisees, Ewald and Blandine Kriegel, find their way to liberalism through him but by diametrically opposed paths—the latter through the 1976 lectures and the notion of the state and its sovereignty, the former through the analysis of liberalism in the 1978 and 1979 lectures. One path revalues absolutism's authoritarian liberalism and its legacy; the other revalues the neoliberalism of the contemporary United States.

The wash-up of radicalism after the May '68 uprisings, and the various forms of extraparliamentary militancy in France, Italy, and Germany, which included terrorist action, certainly shaped aspects of the political orientation of Foucault and his associates during the 1970s. It should not surprise us that Foucault and his closest associates would shift toward more conservative, if not mainstream, traditions of political thought during that decade. What is surprising is that these shifts maintained, at least for Foucault, a fundamental set of continuities. These included an analytical and theoretical antistatism, a rejection of a humanist form of political liberalism, a focus on the creation of subjectivity and identity as the central political stakes, and a denial to the state of its constitutive claim to transcendence. In his search for an immanent analysis that would dissolve the state, Foucault would look toward the field of battle and tactics, the microphysics of power, the rationalities of government, administrative technique, and the plane of civil society. Where his political thought came to rest, at least provisionally and not without reservations, was close to the vision of the subject as self-creation and of a kind of power that left the maximum space for that self-creation and tolerated, worked through, and facilitated difference. This was a model he encountered in the utopias of economic liberalism. Foucault can truly be said to anticipate our present in one crucial respect: a desire to deny the claim to transcendence, constitutive of the innovation that is the modern state—that is, the claim to supreme authority in a particular domain.

One of Foucault's students, Pasquale Pasquino, noted long ago (Pasquino 1993, 84) that while Foucault "affected each one of us very deeply, he kept those closest to him from remaining faithful." Today, those of us who try to be students of Foucault should keep ourselves from being faithful and learn to be unfaithful in our own way. In this spirit we are prepared to be cast out as heretics. So be it!

CHAPTER I

STATE AND CIVIL SOCIETY

At the end of The Birth of Biopolitics lecture series Foucault states that the liberal art of government is founded on the very rationality of the governed themselves: "This, it seems to me, is what characterizes liberal rationality: how to model government, the art of government, how to found the principle of the rationalization of the art of government on the rational behavior of those who are governed" (Foucault 2008, 312). This is a fundamental conclusion for Foucault. He arrives at it after a key analysis of the emergence of "civil society" at the end of the eighteenth century, especially the late eighteenth-century "protosociologist" Adam Ferguson's *An Essay on the History of Civil Society*, which was first published in 1767. In that analysis Foucault finds civil society populated by economic subjects and argues that "*homo œconomicus* and civil society belong to the same ensemble of the technology of liberal governmentality" (2008, 296). Foucault does not elide civil society and the economy in these final passages of his lectures on governmentality, but he emphasizes civil society as the environment of economic agents.

This emphasis has been repeated in some of the standard accounts of what is now known as "governmentality studies" (Sennelart 2007, 390). In this respect it would be straightforward for thinkers such as John Keane (1988) and Jürgen Habermas (1996) to reproach the Foucauldian school for a failure to understand the broader history and significance of civil society as a domain of value-based dialogue and instructive ethics that constitutes another source for telling the truth about society against market exploitation and state domination.

Yet this is certainly not a devastating critique of Foucault. He also stresses that the economic subject "inhabits the dense, full, and complex reality of civil society" (2008, 296) and that this places civil society within a broader story about the "governmentalization" of the state. He locates the problem of how to govern civil society as one version of the emerging general problematic of government through self-government and thus of a piece with liberal and Enlightenment thought. However, given the reemergence of *civil society* as a key term in the lexicon of contemporary governance, it remains to be explored more fully as, in Foucault's terms, "something which forms part of modern governmental technology" (297).

When interrogating the status of civil society, we are immediately faced with its other side: the concept of the state. We know that Foucault was concerned to distinguish his approach from a certain style of analysis of the state. At the beginning of these same lectures he argues for a method that, rather than focusing on already given "universals," as he calls them, such as the state and civil society, would assume that they do not exist and then ask how they are formed through a grid of "concrete practices" (Foucault 2008, 3). This, we might note, is a different project from the one that has so far concerned the most influential of Foucault's governmentality followers: "The analytical language structured by the philosophical opposition of state and civil society is unable to comprehend contemporary transformations in modes of exercise of political power" (Rose and Miller 1992, 173). While all conceptual distinctions have their limitations, this claim manifests a certain ambiguity in the writings on governmentality. On the one hand, as Colin Gordon (1991, 4) has argued, the concept is introduced by Foucault as a way of bridging his "microphysics of power" pioneered in *Discipline and Punish* with a concern for the governing of populations "at the level of the exercise of a political sovereignty over an entire society." On the other hand, this analytical move has been taken by some governmentality writers to imply that analysis of political power should move from macropolitical concerns (with their questions of the conditions of social order, the distribution of power and resources, and the regulatory role of the state) to the "humble," the "local," and the "mundane" technologies and practices of governing.

Such a turn in governmentality studies to minor practices and powers, the small technologies aimed at "producing subjects," has even been grounded on the claim that this is where politics is really at stake: Barbara Cruikshank (1999, 124), for example, has argued that "democratic politics is not so much out there, in the public sphere or in a realm, but in here, at the very soul of subjectivity. Politics is also down there in the strategic field of small things." Foucault certainly focused on the soul of subjectivity. But did he envision the ways in which his analytics have been taken with regard to the state and state-centered power? As we will see, Foucault insisted on a method of decentering the state similar to his earlier displacements of the institutions of psychiatry, the prison, and medicine so that we might better understand our modern experience of the state. He sought, whether successfully or not, to avoid the macro-micro division, but it remains to be seen whether he sought an analysis *beyond* the state and the distinction between state and civil society.

Civil society and the state are key components of the vocabulary by which politics has been discussed for several centuries in the societies of the Occident. But statements concerning such terms not only can have analytical purposes; they also constitute forms of actions in definite political contexts. In this respect Foucault's statements focusing on the state cannot be properly understood without understanding their context, and to do that, we need to understand to whom and against whom or what they are addressed.

Foucault's own work makes this methodological point in several ways. From the analytical perspective of his archaeology (1972), statements should be understood not in terms of what they signify but in terms of what they do. They are hence a form of action that can only be understood within a field of dispersion of statements, a "discursive formation." The term *discursive practices* captures this feature of statements as a kind of action. From the perspective of his genealogies of power-knowledge Foucault employs a series of terms that emphasize the intelligibility of statements and forms of knowledge as actions rather than as mere semantic decodings: strategy, programs of conduct, regimes of truth, and so forth (see, e.g., QM). Applied to his own work, Foucault speaks of it as a "critical ontology" of ourselves and our present with the objective of questioning what is necessary and what is contingent in the identities by which we have come to know ourselves and the relations of power in which we find ourselves and thus to open up the possibilities of thinking and acting differently (Foucault 2010, 20–21).

A similar point has been made in a more straightforward way by Quentin Skinner in his classic paper "Meaning and Understanding in the History of Ideas" (1969). For him political thought cannot be understood purely through the meaning of terms but rather (following John Austin's theory of the speech act) by what form of action is performed by them. To understand what is meant by an utterance, it is necessary to understand the field of utterances of which it is a part, what Skinner regards as its context (Tully 1988). While there are serious differences between Foucault's critical comments on the history of ideas and its focus on authorial intention, and Skinner's attempt to recover intention by locating utterances in context (Walter 2008), they both agree that speech acts should be understood as illocutionary, as forms of performance that seek and have definite consequences. Skinner expressed his central insight in this way: "the grasp of force as well as meaning is essential to the understanding of texts" (1969, 46).

Following this basic insight, we should regard statements concerning the state and civil society as ones made in a particular context or field of dispersion of statements. While some statements might be exegetical, heuristic, or methodological in character, others are clearly addressed to a range of different interlocutors and seek to intervene in a particular field. It is, then, worth examining the context of the *locus classicus* of many of Foucault's statements about state and civil society, and by implication, much of poststructuralism's approach to power, what now might be called his "governmentality lectures" (2007b, 2008).

For our present purposes here the most important thing to note about these texts on governmentality is that they are lectures. This does not mean that they are less than fully reliable sources or that their readers today can take greater interpretive license (see Gordon 2013, 10–13). It does mean, however, that they were likely composed in a single, rapid draft rather than through a number of drafts and that their writing and delivery is often punctuated by present-day concerns more directly than Foucault's monographs. This is a point we find well-put in the foreword reproduced in all these lectures by François Ewald and Alessandro Fontana, their general editors: "The courses also performed a role in contemporary reality. Those who followed his courses were not only held in thrall by the narrative that unfolded week by week and seduced by the rigorous exposition, they also found a perspective on contemporary reality. Michel Foucault's art consisted in using history to cut diagonally through contemporary reality" (Foucault 2008, xv). This primary point is not so much of context as of the nature of the text. The act and immediacy of writing and giving lectures underlines, if anything, the performative and illocutionary aspects of Foucault's thought in its present. This is redoubled by the 1979 lectures, where Foucault, for the only time in his analyses, directly addressed that present. This means that context becomes, if anything, more important.

That context for these lectures is certainly a difficult one to reimagine from our current perspective (Tribe 2009). But to understand his statements on the state, civil society, and related subjects such as socialism, it is necessary to list his possible interlocutors. First, we could name Marxist "state theory," given the then-receding dominance of Marxism in social and political analysis in France. If Marxism was by the mid-1970s waning as a theoretical framework, it was in part due to the diminishing viability of "really existing socialism" with the controversies that followed the publication of books such as Aleksandr Solzhenitsyn's *Gulag Archipelago* in France in 1973–74 (Macey 1993, 383–84). Second, certain statements addressed institutional socialism both as a form of state in Eastern Europe and as a kind of party politics in contemporary liberal democracies. In France this took the form of the long-expected and -delayed ascendancy of the Left to government and the alliance between socialists and the French Communist Party. Third, Foucault is concerned to distance himself from a certain kind of politics of the ultra-left, which views the state as the embodiment of evil that must be attacked at all costs. This may well be related to his own relatively recent collaboration with the Maoists in France, particularly in the Groupe d'information sur les prisons and the more current discussion of left-wing terrorism, particularly in Germany but also in Italy. As a participant in his seminars during this period, Pasquale Pasquino (1993, 79) noted that Foucault's lectures on government were an attempt to break with his earlier language of war and battle, which he now viewed as leading to "an extremist denunciation of power" as a repressive force.

The context of the lectures becomes clearer by considering an episode in November 1977 that occurred just before the start of the "governmentality" lectures. Foucault had protested the extradition from France to Germany of a lawyer, Klaus Croissant, who had represented members of the Baader-Meinhoff gang (officially the Red Army Faction). For his troubles he had received a fractured rib from a police baton (Eribon 1991, 260; Sennelart 2007, 371–77). He also did not want, however, to be identified with a certain style of leftist critique, which confirmed the analysis of those he regarded as "terrorists" by partaking of the denunciation of the German state as a police state or, worse still, a "fascist" state (Eribon 1991, 259–61). This was manifest in his refusal to sign a petition that made precisely such claims. A month later in Berlin he suffered official harassment both while trying to cross into East Berlin and while staying in West Berlin, where he had been denounced for mentioning a book about Ulrike Meinhoff. In *The Birth of Biopolitics* a year later he would speak of this crossing the border in Berlin, where "the question every good Western intellectual asks himself is, of course: Where is true socialism? Is it where I have just come from, or there where I am going?" (Foucault 2008, 93).

While this statement addresses itself to the problem of the choice between Soviet-style socialism and social democracy, others address themselves to the problem of how a socialist government might approach governing, then an imminent possibility in France:

> I would say that what socialism lacks is not so much a theory of the state as a governmental reason. . . . I do not think there is an autonomous socialist governmentality. There is no governmental rationality of socialism. . . . Socialism can only be implemented connected up to diverse types of governmentality. It has been connected up to liberal governmentality. . . . We have seen it function . . . within governmentalities that would no doubt fall more under what last year we called the police state. . . . Maybe there are still other governmentalities that socialism is connected up to, it remains to be seen. But in any case, I do not think that for the moment there is an autonomous governmentality of socialism. (Foucault 2008, 91–93)

If these statements evidence Foucault's concern with institutional socialism and its variants, both the third (ultra-left) and first (theoretical Marxism) of his interlocutors are addressed in the well-cited passage on the two forms of "overvaluation of the state" in *Security, Territory, Population*. The first overvaluation taking an "immediate, affective and tragic form is the lyricism of the cold monster confronting us" (Foucault 2007b, 109). While the immediate target of this are those on the extraparliamentary ultra-left, Foucault will reveal (over the following two years) strange bedfellows of those who suffer from "state phobia," including several types of liberals and advocates of the virtues of civil society (2008, 76). The second is the "paradoxical" reduction of "the state to a number of functions like, for example, the development of the productive forces and the reproduction of the relations of production" (Foucault 2007b, 109), which refers directly, if somewhat crudely, to the Marxist functionalist theory of the state.

At the same time, of course, "neoliberalism" was nothing like the accomplished and embedded program of national and international government it would be by the 1990s, the controversial legacy with which we are still dealing (Peck, Theodore, and Brenner 2009). It was more a rationality that remained on the horizon during a time of significant economic and political transformation. Indeed it is his diagnosis of what he calls "state phobia" (Foucault 2008, 76;

Tribe 2009, 687) that leads most directly to a recovery of German Ordoliberalism and Austrian neoliberalism and the genealogy of a form of rule that sought to limit the extent of the state in the face of a notion of civil society.

The discussion of state phobia appears at the start of the fourth lecture of 1979 as a kind of prolegomena to the historical analysis of forms of neoliberalism. Foucault (2008, 75) begins by citing, rather freely, the art historian Bernard Berenson, to the effect that he feared the invasion of humanity by the state more than the destruction of the world by the atomic bomb. He then proceeds to discuss the coupling of the two fears of the state and the atomic bomb, of the sources of state phobia in the experiences of the Soviet Union of the 1920s, of Nazism, and of English postwar planning and its multiple agents and "promoters" (76). Among the latter are Austrian economists from the 1920s onward and political exiles and dissidents. He concludes by comparing the critique of despotism in the second half of the eighteenth century with the anxiety concerning the state in his own time.

The idea of state phobia serves, then, as a kind of preface to the genealogy of neoliberalism that will follow, beginning in the next four lectures with German Ordoliberalism. It is only after these four lectures that Foucault returns to the theme. What is of contemporary significance about their analyses, he suggests, is that they introduced two themes that amount to a contemporary "critical commonplace" (Foucault 2008, 187): the unlimited expansion of the state in relation to civil society and the inherent dynamism that is specific to the state. These themes allow an unproblematic and barely considered linkage of the "administrative state, the welfare state, the bureaucratic state, the fascist state, and the totalitarian state." What results is an "inflationary critical currency" that deprives analyses of specificity, conducts a general disqualification by the worst and confuses the actual situation with "the great fantasy of the paranoid and devouring state" (187–88). As a critical consequence state phobia deprives its subjects of the capacity to identify the real sources of this kind of suspicion, something Foucault identifies in the formation of neoliberalism in the years 1930 to 1945 (189).

State phobia occupies an important place in these lectures because it suggests that Foucault's project is not so much to do away with the state and its language, as some of his interpreters seem to suggest, but to raise the problem of the denunciatory commonplaces often directed to the state that result in the authority of the state itself being called "fascist" (2008, 188). Foucault's exploration of it is crucial because it shows anxiety about state phobia to be not only the province of his contemporaries on the ultra-left but also to have many versions across the political spectrum. In fact, his analysis shows that the sources of the antistatism of his own time were to be found in a radical conservative movement—neoliberalism. Thus, the Freiburg school of Ordo-liberalism, according to Foucault, diagnoses the history of Germany not as one of market failure but of state failure in which the market has never really been tried. They find the sources and examples of this in List's national economy, Bismarckian state socialism, the planned economy, and Keynesian-style interventionism (Foucault 2008, 107–9). These are all so many versions of the "anti-liberal invariant" (111), which, in what Foucault regards as an intellectual *coup de force*, they find epitomized in Nazism. Indeed Foucault spends some time on the relation between National Socialism and the state in the Ordoliberals' arguments and considers how the latter rejected a possible alternative analysis of this regime, which would be that it initiated a "withering away of the state" by placing the *Volk* above law and right, the *Führer* above authority and administrative hierarchy, and the party above the state (111–12). If one accepts this analysis, Nazism might be considered less an instance of the extension of the rational-legal authority of the state and its bureaucracy (Bauman 1989) or of the "despotism of the state" immanent in governmental rationalities (Rose 1999, 23) and more the appalling consequence of a kind of radical antistatism.

Foucault draws up a similar state-phobic list of opponents for the Chicago School of economics and law of the 1960s: this time "the New Deal, wartime planning, and the big economic and social programs mostly supported by postwar Democratic administrations" are added to the list (Foucault 2008, 323). His genealogy, however, indicates even earlier sources for this antistatism. In *Security, Territory, Population* Foucault already mentions forms of counter-conduct to *raison d'État* that would appear with liberal notions of state and civil society that affirm "an eschatology in which civil society will prevail over the state" (2007b, 356). At the end of the next year's lectures he locates this antistate eschatology at the founding of the American republic, and in the idea of the Third Estate in France (2008, 310–11). State phobia, for Foucault, is thus inscribed deeply in liberal and neoliberal ideas of civil society, assertions of the nation against the absolutist state (Abbé Sieyès), republican ideas of human wickedness leading to government against the inherent goodness of civil society (Thomas Paine), and revolutionary Marxist aspirations for the "withering away of the state."

There are many other possible aspects to the political context of these lectures, including Foucault's growing involvement with the events in Iran and his later journalism on the revolution there (Afary and Anderson 2005; Sennelart 2007, 375–77). This initial exploration of their context, however, allows us to make a central claim: the illocutionary force, as Skinner puts it, of at least some of Foucault's statements is as an intervention in current political concerns. Thus, it is possible to distinguish broadly between three kinds of statement in these lectures: an intellectual practice of the exegesis of primary texts (and the use of secondary sources) that forms the main body of these lectures, the occasional methodological and heuristic statements that often appear as a summing up and attempt to define the possible analytical path Foucault proposes to take, and those statements that address themselves most clearly to the present and to his interlocutors.

These statements are distinct, but we cannot understand them in isolation. If we detect an analytic concern to decenter the state, it is not to overcome the state but to analyze it in a fashion that checks the pervasive tendency to denounce the state in its everyday operation. "Governmentality" appears as the very means by which Foucault proposes to analyze it:

> Just as for the prison we tried to go behind penitentiary institutions in the strict sense to seek out the general economy of power, can we carry out the same reversal for the state? Is it possible to move outside? Is it possible to place the modern state in a general technology of power that assured its mutations, development and functioning? Can we talk of something like a "governmentality" that would be to the state what techniques of segregation were to psychiatry, what techniques of discipline were to the penal system, and what biopolitics was to medical institutions? (2007b, 120)

Governmentality, for Foucault, first appears as an analysis of the state, not something that lies beyond the state. It shows the conditions of an experience of "state" as that which is confronted with an external domain, civil society, to which it must grant a measure of free action in order for government to function. It grows out of a diagnosis of the present as a period in which the state, even in the exercise of the very authority that defines it, according to Max Weber, has come to be regarded as essentially despotic, the source of evil in the world, and as a repressive force that deforms our subjectivity, from the inside as much as from the outside, and limits our potentiality in the world. For Foucault this is a view shared by not only the ultra-left, seeking to overthrow the state by violent action, but also by variants of neoliberalism in the twentieth century. This view has its source in the antistate eschatology of the nineteenth century, which has the notion of civil society at its core.

As we will see, however, there remains the question of whether Foucault escaped the antistatism he had identified. We might also want to ask what the effects of the simple repetition of certain noncontextualized axioms concerning the need to go beyond the state today may be. For not only do such statements not take into account Foucault's context, but they fail to take into account their own. In respect of the latter it is worth reflecting on the differences between Foucault's context, that of the initial widespread reception of his political writings and lectures in the final decade of the twentieth century, and the one we find ourselves in today.

First, consider the reception of Foucault in the 1990s. At least in Europe, state socialism no longer effectively existed and had been symbolically cleansed from the minds of intellectuals by the incantation of a single date, 1989, and event, the fall of the Berlin Wall. Second, Marxism has ceased to have anything like the intellectual hegemony it held a generation ago, despite the fin de siècle reemergence of poststructuralist versions such as those of Michael Hardt and Antonio Negri. There was then no such thing as a Marxist state theory, at least not one that reached a broad intellectual public. Third, neoliberalism had shifted from a marginal intellectual movement to a dominant framework of public policy in many advanced countries and was, in one form or another, exported to or implemented in the Global South and in the former socialist states (Mirowski and Plehwe 2009). Above all, if we were to sum up the key difference between Foucault's conjuncture and this period of the reception and analytical activation of his political thought, it was that in the latter state phobia has migrated from the fringe of the Left to the mainstream to infect socialism and social democracy, such as in the American and British versions of the Third Way under President Clinton and Prime Minister Blair.

In Foucault's context, to reject a theory of the state was to reject a Marxist theory of the state and to take note of anti-institutional movements both within liberal democracies and within those opposed to state socialism. Twenty years later, the rejection of an analysis in terms of the state was made in a context of the repeated mantra of "governance" theorists who diagnosed a shift from government to governance and a "hollowing out [of] the state." It was made amid conceptions of globalization that claimed that global flows of trade, finance, information, and culture have undone the "container" of the national state (Beck

2000, 23) and amid political analyses that claimed that struggles directed toward the state had been displaced by grassroots movements conducting sub-, micro-, and transversal politics underneath, across, and above the territorial state. In short, in the 1970s the rejection of a theory of the state in favor of the analysis of local struggles marked a break with a prevailing Left intellectual problematic and an attempt to open up the discussion of government and state. By the end of the twentieth century, to dissolve the concept of the state came to have the opposite effect: of merely reinforcing what had become a kind of antipolitical orthodoxy that has rendered *the Left* a meaningless term and to accede to a political agenda fatally shaped by the militant intellectual and political "thought collective" of which Foucault was an early analyst: "neoliberalism" (Mirowski and Plehwe 2009).

This is the legacy with which we are still dealing. Recently, Slavoj Žižek has even argued that a fear of the state haunts the contemporary Left: "Those who still insist on fighting state power, let alone directly taking it over, are immediately accused of being stuck in the 'old paradigm': The task today is to resist state power by withdrawing from its scope, subtracting oneself from it, creating new spaces outside its control" (2008, 339). This is an analytical fear of the state and a disdain of political projects aimed at contending for state power. We differ from Žižek here in viewing the state not only as something to be fought but also as a condition of the order and security, and the development of individual and collective capacities, that makes possible such struggle. But what are the elements that constitute our own context today?

First of all, the full publication of Foucault's relevant lectures only occurred in France in 2004 (2004a, 2004b) and in English in 2007 and 2008. The latter date is significant because it is now associated with what is sometimes referred to as a period of "global financial crisis" that led to sharply increased poverty and unemployment in the United States and Europe and is still having major ramifications almost a decade later. In Europe the future of integration has been put in question, and financial regulation is a key issue at stake. In the background are the questions of catastrophic climate change; the emergence of major new economies such as China, India, and Latin America; and the still problematic distribution of global resources. We have been through two major wars in Afghanistan and Iraq; the long-term legacy of the events of September 11, 2001, including the "war on terror" initiated in its aftermath; the international impact of radical political Islamism; and the questions of security and the often exceptional means and emergency powers they have raised.

Certainly in these areas of financial regulation, economic crisis, national inequality, global poverty, climate change, and security, the problem of the state, acting alone or in concert with other states, and the exercise of its political sovereignty, remains at the heart of politics today.

Today this politics not only has a formal shape within the institutions of parliaments and other representative bodies. It is fought out between new radically antistatist grassroots (and "astroturfed") movements, such as the Tea Party in the United States, and new oppositional movements questioning inequality, such as the Occupy protests, or demanding new forms of accountability and regulation of financial institutions, from Greece to Spain. The mere mention of these developments in political struggles and challenges for political sovereignty suggest the urgent need to approach once again these key problems of state and civil society, modulated through contemporary radical political analysis and practice.

.   .   .

We close this chapter with a note on the terms *state* and *regime*. The classic characterization of the modern state, which we think still holds, was provided by Max Weber in his *Economy and Society*:

> The primary formal characteristics of the modern state are as follows: It possesses an administrative and legal order subject to change by legislation, to which the organized activities of the administrative staff, which are also controlled by regulations, are oriented. This system of order claims binding authority, not only over the members of the state, the citizens, most of whom have obtained membership by birth, but also to a very large extent over all action taking place in the area of its jurisdiction. It is thus a compulsory organization with a territorial basis. Furthermore, today, the use of force is regarded as legitimate only so far as it is either permitted by the state or prescribed by it. (1978, 56)

One might wish to add or modify features to this definition, but it does offer many of the enduring characteristics of the state as an object of knowledge: its law-governed and organized form, the existence of its administrative staff, the nature of the membership of its population, its compulsory character for all who reside within its territory, and its specification of the coordinates of the legitimate use of force. For our purposes we view the modern concept of the state in this form to be a historically improvised artifact with its roots in the overcoming of the confessional conflicts of early modern Europe. It is this entity that made possible further elaborations such as the nineteenth-century constitutional state and the twentieth-century welfare state. We would add that the state has remained the central locus of organized political action during these centuries.

We would also distinguish, however, between *regime* and *state*, following on and extending a distinction made by Raymond Aron (1968). For Aron *regime* refers to the embeddedness of the state in social life and the way the state incorporates multiple externalities into its sphere of action (Du Gay and Scott 2010, 16; Scott 2011). Bearing this in mind, and incorporating the insights of Foucault and the governmentality literature, we have proposed an extension of this notion to speak of a distinction between a "regime of government of and by the state" and the state itself (Dean 2014, 161). The regime of government is the terrain of the rationalities, technologies, programs, and so on that try to influence the conduct of the state—its agencies and agents—and to shape the conduct of individuals and populations within the state. Needless to say, the law-governed and regulated territorial state has proven more enduring than any of its different regimes of government. Liberalism, neoliberalism, communitarianism, and welfarism are examples of general rationalities of the government of the state, but they are not different states or forms of state. In this sense one can speak of a neoliberal government of the state rather than a neoliberal state itself.

This more robust conception of the state has the benefit of guarding against the radical antistatism of neoliberal rationalities while allowing for the possibility that neoliberalism is a political movement with statist objectives. In this sense it is a form of what Weber (1978, 54) called "politically oriented action" that "aims at exerting influence on the government of a political organization; especially at the appropriation, expropriation, redistribution or allocation of the powers of government." We note here also that Weber's notion of government goes beyond a focus on the state and in this respect is like Foucault's in that it includes the government of other organizations of different scales, from families to universities and international organizations.

It is our view that a concept of the state similar to the one advanced by Weber, and a distinction between the state and its regime of government, provides sufficient scope for the deconstructionist maneuvers of Foucault and his followers and at the same time provides limits to their analytical, normative, and political antistatism.

CHAPTER 2

EMPIRE WITHOUT STATE

In this and the following chapter we explore two ways of overcoming the distinction between state and civil society in contemporary radical thought: Michael Hardt and Antonio Negri's theory of Empire and Nikolas Rose and his colleagues' diagnosis of advanced liberalism. In their grand edifice on global-ized postmodern capitalism Hardt and Negri draw on ideas from many think-ers, in particular Foucault, Marx, and Gilles Deleuze, whereas Rose (often with his coauthors) emphasizes the empirical analysis of programs, rationalities, technologies, and strategies of the management of human conduct.

At first sight these two positions could hardly be more different. Hardt and Negri locate themselves explicitly within a Marxist framework, emphasizing labor and its reproduction, whereas Rose rejects the Marxist theoretical sche-mata of state and economy. Hardt and Negri invoke an overarching historical narrative and seek to offer a conceptual intervention at a distinctly philosoph-ical level, while Rose sometimes speaks of his work as a kind of Deleuzian-inspired empiricism that distinguishes itself from theory and sociological thought (see, e.g., Rose 1999, 11–12). Moreover, Hardt and Negri (2000, 328) invoke a classic institutional concept of civil society, populated by labor unions, free associations, and nonstate agents, whereas for Rose and Peter Miller (1992, 179–80) "civil society" is a component in a liberal mentality of government that makes rule operable through a domain outside formal politics. Hardt and Negri recognize that any attempt to overcome the state/civil society binary is inherently political, whereas Rose and his colleagues work with a "diagnostics" that only allows for the subdued normativity of increasing the contestability of regimes of authority. If that task has a political function, states Rose, it is to provide resources for those who have a right to contest their constitution as subjects of government (1999, 60–61).

Hardt and Negri launch a sweeping attack on poststructuralist, postmodern, and postcolonial critics for not merely being out of touch with the present ("they mistake today's real enemy") but unwittingly reinforcing postmodern globalized capitalism in their celebration of "hybrid and fragmentary subjectivities" through which contemporary imperial power rules (2000, 137–38). Rose (with Paul Rabinow) in turn has criticized Hardt and Negri for applying a totalizing and simplistic approach that simply provides "a superficial description of certain aspects of the present, framed within the kind of grand narrative of history that other theorists of postmodernity had proclaimed a thing of the past" (Rabinow and Rose 2006, 199). There are, however, more affinities than either party is willing to allow.

Let us now focus on the route by which Hardt and Negri arrive at the demise of the nation-state and a celebration of the creative, revolutionary potential of their proxy for a new form of civil society—the multitude. This route has three dimensions. First, Hardt and Negri break with state-centered political theory by reconceptualizing and radicalizing the meaning of *globalization*. Second, they invoke Deleuze's (1992a) thesis about the transition from disciplinary to "control societies" that dissolves modern institutional boundaries—their distinctiveness and enclosures—including the state and civil society. Third, by applying an "immanence" perspective, in which resistance is immanent to power, productivity is immanent to being, revolutionary potential is immanent to capitalism, and Empire is immanent to all social relations, Hardt and Negri affirm the ever-present transformative potentiality of the dispersed multitude of living and productive human beings.

Globalization is first of all reconceptualized as an explicit form of political agency, Empire, which suspends the key foundations for conventional political analysis: the sovereign state and the interstate system. While the sovereign state constructed and maintained itself by drawing boundaries and denigrating its outside, Empire operates by integrating and assimilating all "outsides"—the entirety of social relations—into its expanding network. The structures of national states serve only as obstacles to the processes constitutive of Empire— that is, the intensified flow of capital, goods, and information; the recognition of cultural differences and minorities; and the linking up of nongovernment organizations, interstate agencies, and multinational corporations. This new "global constitution" has begun to exert a political agency that does not need nation-states for its exercise of sovereignty (Hardt and Negri 2000, 151). It is not that nation-states are no longer important political actors, or do not exert significant powers, but that "the nation-state is no longer the ultimate form of sovereignty, as it was during the modern era and that nation-states now function within the imperial framework of sovereignty" (Hardt and Negri 2002, 182). Imperial sovereignty still creates lines of division, but these cannot be adequately conceived along national boundaries.

The sensation of a hyperexpansive, globalized, and omnipotent form of power, the new Leviathan of Empire, is counterbalanced by the inherent possibilities, or even revolutionary potentials, within the monster itself. By this move they offer an alternative to the fear on the Left that finds in the sweeping indifference of globalization only a clear-cut threat to the welfare state and to democracy. It is from within the dynamics of Empire that progressive actions must be taken, and not by invoking a nostalgic return to the protective walls of national and welfare states (Hardt and Negri 2002, 184). After having dissolved the state as an analytical object, Hardt and Negri thus give a more explicit political negation of state-centered politics.

This is where the Deleuzian concept of "control societies" comes in. The dissolution of the state is repeated in regard to the division between state and civil society. For Hardt and Negri it is again the hypertransgressive forces of Empire that cause civil society to dissolve or "wither away" (2000, 328–32). To be sure, the dissolution of civil society takes place through the dismantling of the former dialectics between the capitalist state and the forces of labor, which is manifest in the declining influence of labor unions and collective bargaining power (328). But the withering away of civil society also follows more fundamentally the passage from disciplinary society to control societies. The forms of subjectivity formerly shaped by disciplinary institutions escape institutional barriers and are now spread out and generalized across the social field (329). Hardt states, "The logic of capitalist production perfected in the factory now invests all forms of social production. The same can be said also for the school, the family, the hospital, and the other disciplinary institutions. . . . Social space has not been emptied of disciplinary institutions; it has been completely filled with the modulations of control" (Hardt 1995, 3). To the disappointment of those who hoped that the critique of power would come from labor unions, interest organizations, and local groups, Hardt proclaims, "Not the State, but civil society has withered away! In other words, even if one were to consider civil society politically desirable . . . the social conditions necessary for civil society no longer exist" (5).

Since a traditional institutional concept of civil society is clearly of little relevance in the passage to Empire, Hardt and Negri envisage a kind of substitute, the multitude, which serves many of the functions that civil society does for other critics. Although they state that the multitude is intended as a successor concept for class (Hardt and Negri 2000, 52), there are a number of fundamental structural similarities between the multitude and the concept of civil society offered by its key thinkers, especially those who emphasize a "checks-and-balances" relationship between civil society and the forces it opposes (e.g., Hegel, de Tocqueville, and, more recently, Jürgen Habermas).

Multitude and civil society stand in a relationship of codependency, if not immanence, to their counterpart (the state, bureaucratic apparatuses, globalized capitalism), which both realms rely on and challenge. Both are constituted by relationships of personal allegiance rather than formal juridical and contractual relations. Both rest on human creativity and communication as their fundamental activity—instances of which cannot be restricted to any circumscribed sites but may take diverse and sometimes unexpected points of emergence. Finally, some of the key concrete exemplifications of the multitude in Hardt and Negri, such as the new social movements, are also viewed as proof of the coming of a "global civil society" by the latter's proponents. In brief, like civil society, the multitude is a domain of emancipatory potential constituted in relation to structures of domination but nonetheless exceeding them through its energies, creativity, and learning.

The invention of the multitude thus allows Hardt and Negri to dream of a moment where the structures of domination will be rewound to serve progressive goals, since the creative force of the masses may be unleashed within the very relays of globalized capitalism itself (Hardt and Negri 2004, 101). Crucial to this point is Hardt and Negri's reelaboration of Foucault's concept of biopolitics so that it emphasizes the productive potentiality of human life, conceiving of human beings "at once as artificers and tools" (Casarino and Negri 2004, 165). The progressive overlapping of material production and human reproduction turns social relations into the essence of production, and this in turn opens up the multitude's constitutive agency: "Biopolitics becomes fully realized precisely when production and reproduction are one and the same, that is, when production is no longer a distinct activity but resides in social relations themselves—in living labor, in language, and social exchange" (167). This form of capitalism, with its global flows of digitized information, makes possible a decentralized multitude whose activities are simultaneously productive and resistant, reproductive and subversive. One illustration of this is how flows of digitized information can be accessed by collectives whose activities are simultaneously productive and subversive.

As their joint work developed, Hardt and Negri's concept of biopolitics becomes more fluid and polyfunctional. In *Commonwealth*, the third volume of the trilogy initiated by *Empire*, biopolitics comes to be identical to life itself or the power *of* life rather than the power *over* life. Here the former represents the "minor current" in Foucault and the latter the major one (Hardt and Negri 2009, 56–57). Life itself tends to be identified with resistance, and biopolitics is associated with the production of subjectivities: "Our reading not only identifies biopolitics with the localized productive powers of life—that is the production of affects and languages through social cooperation and the interaction of bodies and desires, the invention of new forms of the relation to self and others, and so forth—but also affirms biopolitics as the creation of new subjectivities that are presented at once as resistance and de-subjectification" (58–59). The notion of biopolitics thus becomes a kind of shifting signifier in their work: it first specifies a new form of power that escapes disciplinary institutions; it then becomes a new political economy or form of production; and it finally indicates the very forces of resistance that well up from within the multitude. The term thus links a political actor with a form of economy and a form of political institution. In doing so much work, it becomes vague and loses touch with its Foucauldian sources and ultimately derives its content from a kind of metaphysics of life, a kind of vitalism.

This brings us to the postulate of the immanence of resistance to Empire and the transformative potential of the multitude. The fact that Empire harnesses and depends on life itself constitutes the fundamental condition for the multitude to exercise insubordination, resistance, or even sabotage in various forms of micropolitical practices. Such contestation takes on an increasingly dispersed and uncoordinated character. Yet for Hardt and Negri this is not necessarily a problem since the open and expansive networks of Empire can be interrupted from multiple sites, and a single uncoordinated attack can be highly effective. Perhaps the more capital extends its global networks of production and control, the more powerful any single point of revolt will be. These serpentine struggles, simply by focusing their own powers and concentrating their energies in a tense and compact coil, strike directly at the highest articulations of imperial order. The notion of Empire indeed presents a superficial world, the virtual center of which can be accessed immediately from any point across the surface (Hardt and Negri 2000, 58). Thus the multitude does not need the worn-out modernist forms of support such as the welfare state, labor unions, political parties, or formal associations for it to exercise real transformative actions. A resort to these institutions would also block the space necessary for the elaboration of utopian and alternative projects.

In the later iteration of their thesis Hardt and Negri (2009, 355) adopt a rigorously antistatist position and pose the multitude in direct and simple antagonism to the state: "The multitude . . . has no interest in taking control of the state apparatuses, not even in order to direct them to other ends—or, better, it wants to lay its hands on state apparatuses only to dismantle them. It regards the state as not the realm of freedom but the seat of domination, which not only guarantees capitalist exploitation and defends the rule of property but also maintains and polices all identity hierarchies." In a manner reminiscent of classical Marxism they thus reject any focus on "transcendent authority and violence" as something that "eclipses and mystifies" what are the dominant forms of power rooted in regimes of property and capital.

With the emergence of Empire the welfare state becomes impossible since it requires a foundation for its values in national citizenship rights. While throughout modernity the immeasurable was the object of an epistemological ban, this metaphysical illusion disappears today—it is now the *transcendent* that has become unthinkable (Hardt and Negri 2000, 355). Are Hardt and Negri then postmodern thinkers? Perhaps not. They are highly critical of postmodern theorizing, which they see as stuck within a critique of modernity and thus unable to grasp the present conditions. In fact, they hark back to a pre- or protomodernity to find a potential of a form of direct, "immanent" democracy: "There were two modernities in Europe: a first characterized by immanence and absolute democracy of the multitude and a second, which arose in reaction to the first, that culminated in the construction of the nation-state and its colonial projects. The latter path of European modernity won, but the potential of the former has always remained" (Hardt and Negri 2002, 187–88). In this quest for a nonmodern, nonstate form of democracy Hardt and Negri display an oddly anti-Enlightenment stance. Perhaps recognizing this possibility, they later coin the expression "altermodernity" to capture a political process grounded in antimodernity struggles but that transforms these resistances into the provision of alternatives. "In short," they conclude, "altermodernity constitutes a *dispositif* for the production of subjectivity" (Hardt and Negri 2009, 115).

Empire had been extensively criticized by various commentators (Dean 2003; Rabinow and Rose 2006; Žižek 2008), particularly because its totalizing metanarrative was of little use for empirical analysis. Here, we emphasize two points related to Hardt and Negri's dismissal of the state and state-centered politics. First, we question, in line with Žižek, whether Hardt and Negri's proclamation of a society of unmediated expression of the multitude's creative agency is possible. This is the idea of a society without representation, one of "absolute democracy"—that is, "a society fully organized in terms of expression of the multitude" (Žižek 2008, 364). This illusion is, according to Žižek (364–65), a version of the philosophical problem of "becoming versus Being (living productivity versus the sterility of an inert structure of representation), where every re-presentation is parasitical upon productive expressivity." Rather than accept the opposition of "real" productivity versus the state as sterile representation, it should be seen as expressing interdependence, that is, no "self-organized" multitude without state power. There would be no productive multitude and no diversified creativity (such as found in social movements and processes of innovation) without the structure of mediation and representation. Thus says Žižek, "What if Mao was aware that the very flourishing of movements of the multitude always-already had to rely on some dispositive of Power which structures and sustains the very space within which they operate? Today, the movements for gay rights, human rights, and so on, all rely on state apparatuses, which are not only the addressee of their demands, but also provide the framework for their activity (stable civil life)" (371). We contend that Hardt and Negri's conceptualization of power allows them to eschew any consideration of the extent to which the territorial state and its institutions provides the necessary conditions for a civil society, even as they themselves define it. Thus, by their use of Empire—the virtual omnipresent logic of postmodern, postbinary, posthierarchical, and postnational forms of organizing—they succeed in abandoning completely the state or a system of states as an enduring analytical problem and political issue. At the national or international level the state or state system only appears as something to be opposed or overcome. This is because, for them, all of the movements are immediately subversive in themselves and do not require any sort of external assistance and social support to guarantee their effectiveness (Hardt and Negri 2000, 58) or conditions of order, peace, and stability in which to achieve their ends.

Second, and more disturbing, what are the implications of the multitude, which appears as a new form of civil society "on steroids"? The image of an unorganized collective subject that momentarily expresses its creative political potential seems to share characteristic features with extreme variants of eschatological politics such as libertarian liberalism, communism, or even the fascist use of crowds and their expressive acclamations, recently analyzed by Giorgio Agamben (2011). This is no doubt why Hardt and Negri (2004, 99–100) seek to distinguish the multitude in terms of its ability to maintain difference rather than dissolving it into the mindless indifference of the mass or the fabricated unity of the people.

Yet this remains a purely theoretical set of distinctions. After the demise of modern and enlightenment values, we seem to be left with paradigmatic postmodern features, that is, aestheticized forms of communication, organization, and identity in which "differences express themselves freely" (Hardt and Negri 2004, 101). But is the aim of the free expression of all difference political or aesthetic, and what are its consequences? Thus, Levinson instructively observes: "Indeed, is not the movement of a spontaneous and 'bodily' multitude, without plan or communication, the very formula for the most aestheticized political models, above all populism, even fascism?" (Levinson 2001, 213). Could it be that Hardt and Negri's way of opening up the space for political innovation runs the risk of a crushing limitation of our political choices?

It is interesting that Hardt and Negri seek in *Commonwealth* to address a range of thinkers who question either the capacity of the multitude to act as a political actor (Pierre Macherey, Ernesto Laclau) or question their supposition of its progressive and liberatory political character (Paolo Virni, Etienne Balibar, Žižek, and Alain Badiou) (Hardt and Negri 2009, 166–69). Despite the at times repetitious and dare we say a little desperate reiteration of key theses (of the primacy of resistance, of the creative acts of the multitude) they admit that all this is not enough to establish the political orientation of the multitude. Their language turns toward an increasingly pious and normative wish-list in which the multitude *must* act outside the corruption of existing institutions (the family, the corporation, the nation) or *should* produce the commons and *needs* a theory on the "terrain of organization" (178).

Unfortunately, when we search for that theory of organization, particularly in the final chapter of *Commonwealth*, called "Governing the Revolution," we find only the admission of a series of self-described "impasses," such as finding an answer to the question "What or who draws the political diagonal that guides the transition?" or on the nature of the governmental, constitutional, and juridical framework that comes from the revolution (Hardt and Negri 2009, 363). These are hardly minor issues given the ambition of their work as revolutionary political theory. It turns out that the authors are best at specifying conceptions of revolutionary organization they oppose—that is, the ones that are ready to seize the state, to establish a counterpower and a newly constituent power, or to found some form of dictatorship. They are less interested in elucidating revolutionary organization itself. When they gesture toward an alternative conception of organization it is one that appropriates current notions of "governance without government" and hopes to subvert and reformulate them (372–75). While the antistatism of this literature can be taken as given, it remains to be seen whether this focus on governance can in any way be viewed as an adequate way of displacing a conception and theory of the state.

Radical antistatism unites the militant Left with a libertarian or neoliberal Right, autonomist post-Marxists with centrist social democrats and students of public administration. Yet Hardt and Negri are legitimate students of Foucault in one sense: they pronounce the anticipated end of a transcendent form of power and a reign of immanence. They thus foresee the end of the form of power that is constitutive of the state: sovereignty. This is due to the rise of the multitude: "The autonomy of the multitude and its capacities for economic, political and social self-organization take away any role for sovereignty. Not only is sovereignty no longer the exclusive terrain of the political, the multitude banishes sovereignty from politics. When the multitude is finally able to rule itself, democracy becomes possible" (Hardt and Negri 2004, 340). This, we note, is the classic dream of civil society, to finally become one with itself outside the alienated condition it suffers under the domination of the state. It is the form that many modern political eschatologies take.

Sergei Prozorov offers us the insight that the end of sovereignty here entails an immanentist metaphysics discerned by Foucault himself:

> Ironically, this vision of a purely immanent self-organising and self-governing community of men may be read as a *manifesto* of biopower rather than an articulation of resistance to it. . . . Indeed, at the risk of oversimplification, we may reduce Hardt and Negri's formula to "biopolitics without sovereignty," which entails that this project belongs squarely to the immanentist metaphysics that in Foucault's argument conditioned the possibility of the rise of biopower. From this perspective, Hardt and Negri may be read not as the *critics*, but rather as

the great *metaphysicians* of the age of biopolitical immanence. (2007b, 64, 74; emphasis in the original)

The question remains, however, about how faithful Hardt and Negri have been to Foucault on this point. Should we read Foucault as a critical diagnostician of the claim that we have entered a great age of biopolitical immanence or as merely the messenger of this age? Before considering this question we first explore the immediately contrasting reading of Foucault in Nikolas Rose's politics of life.

CHAPTER 3

POLITICS OF LIFE

The influential post-Foucauldian analyst Nikolas Rose is skeptical of approaches of "the epochal sort" like those of Hardt and Negri, preferring "to examine changes at the more modest level, not in terms of cultural shifts but as empirically identifiable differences in ways of thinking and acting" (Rose 1999, 173). Rose sees his work as "more empirical than theoretical," thus establishing a clear demarcation between those who are concerned with "the waning of an epoch of modernity and the hesitant birth of another" and those who, like himself, are attentive to "the humble, the mundane, the little shifts . . . the small and contingent struggles" (11). Nothing it seems could be further from the grandiose project of the theorists of Empire and multitude.

On closer inspection, however, there are some compelling similarities between Rose and Hardt and Negri. Rose also succeeds in writing the state out of his historical narrative, although by a slightly different route, referring to the demise of "the social" as a key logic of contemporary government and the emergence of a new multiplicity of territorialities around the notion of community. He argues that "community" is about to or has become the key reference point, or "plane," of government at the expense of "the social" as the core sector that conditioned the emergence of the modern welfare state as ethos and practice (Rose 1996a). Rose's approach is not exactly an immanence perspective, but he offers a parallel view of the blurring between those who govern and those who contest governing within a sphere somewhat akin to civil society.

This key observation rests on the approach to liberalism shared by Rose and other students of governmentality. This literature emphasizes the capacity of liberal forms of governing to continuously accommodate itself to critique in the quest to govern more wisely, prudently, and efficiently. Liberalism is hence understood as "a restless and dissatisfied ethos of recurrent critique of State reason and politics" (Barry, Osborne, and Rose 1996, 8). Liberal government, in this view, has an internal self-problematizing impetus that makes it skeptical toward state planning, in-depth regulation, and control of human affairs, while it nevertheless intervenes to "secure the natural processes" of society. This double gaze, which observes its objects as at the same time natural and cultivated, gives liberalism a permanent creativity in criticizing existing forms of governing and inventing new ones (Foucault 2007b, 349).

The Rebirth of Community

Rose uses this figure of nature/artifice in his analysis of how by the 1990s "community" had emerged as a key terrain of government in "advanced liberal societies." This emergence promised a reawakening: "Community is to be achieved, yet the achievement is nothing more than the birth-to-presence of a form of being which pre-exists" (Rose 1999, 177). He demonstrates how a category that is first utilized as a means of social critique by activists became appropriated by governmental authorities for various regulatory strategies such as the management of risk. These strategies revolved around the imaginary of a "lost community" with potentials for crime prevention, health promotion, neighborhood revitalization, and more (Rose 1996a, 332). Thus what began in the 1960s as a category of resistance was transformed into a governmental tool to represent and intervene in risky cultural zones and geographies. Indeed, Rose suggests that the mutation in political rationality, from national planning to governing through diverse communities, should not be seen as the result of either centralized authorities implementing "from above" or as the action of interest groups, local communities, and regions arising "from below." Instead, he indicates a reciprocal action between the strivings of activists and the authorities and experts who seek to govern in a more culturally sensitive and empowering fashion. Rose then shows that there is not *one* civil society but rather numerous "fictions" of it, each inscribed and mobilized within different, and to some extent heterogeneous, governmental strategies. It follows that we need to examine in detail how concepts of community or civil society appear and which tactical function they play in each instance.

This perspective on political power as reversible, shaped in networks of state and nonstate agents, echoes Rose and Miller's (1992) decentered analytical approach to the state. Opposing themselves to theories that explained the exercise of power over a territory or in geopolitical relations with reference to the specific form of state, they argued for an antistate-centric approach to political power that they found in Foucault. They argued that the way power is exercised in advanced liberal states could not be comprehended within the binary logics of political theory: "But the political vocabulary structured by oppositions between state and civil society, public and private, government and market, coercion and consent, sovereignty and autonomy, and the like, does not adequately characterize the diverse ways in which rule is exercised in advanced liberal democracies. Political power is exercised today through a profusion of shifting alliances between diverse authorities in projects to govern a multitude of facets of economic activity, social life and individual conduct" (Rose and Miller 1992, 174).

We have already noted that Foucault's observations on the state and state power should be viewed as an attempt to afford an analytical reorientation and were made in a specific context. They are neither an elaboration of a new theory of politics nor a set of substantive claims about how political power actually functions. Yet reading this programmatic statement, one gets the impression that an actual transformation has taken place in the field of power relations. It is as if advanced liberal-democratic states are *today* governed through the mobile alliance of diverse actors in network-like complexes of power. These power relations align state agencies with nonstate actors, thereby rendering the distinctions between state/civil society, public/private, and so on obsolete. What starts out as a variety of contingent and fragmentary statements against state-centered views of power is turned into a methodological framework suited to understanding our contemporary forms of political power. By blurring the boundaries between analytical provocations and representations of actual changes, Rose and Miller succeed in making Foucault's heuristic precepts serve as an adequate diagnostic of the present.

Rose's claim for a mutation in the relations of power is also substantiated by another path on which he shifts from second-order observations to observations of the first order. To be sure, he generally operates at the second-order level insofar as he observes how objects of government are made thinkable and actionable by means of governmental rationalities and technologies (Rose 1999, 35). Yet when he drifts to a more positive characterization of "our plural present" (195), Rose replicates some key claims offered by the stories of contemporary cultural theorists and sociologists about cultural differentiation, subpolitics, and aestheticized consumerism. While his approach does not rule out a critical perspective on postsocial, advanced liberal forms of governing, Rose nevertheless emphasizes their positive potentials with respect to social experimentation and alternative forms of political agency: "Within these spaces [of communities], it is possible for subjects to distance themselves from the cohesive discourse and strategies of the social state—schooling, public service broadcasting, municipal architecture, and the like. They can now access a whole range of resources and techniques of subject formation in order to invent themselves, individually and collectively, as new kinds of political actors" (179). This is the precise point in the argument at which Rose does not remain merely diagnostic but explicitly affirms a particular kind of self-inventing subject. The shift from detached second-order observation to affirmative first-order description is complemented by Rose's invention of what he terms "ethico-politics" (188) to designate the emergent field of contestation and experimental self-creation opened up after the withering of the social perspective and the critique of the welfare state.

What is at stake in the view that society as a knowable totality gives way to a form of a sociality constituted by multiple forms of expertise, networks, or communities? What are the costs for political analysis of privileging politics as the "active art of living" that opposes all obstacles to the vital self-assertion of the will to live through active self-creation? (Rose 1999, 283). First, there are of course political costs of what is conceived as no longer possible. They center on the difficulties, to say the least, of referring to the kind of knowledge of society or social structure that has been essential for public policy and provision as remedies against social inequality and its ills and as a condition of exercising civil, political, and social rights. There is a dual displacement occurring: of forms of social knowledge and of questions of the role of the state in resource allocation and the securing of minimum and universal standards. The emphasis on the identifications that form communities, or on aestheticized forms of self-creation through "somatic individuality" and an "ethic of vitalism" (Rose 1999, 283; 2001, 18) appears to sideline, if not to rule out, the salience of this kind of knowledge and these political questions.

In this respect the "birth of community" seems to manifest the long-noted affinities between postmodern discourses on cultural diversity and societal differentiation, on the one hand, and neoliberal strategies for dismantling and transforming welfare services and ossifying and exploiting differences (Taylor-Gooby 1994). Arguments for granting more space to the diversity of civil society, for instance in the shape of "ethico-political movements," run the risk of ossifying differences of a social nature. While Rose would no doubt insist that differences are in part governmental artifacts and identity the result of active identifications, this still leaves open the wider political ramifications of the enthusiasm for a politics of plural communities beyond the state.

There are also analytical costs, as pointed out by urban sociologists and geographers (Brenner, Peck, and Theodore 2010). It is simply very difficult to move from the local, the unique, the contingent, and the relatively unstructured to extralocal contexts, systems, and institutional frameworks or to the vectors, logics, and pathways that constitute more solid and enduring kinds of power and regulation. There is a risk here of fetishizing the localized and empirical through a methodological commitment to always study power in its particular manifestations. A set of in-principle useful methodological gestures thus becomes an untenable ontological commitment to a particular vision of social and political life as unstructured flux and fluidity (206).

As it is, Rose's ethicopolitics is a politics of self-creation that appears after the displacement of the social state. It is striking, however, that Rose, similar to other post-Foucauldians such as William Connolly (1993), comes very close to privileging civil society and its multiple identities over the state. Thus, Rose's conception of politics shares the same space as civil society; it is an extrastate space of innovation and creativity and of critical contestation of state-centered politics and administration. While Rose may share with critical theorists and liberal philosophers a celebration of this realm and its self-creating agents, he brackets out the enduring problematic of the conditions of a thriving civil society. This includes the fundamental question of what kind of active, sovereign state power needs to be exercised for the potentially lethal conflicts of civil society to be kept in check and for individuals to gain the capacities to participate and engage in social and political life. We are left with only a fluid and experimental form of postsocial politics.

In Rose's more recent writings the bracketing of the state is sustained, although the concept of ethicopolitics seems to have receded. In their introduction to the collection *Governing the Present*, Rose and Miller (2008) make clear their initial ambitions with these studies. The republication of these works, they explain, aims "to counter some of the abstract forms that some of these ideas have taken, and to demonstrate how our conceptual tools were forged in the analysis of some very specific problem fields" (21). Hence, the emphasis on localized and empirical analysis is repeated and thereby underlined. Rose and Miller also state their ambition to avoid economic reductionism and all-embracing, epochal descriptions, and their desire to develop a non–state centered perspective on power. In the place of structural analysis (derived from Louis Althusser) and its tendency to reduce social relations and subjectivities to their function in reproducing economic relations, they claim that they wished to open up more sophisticated ways of addressing "the multiplicity and variability of modes of subject formation" (4) and the specificity and irreducibility of programs of governance operating within various domains.

One way of doing this is by concentrating on "minor figures" and their specific activities since it is "only through their activities that states, as they were termed by those who seemed untroubled by the meaning of this term, could govern at all" (Rose and Miller 2008, 5). Rather than the state apparatus as point of origin, the focus should be on "a power without a center, or rather with multiple centers" (9). While such an approach could be read as a fruitful way of supplementing or extending the analysis of state politics and policy, it becomes a substitute for it or alternative to it. Under the aegis of this approach studies of governmentality mistake the analysis of regimes of governing—with their rationalities, technologies, modes of subjectification, and different aspirations and ends—for a study of the state itself.

Vital Politics and the Art of Living

Rose's subsequent work (2001; 2007) becomes more focused on life and the neurosciences. He first shifts from governmentality to biopolitics in its several contemporary manifestations, instanced by genetics and genomics, risk screening and pharmacology, and all the way to aesthetic interventions on the body. There he finds that the days of state-administered biopolitics, exemplified by the eugenic drive for biological and moral perfection, are over, succeeded by alliances between, for instance, self-creating consumers and pharmaceutical companies, and a biomedicine that offers products for voluntary bodily improvements and services for risk minimization. Rose is at pains to avoid a purely negative view of this novel "somatic individuality" and its ethics and recognizes the expanded possibilities for autonomy and self-formation offered by biotechnology that "enables us to intervene upon ourselves in new ways" (Rose 2007, 8). The passage from "the social state" to "advanced liberalism" thus holds the promise of more diversified experimentation and contestation of truth claims about biological normality: "Our somatic individuality has be-come opened up to choice, prudence and responsibility, to experimentation, to contestation—and so to a 'vital politics'" (Rose 2001, 20).

The phrase "art of living" is here given a more substantive anchorage in the very materiality of the body, and the concept of ethicopolitics has been transmuted into "ethopolitics": "By ethopolitics I mean to characterize ways in which the ethos of human existence . . . have come to provide the 'medium' within which the self-government of the autonomous individual can be con-nected up with the imperatives of good government. . . . While ethopolitical concerns range from those of lifestyle to those of community, they coalesce around a kind of vitalism. . . . In this highly contested domain, somatic in-dividuals are the key actors" (Rose 2001, 18). None of this escapes the earlier dilemmas we have raised. If we follow Rose and regard a politics of "life itself" as a fundamental form of contemporary agency and contestation, then it is dif-ficult to understand how active choices of self-creation can be available without raising the question of the role of the state in ensuring access to a health-care system that includes the innovations of biomedicine, surgery, and the phar-maceutical industries and in ensuring a set of universal standards so that life can be lived in this self-governing way. Otherwise, ethopolitics becomes the preserve of a privileged caste (on either national or global scales) or, at best, highly unevenly distributed. If we admit this, then the conventional charac-ter of politics has not been displaced by the discovery of the ever new forms of biopolitics but will be played out in those old appropriation and allocation struggles, which have been at the core of the territorial state's quest for civil peace and the welfare state's establishment of social rights.

Without the conventional domain of social politics, typically framed in terms of questions of access and equality, ethopolitics is confined to its vitalist, consumerist, technological, and lifestyle elements. It simply amplifies a kind of narcissistic lifestyle concern with the self's corporeal perfectibility and vital capacities. It is at these intersections that Rose sees the emergence of a new kind of ethical subjectivity in terms of active self-creation in relation to the plasticity of life and corporeality. At such moments the Foucauldian project reminds us of nothing as much as mainstream sociological assertions of "life as a planning project" and of the self-creation of identity in late modern life-politics advanced some years ago by theorists such as Ulrich Beck (1992) and Anthony Giddens (1991; Beck-Gernsheim 1996)—with the added stratum of a plastic biological materiality. Paradoxically, the demise of the social state leaves us not with the positive conception of power advanced by Foucault but with resistance to a highly negative or repressive power, as "all that which blocks or subverts the capacity of others asserting for themselves their own vitalism" (Rose 1999, 283).

We can identify four key aspects of the ethical subjectivity associated with ethopolitics. First, it is located outside or at the fringes of the "social state" and is shaped by the multiple, personal identifications with diverse communities. Second, it breaks free from or contests the conventional "welfarist" institutions and their authorized knowledges. Third, it takes the form of "freedom from" conventional political structures and action and formal organization. Finally, it is particularly intense and innovative in the experimental practices of self-creation, where human and nonhuman forces intersect—such as those discovered by the life sciences or the brain or neurosciences.

Most recently, Rose has moved on to address the growing centrality of the brain as the explanatory instance for knowing ourselves and how it has become a key focus for improving individual and collective human life (Rose 2009, 2013; Rose and Abi-Rached 2013). Within pharmacology, neurogenomics, and neuroplasticity there has been an explosion of research paving the way for a new and widely accepted conception of the "plastic" human brain. There is a certain restraint in these writings and a rejection of the more exaggerated claims made on behalf of brain research learned perhaps through the earlier engagement with the "bio." The "neurobiological age," as Rose calls it, is full of "inflated expectations, exaggerated claims, hopeful anticipations and unwise predictions" associated with prestige large-scale scientific endeavor (Rose and Abi-Rached 2013, 232). Nevertheless, Rose and Joelle M. Abi-Rached suggest the possibility that the brain will take over from, or at least side with, the central role occupied by the psyche throughout the twentieth century. This possibility arises because "the twenty-first century brain is not an organ whose fate is fixed at the moment of conception or birth, but is plastic and open to external influences throughout development and indeed throughout life" (217). The conception of the brain as modifiable and in constant transaction with the environment has made possible new preventive strategies and interventions and extends the "bio-medical prudence" that had developed in the life sciences, for instance, in the growth of genetic predictions, the promotion of self-education, and the calls for individuals to take responsibility for their personal genome (Rose 2009, 69–72).

In these recent works Rose's principal aim seems to be to advocate a positive dialogue between the biological sciences and the social sciences. At the least this seems to be a strange trajectory for Foucauldian thinking in a number of very basic ways. Foucault's work presented itself as an "antiscience," highly skeptical of institutional knowledge and the forms of truth it promoted and intent on uncovering "subjugated knowledges" (Foucault 2003, 8–9). Indeed, it would be commonly assumed that this is why he wished to bracket scientific truth claims in order to investigate "power-knowledge" relations. Instead of this critical genealogy of truth we have a rather assiduously descriptive approach to the kinds of truth that assume the status of human nature in the currently most fashionable parts of the natural sciences. Genomics and brain science would seem to be the very opposite of the search for subjugated knowledges; they are heavily funded and highly institutionalized Big Science, often found within private corporations and research institutes. Moreover, whatever its intent, a relentlessly descriptive account of such forms of knowledge naturalizes their very status and accounts of human subjectivity as fundamentally conditioned by Nature that Foucault would have seemed to be have wanted to problematize.

Rose has recently suggested we should take an "affirmative relation" with the new genomic and neuroscientific paradigms. Referring to Canguilhem, he specifies the affirmative relation: "At every historical moment, the ways in which we *think about* how to think about vitality must be informed by, underpinned by, shaped by, premised on, the very way in which vitality itself is understood in the contemporary sciences of life" (Rose 2013, 22). Granted this is Canguilhem's normative doctrine, not Rose's, but why should this be so? Life, vitality, and so on can and have been thought about extensively from political, aesthetic, philosophical, economic, and theological points of view as well as scientific ones. Should we not think about how vitality is thought about in all these ways? This position cannot account for the privilege it wishes to give to the life sciences. And it thereby forecloses the possibilities of critique, which becomes a decidedly immanent activity that affirms and further articulates an already ongoing production of knowledge (Raffnsøe, Gudmand-Høyer, and Thaning 2014, 10). This stark formulation of immanent critique (in which the object under description sets the parameters for the observer's critical reflection) would seem to limit the terrain that the humanities and social sciences can address. They can live in the reflected glory of the natural sciences and contribute to the latter's quest for cultural hegemony.

The affirmative attitude to the biological age leaves very little space for critical engagement with the truth claims of these sciences. In fact, it appears to cede the possibility of critique to neuroscience itself. On the one hand, such science must be reminded that the brain and its capacities, affects, and powers are "enabled by a supra-individual, material, symbolic and cultural matrix" (Rose and Abi-Rached 2013, 233); that is, it is culturally, socially, and economically embedded. On the other hand, such science will help decide our models of true subjectivity, such as when we must hope for "unpredictable conversations" in which the neurosciences could provide the evidence and "disprove" the view that humans are self-maximizing and that they should be governed by requiring each individual "to bear the responsibilities and culpabilities of his or her selfish choice" (234). The conversations with the neurosciences "enable us to begin to construct a very different idea of the human person, human societies, and human freedom" (234). Again, we might ask, why is this privilege being handed over to the neurosciences? Is it because in them human being is most satisfactorily naturalized today? Or is it simply because they are big and powerful? And why should a Foucauldian, initially concerned with the different ways in which we are made and asked to view ourselves as subjects, suddenly switch to wanting evidence and proof as to who or what we really are as subjects?

The mention of the self-maximizing individual, associated broadly with neoliberalism, reminds us here that one of its most famous progenitors, Friedrich Hayek, would also understand the development of societies in terms of notions of complexity taken from a branch of biology—the field of systems ecology pioneered by C. J. Holling (Hayek 1967; Walker and Cooper 2011). The themes of the limits of human knowledge of complex systems, of the spontaneous and vital nature of change and development, and, above all, of the rejection of the "pretensions" of an *autonomous* social science are among the fundamental truths of Hayekian neoliberalism. But here a contemporary Foucauldian analysis points in similar directions to argue that the biomedical knowledge of vitality (understood as the self-organizing capacity of living organisms) must be recognized by the social sciences: "Vitalism will remain as a constant reminder of the self-organizing, dynamic, self-regulating complexity of living systems, the fact that, unlike machines, they exist and develop in time and space, and of the inseparability of organism and milieu in life in the real world. The social and human sciences need to grasp these operative philosophies of biology and biomedicine, to explore the 'philosophies of life' which they embody and the potential forms of life to which they may be linked" (Rose 2013, 23). This invocation of an indeterminate vitality, no matter how drawn from the contemporary life sciences, resonates not only with Rose's earlier adventures in Deleuzian vitalism but also with the Hayekian model of social systems. It is possible that Rose, in principle, ascribes an equal importance to knowledge of the social, cultural, and political conditions of human life. But his "affirmative" attention to the discoveries of vital factors in human life in his most recent work not only resonates with a general metaphysics of life but also appears to set a priori limits on anything like a critical ethos toward the claims of these now dominant sciences.

Political Vitalism

At a distance there are, of course, vast differences between Rose's meticulous empirical work and the messianic narrative of Hardt and Negri with its dual universe of Empire and multitude. While the multitude is the vast, unmediated, immanent, and dispersed social subject permeated by, but nevertheless potentially subversive of, imperial domination, Rose's remedy to avoid the binary around power and resistance is to point to a set of mobile and multiple "conflicting points of opposition, alliance and division of labour" (1999, 277). Moreover, these communities and somatic individuals are not spontaneous foci of resistance but are themselves products of engagement with governmental practices and strategies and with new forms of knowledge and technologies— although, as we have just seen, the more recent affirmative relationship to the biological sciences seems to naturalize quite a significant part of human existence.

There are, however, deep and unexpected affinities. There is the fascination with the "bio," no doubt related to the public success and branding of biomedicine and biotechnology around the threshold of the twenty-first century and the ethical and political problems these forms of knowledge raised. Biopolitics becomes central in its different ways to both projects. But beyond this is a common desire to discover a politics based on life and the living, as well as on the energetic, the creative, the vital, and the nomadic. In Hardt and Negri this vitalism takes the form of the "lived experience of the global multitude" that incarnates without object or qualification *"the will to be against"* (2000, 210; emphasis in the original). For Rose (1999, 283), quoting Deleuze, "we should oppose all that which stands in the way of life being its own telos . . . in favor of life, of 'the obstinate, stubborn, indomitable will to live.'" Both privilege a politics that indicates "lines of flight" that are always in danger of becoming recuperated, organized, systematized, and programmed by regimes of power and domination. We can hardly miss the similarities to the expressive and diverse singularity of the multitude when Rose indicates "moments of minoring, of breaking away, creating something new within the most traditional political forms, as when new practices of mobilization and protest are invented within the most organized forms of strikes, where new and mobile subjectivities form, swarm and dissipate in mass mobilizations, marches and demonstrations" (280). Where Hardt and Negri incarnate the vital in the multitude, Rose discovers it in a certain nomadic attitude to forms of struggle and contestation or even to the vital self-creative forces found in them. We might ask whether and to what extent Rose joins with Hardt and Negri in invoking the Deleuzian "creative plenitude of a singular vitality" (Hallward 2000, 101).

Both approaches claim to dissolve the traditional state/civil society binary to indicate a new kind of politics beyond the state. However, they both oddly reinvent the traditional privilege given to the inventiveness, creativity, and mobility found not in the "rigidities" of the state and formal political organizations but in a domain of energy, expression, and vitality that lies beyond them, opposes them, or occasionally breaks forth inside them and which they seek to recode, reinscribe, discipline, and organize. Although we might characterize the multitude as a kind of hypercivil society, Rose's (1999, 195, 280) "non-conventional communities" and "moments of minoring," which can be found even in the interstices of conventional political action and forms, more closely resemble the quasi-natural creativity and vitality of a liberal civil society. As his work has developed, this vitality has come to reside in organic materiality itself.

The dissolution of the state and state-based politics shared by Rose and Hardt and Negri may rest on a parallel inspiration from Gilles Deleuze and his discovery in Foucault of "a certain vitalism" in which life is "the capacity to resist force" (1988, 93). Lying outside the limitations and forms of the Foucauldian trinity of knowledge, power, and subjectivity, this vitality is, as we will see in Chapter 7, an ever-expressive reservoir of the virtual. One reason why these authors are less concerned about problems of state organization and formal politics is that the forces for which they wish to pave the way concern the irruption of these virtualities. Indeed, "multitude" and "Empire" are for Hardt and Negri not representations of really existing, ontological entities; they are tools "for identifying tendencies and imagining projects of constitution" that the authors believe already exist "in potential in the real" (Casarino and Negri 2004, 168–69). For Rose "an explicit and agonistic ethico-politics" is similarly a potentiality inherent in our "plural present," in which "creative ways of thinking and acting" offer "some limited grounds for optimism" (Rose 1999, 195–96).

Certainly Rose's occasional inspiration from Deleuze is not of the same order as the full-blown metaphysical immersion of Hardt and Negri. Yet for both cases Deleuze's philosophy does not seem to offer clear criteria for which forms of virtuality should be actualized, the principle being that any act of actualization produces new virtualities and thus possibilities. Negri explains: "the actualization of the virtual never constitutes an impoverishment or mortification of the virtual, because such an actualization always produces in its turn still other virtual realities." (Casarino and Negri 2004, 179). The assertion of the existence of an inherently creative force means that any arrangement or system is pregnant with more possibilities than are ever realized. Hence, the virtual presses against the borders of our present reality, challenging its order, and inciting it to transcend itself. At the level of subjectivity this affirmation of creative vitality entails, as Badiou observes, an injunction to dissolve the bounded pretentions of our actual being (2000, 195). Some have found this kind of self-transgressive activity based on a vital energy to constitute "an ethics of the strong" (Badiou 2000, 196). Others have linked it to the very image of modern capitalism offered by Hardt and Negri. For Žižek (2004, 163) "the need to reinvent oneself permanently . . . opening oneself up to a multitude of desires" is congruent with the fundamental outlook of contemporary capitalism.

The ontology of potentiality, when mobilized by Hardt and Negri, and in a minor register by Rose, seems to privilege a world with little fixity and no structure, a suspicion of formality, and a politics that is mobile, fluid, and nomadic. In Rose it follows from his diagnosis that a return of the "social state" would threaten to foreclose the new potentials and diversity of ethopolitics under the weight of an old-style biopolitics of the population. Hardt and Negri see themselves as capable of distinguishing between the progressive versus the reactive—and, indeed, reactionary—forces within Empire. The first represents nonstate forces; the latter includes the structures of nation-states. For both positions the modernist framework of the nation state is envisioned as a stumbling block for the self-unfolding of the new energies that they depict. The history of political vitalism is of course a much longer one, but we are reminded here of the "political romanticism" of the young revolutionaries who viewed the French Revolution as simply an *organic* expression of the free spirit (Schmitt 1986, 24).

CHAPTER 4

SAINT FOUCAULT

In 1995 David M. Halperin, a Massachusetts Institute of Technology professor of literature, published a book called *Saint Foucault: Towards a Gay Hagiography*. The phrase "Saint Foucault" was used at least half ironically as a response to an unsympathetic reviewer who had accused Halperin of "generic worship of Saint Foucault" (Halperin 1995, 4). But his ironical appropriation of an insult had its limits, as Halperin states: "As I have watched the cautionary spectacle of Foucault's demonization unfold, and noted the specific terms in which it has been carried out, my attitude to Foucault has gradually changed, correspondingly, from one of distant admiration to one of passionate personal identification" (6). Part of Halperin's identification is with Foucault as a gay scholar, critic, and activist who can act as something of a role model for other gay scholars. A second part is the need to passionately defend him against charges of political quietism and that his activism amounted to what Richard Rorty described as a kind of French-theoretical "self-indulgent radical chic" (Rorty 1986, 47; Halperin 1995, 24).

We are certainly sympathetic to the idea of Foucault as displaying a kind of exemplary comportment that might inspire other scholar-activists. We are more skeptical of passionate identification in political and intellectual life. Foucault himself was inclined to endorse such an impassioned approach to politics. Speaking in October 1982 in relation to the suppression of the Solidarity movement and trade union in Poland, he said: "As for the emotional aspect, it is, after all, the role of the governed to take offense and put passion into their reactions. I do believe in the importance of political affect" (MSP, 470–71).

It is a third part of Halperin's identification, however, that is most directly relevant to our concerns. He detects a kind of fundamental affinity between Foucault's writings and a certain kind of grassroots politics. He cites New York AIDS activists around 1990 who responded to the question of their key theoretical text with a unanimous answer: "*History of Sexuality, Volume 1*" (Halperin 1995, 15–16). In short, without giving Foucault too much credit, and without judging cause and effect, or neglecting the role of intermediary studies drawing on Foucault, Halperin asserts a close connection between Foucault's work and "contemporary styles of direct-action politics" and new social movements: "At least some of Foucault's most important theoretical reflections on power were directly inspired by political struggles that he saw already going on around him—political struggles waged . . . by the student movements, the children's rights movement, the antipsychiatry movement, the women's movement, and the gay and lesbian movement" (25–26).

In this chapter we explore this thesis, summed up by the image of Saint Foucault as the thinker of new powers and resistances, new forms of struggles, located not in the conventional domain of politics and the state but in something akin to what has been conventionally called civil society. We intuit that it is this image that is behind the overwhelmingly positive status ascribed to Foucault and his work by many students and faculty today. We begin to investigate the proposition that Foucault was an advocate of a kind of antistate and antiauthority politics located in civil society. We do so from three angles: the literature that would claim his support for a politics of difference or identity politics; his own enthusiasm for localized struggles and the excavation of subjugated knowledges; and his consideration of the relationships between critique, truth, and power.

Hero of Identity Politics and the Grassroots

Let us consider Foucault's apparent advocacy of a politics of civil society. Following Halperin, it would seem self-evident to locate Foucault positively as an advocate of civil society, purely on the basis of his own commitments to various protest movements, for example prisoners' rights, the antipsychiatry movement, and his apparent sympathy with "abnormals" caught up in bureaucratic machines of power. It could also be pointed out that the ideal of providing opportunities for creative self-fashioning, for "nomadic thinking" that challenges the limits of accepted categories and criticizes the way in which state institutions exercise power, chimes with an "identity politics" that defends individuals' and groups' rights to express and live out their particular cultural identity. In this vein Bent Flyvbjerg ascribes to Foucault's thinking a particular sensitivity to diversity and marginality that connects him with nonstate actors such as grassroots movements and local activism: "Foucault's emphasis on marginality makes his thinking sensitive to difference, diversity, and the politics of identity, something which today is crucial for understanding civil society and for acting in it" (Flyvbjerg 1998, 225). Indeed, several political theorists and analysts, including Iris Marion Young (1990, 7), have championed the existence of this kind of normative position in Foucault, which they say can be used along with thinkers such as Derrida, Lyotard, and Kristeva to argue in favor of a "politics of difference" (see also Bevir 1999). Foucault's explicit stance against any unifying, totalizing, and "top-down" theoretical-deductive thinking further supports this view. In brief, a politics of difference may be defined as an intellectual activity that fights for open, pluralistic, and emergent forms of "bottom-up" truth production and aims to nurture the potential in real-life, nonuniversal conflicts and everyday struggles about identity (Trainor 2003, 566).

There is some evidence to support claims of an antistatist, anti-institutional, and prosocial movement orientation in Foucault's work and political activism. In respect to the latter Foucault suggested that he wished to stand beside the oppressed instead of representing or protecting them. He indicated the desire to make room for marginalized groups' self-formulated critiques rather than take on the role of spokesperson for them. In an interview published in 1977, for instance, he famously rejected the idea of the "universal intellectual" who claimed to speak on behalf of others and charted the emergence of "specific intellectuals" who speak on the basis of their own localized expertise and knowledge (TP, 126–28).

He further expressed the wish to exercise an "immanent" or "embedded" critique, in the form of an analytics informed by "the gaps," conflicts, and urgent paradoxes expressed by the specific agents of psychiatry, the hospitals, or the prison service. In an interview with an Italian Marxist journalist published in 1978, Foucault talks about conducting analyses that "shut the mouths" of prophets and legislators by presenting problems in their full complexity and in relation to people's actual lives: "I concern myself with determining problems, unleashing them, revealing them within the framework of such complexity as to shut the mouths of prophets and legislators: all those who speak *for* others and *above* others. It is at that moment that the complexity of the problems will be able to appear in its connection with people's lives; and consequently, the legitimacy of a common enterprise will be able to appear through concrete questions, difficult cases, revolutionary movements, reflections, and evidence" (1991, 159; emphasis in original). This quote can be seen in light of Foucault's dual skepticism toward the practice of representation. First, Foucault opposed the idea of the intellectual as someone who unveils and exposes a reality unknown to the agents acting in it. He explicitly rejected the idea of theorizing as a means to unveil "the codifications which, without our knowledge, rule our behavior" (QM, 230). Second, Foucault was skeptical about acting as a representative of "the weak," partly as a result of his reflections about power and partly because of the inherent risk of contributing to their disempowerment via the act of representing their perceived hardships, needs, and desires for them. This meant that he would cast himself as much more a participant actor than an advocate of civil society.

In a conversation from 1972 that discussed their mutual involvement in the activist group on prisoners' conditions, GIP (Groupe d'information sur les prisons), Gilles Deleuze praised Foucault for being the first intellectual to spearhead the fundamental lesson of "the indignity of speaking for others" (Foucault and Deleuze 1977, 209). Deleuze described the GIP as an attempt to break with representation and let the prisoners' own voices "sound out" while he admitted that they, as organizers, did not in reality avoid speaking on behalf of prisoners: "We ridiculed representation and said it was finished, but we failed to draw the consequences of this 'theoretical' conversion—to appreciate the theoretical fact that only those directly concerned can speak in a practical way on their own behalf" (Foucault and Deleuze 1977, 209).

During this period of Maoist engagement, and contrary to thinking on the role of the intellectual as a vanguard who shapes the consciousness of the working class, Foucault ascribes to the intellectual the function of a mediator who passes working-class knowledge into communication networks. This is because the intellectual does not possess superior knowledge about working-class conditions "compared to the massive experience that the working class has" (quoted in Macey 1993, 317). In 1973 Foucault wrote in *Libération* that "the workers don't need intellectuals to tell them what they are doing; they know perfectly well what they are doing. . . . His [the intellectual's] role is therefore not to shape a working-class consciousness, as that consciousness already exists, but to allow that consciousness, that working-class knowledge, to enter the information system" (quoted in Macey 1993, 317–18). The intellectual is, as Foucault puts it, "plugged into the information network, not the production network" (quoted in Macey 1993, 317). In Foucault's *gauchiste* phase the intellectual can play a critical function in excavating and circulating the knowledge of the working class. Foucault here wishes to attribute particular legitimacy to intellectuals and political activists who have a direct link to ordinary people's problems, especially people who are incarcerated or disempowered in some other way(s) by structures of domination. Just as Deleuze (1988, 98) has observed in him "a certain vitalism," Foucault assigns substantial legitimacy to social movements that are "vitalized" by their contact with disempowered groups (Trainor 2003, 571). We might say that insofar as Foucault has a politics of civil society, it is a performative one rather than one that elevates civil society to a kind of permanent, normative ideal.

We also note the syntagma quoted above: "all those who speak *for* others and *above* others" and its original emphasis. If the "*for* others" captures this political target of Foucault's antirepresentational positions, encapsulated in the Leninist party, the "*above* others" is a metaphor for a transcendent domain of authority, such as that found in expertise and exercised by certified professionals, state bureaucrats, and legislatures. The statement is, on the one hand, in its very elemental metaphorics, pitted against the form of political representation found in either parliamentarist or revolutionary proletarian parties. On the other hand, it also positions itself against something that comes from *above*: against the authority of formal and institutionalized knowledge and against the state and its certified and appointed agents and officials. In this sense Foucault adopts, at least in the more free-form genre of the interview, a fundamentally anti-institutional and antistatist position. He thus presents us with an anti-universalist, antirepresentational, and antiauthority view of political struggle and action and the knowledge on which it is based, which can be read as clearing the space of situated intellectuals, embedded forms of knowledge, and direct action located in civil society.

This argument has been extended in one further direction. Foucault's practical political orientation toward local struggles, and theoretical preference for contestatory and oppositional forms of knowledge and truth, has led some political theorists to argue that he further indicates something akin to formal, procedural principles that enable us to assess the legitimacy of state regimes and institutional arrangements (Connolly 1993; Simons 1995). According to this interpretation, Foucault's position on civil society is that it is guided by the principle of keeping the space of contestation open in the face of perpetual conflicts between antagonistic social groups and attempts to solidify hegemonic state projects. The legitimate exercise of political authority ought to enact a public space in which no totalizing project is able to achieve hegemony. William Connolly characterizes Foucault's "ethico-political sensibility" in a manner that clearly draws him in the direction of a politics of difference that turns away from state-centered politics in favor of diverse subcultures and fluid identity creation. That sensibility is manifest in "genealogies that dissolve apparent necessities into contingent formations; cultivation of care for possibilities of life that challenge claims to an intrinsic moral order; democratic disturbances of sedimented identities that conceal violence in their terms of closure; practices that enable multifarious styles of life to coexist on the same territory; and a plurality of political identifications extending through and beyond the state to break up the monopolies of state-centered politics" (Connolly 1993, 381). Foucault becomes via such a reading a radical democratic theorist who envisaged a pluralist civil society of reciprocally agonistic differences that presents limits to all species of epistemological and moral fundamentalism. Not all commentators would go so far, it should be noted. Contra Connolly, Brian Trainor has suggested that it is extremely difficult to find a normative endorsement of the politics-of-difference position in Foucault. Trainor insists that a "politics of difference project" is "profoundly anti-Foucauldian and the general tone and tenor of his work is adamantly (perhaps too adamantly) anti-normative, anti-metaphysical and therefore 'anti' the project of providing a genuine normative underpinning for the 'politics of difference'" (Trainor 2003, 575). Bearing this in mind, however, let us investigate two concrete examples of how Foucault's work could be said to maintain a positive evaluation of the struggles located in civil society: his valorization of local struggles and his explorations of the critical function of Enlightenment.

Local Struggles and Subjugated Knowledges

The pro–civil society stream in Foucault's thought can be explored through the first lectures from the 1976 series *"Society Must Be Defended"* (2003). There Foucault champions a kind of autonomous knowledge production that counters authorized sciences and formal institutions. Foucault's formulations of his method in this context emphasize the value of excavating and circulating marginalized, disqualified, and subjugated knowledge (6–13). Foucault thus valorizes the dispersed against the "unitary," the informal and local against the "formal," and subjugated and counterknowledges against "scientific theoretical discourse" (10). "I think," he says, "that the essentially local character of critique in fact indicates something resembling a sort of autonomous, noncentralized theoretical production, or in other words a theoretical production that does not need a visa from some common regime to establish its validity" (6). He thus seeks to disrupt the tyranny of a unitary theoretical and scientific discourse by mobilizing a union of local struggles and neglected erudition against it.

There are at least two main aspects of the contemporary context of this opposition between the local and disqualified and the centralized and authorized. The first is the legacy of Foucault's earlier involvement in noninstitutionalized, radical activism, notably his founding role in the GIP, an organization that would be in part a response to the imprisonment of Maoist militants. Although several of Foucault's interpreters have noted his involvement in a range of political issues in the 1970s (Wolin 2010; Kelly 2009), only rarely do they relate these political experiences to his theoretical development (Hoffman 2014). Kelly notes: "In terms of the development of the specifics of his political thought, the most decisive event for Foucault was his leading involvement in the Groupe d'information sur les prisons" (2008, 19). One of the current authors has investigated how Foucault's practical experience in this area significantly marks his tenets on power, critique, and genealogy (Karlsen and Villadsen 2014).

The Maoist-inspired principles for activism developed by the GIP bring to mind a number of Foucault's contemporary formulations of the genealogical method and his rendering of the power-knowledge nexus. Hence, contrary to a Leninist view, the Maoists stressed the role of the masses rather than a party vanguard in creating history. Emphasizing that people themselves should be allowed to speak out their concerns, Maoism adopted an antiauthoritarian, antihierarchical posture and offered a significant critique of the model of representation. Furthermore, the Maoists emphasized that the political activist should not predict or plan revolution on the basis of economic and historical analysis but always have a practical grounding in concrete social situations—as opposed to a mere theoretical understanding of these. Accordingly, the Maoists held a fundamental mistrust of "scientific Marxism" and traditional Leninist forms of party organization, which was evident in their polemics against the trade unions and the French Communist Party.

The extent to which Foucault endorsed these principles is open to debate. Although he did use Maoist terminology, he also expressed opposition to several of their ideas, notably to the demands for "counter-justice" that he believed would function as a remade state-apparatus and hence inevitably divide the masses (Macey 1993, 300). Nevertheless, several of the Maoists' key principles are clearly recognizable in the context of Foucault's formulations on genealogy and power in the mid and late 1970s. These include the close link between knowledge production and social struggle; the emphasis on the local and concrete as starting point as opposed to universal assumptions; and the problematization of representational thinking and the idea that "specialists" can represent the oppressed (Karlsen and Villadsen 2014, 13–14).

A second possible political resonance with Foucault's statements on "local and subjugated knowledge" would be his critical evaluation of contemporary Marxist intellectuals and in particular the French Communist Party. Foucault's critique of what he termed "university Marxism" concerned these vanguardist assumptions of a hierarchical relationship between theoretical truth and people's everyday knowledge (Foucault 2003, 10–13; see also TJF, 15). For Foucault this quest for theoretical truth was characteristic of the party organization, with its hierarchies, dogmatism, and invocation of unifying, scientific discourse. The party organization entailed a strategy for narrowing the terrain of the political to a particular form of privileged and sanctioned arena. In "Truth and Power" Foucault observes a certain collusion and desire in the relationship between Marxist intellectuals and the academic and scientific establishment: "for Marxist intellectuals in France (and they were playing the role prescribed for them by the PCF) the problem consisted in gaining for themselves the recognition of the university institutions and the establishment. Consequently, they found it necessary to pose the same theoretical questions as the academic establishment, to deal with the same problems and topics. . . . It followed that they wanted to take up the 'noblest,' most academic problems in the history of the sciences: mathematics and physics" (TP, 112). As a consequence these Marxist intellectuals would not approach "uncharted domains," in which there were "no ready-made concepts, no approved terms of vocabulary available for questions like the power-effects of psychiatry or the political function of medicine" (112). This critique of the Marxist intellectual project to establish scientific, high-theoretical knowledge helps Foucault explain his own emphasis on mobilizing "disqualified" knowledges and local struggles in his genealogical studies.

According to Foucault, another problem with the party and the prevailing intellectual and political climate of the 1970s in France was the rigid dividing lines and "hostile," but nevertheless quotidian, struggles over affiliation in "a system of allegiance" (Foucault, Gordon, and Patton 2012, 107). He found "it truly striking, the way in which, how could I say, I do not mean Marxist, but the Soviet model, in all its odious character, was diffused through French intellectual groups, and not only French political groups but throughout the whole intellectual world." This resulted in a catastrophic "politicization of human relationships" and a system of enmity. He observes that with it "we are truly in a world of enemies."

Foucault seemed to take this contemporary political context into account in his formulation of genealogy as an effective instrument for contesting the political (and not merely academic) landscape with its frozen orthodoxies, party dogmas, and hostilities. The rejection of Communist Party orthodoxies and scientific Marxism in favor of subjugated knowledges further resonates with the Maoist-inspired tenets that based critique on concrete investigations (*enquêtes*) of the real conditions of the oppressed rather than on the theorizing of these conditions. His comments reflect the idea of exerting a localized, critical practice that would not easily be absorbed by and nurture those power structures, such as hierarchical party-organization and theoretically uniform and institutionalized discourse.

This becomes clear in the first of the 1976 lectures. Foucault persistently cautions the critical intellectual to guard against enrollment in the academic and scientific establishment. He regards genealogies "not as positivistic returns to a form of science that is more attentive or more accurate" but "as, quite specifically, antisciences" (Foucault 2003, 9). Such antisciences are an "insurrection against the centralizing power-effects that are bound up with the institutionalization of and workings of any scientific discourse in a society such as ours" (9). The "centralizing institution" thus includes the orthodox revolutionary party, organized science, and, behind these, the state as a privileged site of struggle and authority. In this phase of his work, at least, there is an elision between the claims to science, which are viewed as totalizing and unitary, on the one hand, and forms of domination that support or contest the legal and political order of the state, on the other hand. And just as the juridical discourse of sovereignty masks the element of real domination in practice, so the social and human sciences recodify knowledge arising from social struggles and hence are detrimental to a critical practice, the objective of which was to facilitate the self-representation of marginalized groups.

These statements certainly are conditioned by Foucault's involvement with leftist politics, particularly those of the Maoist-related GIP, and his fundamental antipathy toward the French Communist Party. They could also certainly be invoked to ascribe to Foucault a position of advocacy for the forces of civil society. There is his emphasis on the local and concrete as starting point, as opposed to universal categories (characteristic both of the juridical-political discourse of sovereignty and totalizing theory). There is also a kind of necessary link between local knowledge and particularist social struggles, and critique of representation in political thought and the preference for the specific over the universal intellectual. Furthermore, Foucault's enduring suspicion of Communist Party politics meant that he would attribute particular legitimacy to extraparliamentary political struggle and social movements that have a direct link to ordinary people's problems. With regard to Foucault's critique of centralizing institutions and scientific and professional authority, this would have the implication of a kind of a priori politics of suspicion of state policies and planning and the forms of knowledge that they rely on. The practical consequence of all this would be a preference for localized, diversified, "bottom-up" kinds of knowledge formation that could perhaps transform public policies into a community-based form of democracy. All this may sound encouraging to those who view Foucault as an advocate of civil society.

The Separation of Truth and Power

There is another possible instance of Foucault's manifest enthusiasm for civil society: the Enlightenment notion of truth against power. This concerns Foucault's positive evaluation of certain elements of the Enlightenment and the emergent liberal governmentality's reconfiguration of the relationship linking power, knowledge, and subjectivity. In a series of texts and lectures from the late 1970s Foucault responded to claims that his thought was an anti-Enlightenment one that left no space from which critique could be offered. In his response Foucault gave a cautiously positive assessment of the opportunities that the Enlightenment offers with regard to the contingent and cultural-historical nature of truth. For Foucault the Enlightenment heralded the point in history at which individuals became able to question the truths by which they are governed and to formulate criticisms of how they are governed in the name of truth.

In "What Is Critique?," a lecture delivered in 1978, Foucault notes that the "governmentalization" of the European West cannot be dissociated from the "critical attitude" that is "like a counterpoint, or rather as at once partner and adversary of the arts of government" and concerned with "how not to be governed?" (1996, 384). This means "How not to be governed *like that*, by that, in the name of these principles, in view of such objectives and by the means of such methods, not like that, not for that, not by them?" (384; emphasis in original). For Foucault this critical attitude emerges in the three fundamental spheres of religious belief and scripture, natural law and right, and the authority of science. Critique, which is very close to the notion of Enlightenment itself, "is the movement through which the subject gives itself the right to question truth concerning its power effects and to question power about its discourses of truth" (386). Foucault does not quite repeat the classic opposition of truth to power but indicates the emergence of a new space from which it becomes possible to speak to and oppose the way we are governed, an opposition certainly redolent of the theme of civil society against the state.

Less well-noted is that Foucault at moments displayed a certain enthusiasm in regard to the division, which emerged in the eighteenth century, between political power and those who would claim to speak the truth about society. Such an attitude can be discerned in his characterization of the state and political economy. The latter discovers a naturalness of an entirely different complexion to that of the sixteenth- and seventeenth-century governmental rationalities such as reason of state and police. It is a nature to be recognized and known in society's intrinsic mechanisms, which are distant from, or even beyond the reach of, political power. This new division marked out an external site from which political power could be contested. In 1978 Foucault noted, "It is not at all knowledge internal to the art of government; it is no longer simply a calculation that should arise within the practice of those who govern. You have a science which is, as it were, in a *tête-à-tête* with the art of government" (2007b, 351). In accounts of the differentiation between political power and science, particularly well described in the historical sociology of Max Weber and Niklas Luhmann, politics and science emerge with modernization as independent systems, each propelled by its own self-referential logic. Thus, the fundamental possibility is afforded to oppose power by reference to truth—a "social truth," established by virtue of forms of knowledge of a domain beyond political authority such as that revealed by the emerging political economy. It is the supposed opacity of this domain and its inherent principles that political economists and others can invoke in demanding the self-limitation of governors. This political principle of self-limitation becomes, in Foucault's rendering, akin to a political equivalent of a Kantian critique of reason. Just as "political economy is able to present itself as a critique of governmental reason . . . Kant too, a little later moreover, had to tell man that he cannot know the totality of the world" (Foucault 2008, 283). Thus, the emergence of political economy, like Enlightenment critique more broadly, inaugurated the possibility of speaking truth to power by stressing the limits of the pretension to sovereign knowledge.

For Foucault knowledge would enter into more mobile and tactically reversible relations with political authority and governmental reason. A kind of checks-and-balances system was established between political authorities and those critics and experts who would advocate the need for restrictions or corrections of the exercise of political government with reference to the truth about society: "So, as you can see, a quite particular relationship of power and knowledge, of government and science appears. . . . An art of government that would be both knowledge and power, science and decision, begins to be clarified and separated out, and anyway two poles appear of a scientificity that, on the one hand, increasingly appeals to its theoretical purity and becomes economics, and, on the other, at the same time claims the right to be taken into consideration by a government that must model its decisions on it" (2007b, 351). This opposition between state power and a truth located in society would mean that modern social and political movements have proclaimed themselves to be the representatives of society, of the people or the nation vis-à-vis the state. On the one hand, there is the immutability of the state and its rationality inaugurated with "the new historicity" of *raison d'État*. This reason of state portended a new era in which there "will always be governments, the state will always be there, and there is no hope of having done with it" (355). On the other hand, movements arose that practiced various forms of counterconduct dreaming of the day when the state would dissolve into civil society; thereby, "revolutionary eschatology constantly haunted the nineteenth and twentieth centuries" (356). (We will take up this theme later.)

In the essay "What Is Enlightenment?" Foucault emphasizes that he prefers gradual and partial transformations to "the programs for a new man that the worst political systems have repeated throughout the twentieth century" (WE, 316). With reference to twentieth-century totalitarian ideologies Foucault says, "In fact we know from experience that the claim to escape from the system of contemporary reality so as to produce the overall programs of another society, of another way of thinking, another culture, another vision of the world, has led only to the return of the most dangerous traditions" (316). If we take into account Foucault's skepticism about revolutionary movements and their promises of a social order in which, it is claimed, power will be annulled and society realized in its objectivity, these comments can be interpreted along the following lines. First, we still face the problematic of the modern state, namely the fact that the exercise of political power can and will be challenged, criticized, and corrected with reference to authorities of truth outside of political power.

Second, this balance involves a series of mechanisms that limit the risk of the emergence of totalitarian regimes. And finally, forms of knowledge that claim to have access to the truth of society, and promise the realization thereof, may play a balancing role vis-à-vis the state but, as we will see, ought not be able to achieve hegemony. Taken together, the ways in which Foucault positioned himself in the above-mentioned contexts indicate that he had a somewhat positive view of the historical moment of division between state and civil society, which had characterized certain streams of Enlightenment philosophy (Fine 1997).

Ian Hunter (1998, 260) distinguished between two broad paradigms in German thought concerned with the emergence of civil society: the first views civil society as the outcome of "the social delimitation of the state," the second as the outcome of the "political neutralization of confessional society." These paradigms are "partly disciplinary and methodological": the first broadly sociological, the latter political-scientific and jurisprudential (261). The first, typified by Jürgen Habermas, is "theoretical and ethical," and "the sociology of civil society tends to see it in terms of a progressive dialectic between social forces and moral imperatives." The second, displayed by Reinhardt Koselleck and Carl Schmitt, is a more disenchanted, empirical political-juridical account in which civil society is "seen as the by-product of political pacification." Hunter then proceeds, surprisingly, to locate Foucault's genealogy of liberal government in the ethical-sociological paradigm—that is, within the first model rather than the second. This paradigm takes a denaturalizing approach to civil society informed by a social constructivist ontology. Here, civil society does not refer to any permanent object but rather to a series of normative principles concerning its self-organization and ability to contribute to the integration of modern society. Thus, its foremost ethical-sociological advocates stress that a viable civil society exists only insofar as certain communicative procedures and institutional-legal standards prevail.

At the time of his writing, Hunter had only the single lecture on governmentality, not the entirety of the 1978 and 1979 lectures; nevertheless, we find the distinction useful. There *do* appear to be elements of both stances in Foucault's discussions of civil society in the 1970s. We will return to the other side of the equation in Chapter 9. But given Foucault's discussion of the critical ethos of Enlightenment, value-orientation toward nonrepresentational local knowledge and anti-institutional struggles, and thematization of his relation to social movements and forces, Hunter's initial characterization remains most apt. The commentaries on Foucault, and texts by him considered in this chapter, would appear to confirm the view that he positively valorized civil society against the state.

Crucially, this valorization of civil society as the locus or force for the critique, limitation, overcoming, or transformation of the state is in evidence when Foucault comments on current political uprisings and displays his own political passions. In October 1978 in his journalism on the Iranian Revolution, he would cite the role of Islam as a force within Persian society against the state. It was "a religion that throughout the centuries never ceased to give irreducible strength to everything from the depths of a people that can oppose state power" (Foucault 2005, 203). Similarly, four years later, in commenting on the Polish situation, he would speak about the "dislocation of society" in Poland and agree that what was happening was the "moral awakening of a whole society" (MSP, 468). Finally, even in contemporary France after the election of the Socialists in 1981, he commends them for grasping the reality that "for a good twenty years, a series of questions have been raised in society itself" (IT, 454). In each case it is "society itself" that generates the political spirituality, the political awakening, and the moral questioning that will lead to political change.

Against this image of Foucault as a thinker of civil society, however, can be placed a strain of deep skepticism, which views the presence of power relations across the social body as indicative of its treacherous and even blood-soaked nature.

EXCURSUS: FOUCAULT AGAINST CIVIL SOCIETY

If Foucault viewed civil society as the outcome of the "social delimitation of the state," as Ian Hunter maintained, then he must have claimed a certain privilege or virtue for it. But certain attentive readers have noted that Foucault often displays a profound distrust of the social ties and mechanisms of civil society. Colin Gordon (1996) pointed out that Foucault's reception in Britain was dominated by disappointment among Left intellectuals because he refused to take the side of society against the state. According to Gordon, Foucault refused to accept the idea that inherent within civil society is a principle of good that is capable of countering the evils of the state. In Gordon's opinion it is possible to read in Foucault "a conception of power, outlined here and there, in which all are in virtual conflict with all; an acute sensitivity to contemporary residues and recurrences in French society of the Pétainist collaboration; a clear refusal, finally, to recognize in civil society—as defined by Left or Right—a principle of good opposable to the evil of the State" (263). Gordon claims that Foucault's attitude toward civil society actually offended "English-speaking moralists." Foucault's position, however, was not one of contempt but of constant vigilance and profound distrust of social ties.

We can consider Foucault's long-standing interest in denunciation as a social practice, a theme running from *History of Madness* to his governmentality lectures. In particular, he made reference to the notorious *lettres de cachet*, the system under the *ancien régime* whereby family members could appeal to the sovereign to have their disorderly and disreputable members removed and interned in one form or another. These strangely obsequious and grandiloquent appeals, with their mixture of formality and rage, are addressed in "Lives of Infamous Men," published in 1977, which Foucault wrote as an introduction to an anthology about the prison archives from the *hôpitaux généraux* and the Bastille (LIM, 157–75; Gordon 1996, 263–64). They form an episode, together with case files and petitions, in the history of denunciation and its mechanisms of recording and provide an oblique view of apparently minor episodes of "small" people who were charged with various petty crimes, morally offensive behavior, and malicious intent.

Foucault uses the *lettres de cachet* to illustrate the transition in the seventeenth and eighteenth centuries from the control of the deviant and the sinful through a religious discourse—not least through the requirement for confession—to the establishment of a modern network of monitoring, internment, and penalties for those who presented minor offences and deviations. Their practice stands as a kind of transitional episode in this movement. As transitional, it was not yet like the "fine, differentiated, continuous, network" of disciplinary normalization; however, like the latter it was indeed "power exercised at the level of everyday life" (LIM, 171–72).

In regard to the system of the *ancien régime* we would like to highlight one element that plays a central role in Foucault's analysis: it is agents on the lowest social level that carry out and, in many cases, actively initiate the exclusion and confinement of neighbors, family members, or others in their own circle by petitioning the king. The king's sovereign exercise of power was orchestrated as if it were an act of his own will, but in reality it was often a response to petitions "from below," from the people. Foucault explains:

> Except in the rarest of cases, the "king's orders" did not strike without warning, crashing down from above as signs of the monarch's anger. More often than not,

they were requested against someone by his entourage—his father and mother, one of his relatives, his family, his sons or daughters, his neighbors, the local priest on occasion, or some notable. The *lettre de cachet* that was presented as the express and particular will of the king to have one of his subjects confined, outside the channels of regular justice, was nothing more than the response to such petitions coming from below. (LIM, 167)

Foucault describes the petitions submitted by ordinary people as being written in a comically formal and clumsily expressed language addressed to a majestic power that often jarred with the insignificant violations they wished to see punished. If the petitions receive royal assent, these warrants, the *lettres de cachet* themselves, would be issued, which entailed that the wrongdoer was sentenced, without trial or defense, to imprisonment, to the custody of a monastery or a general hospital, or to deportation to the colonies. In this way Foucault thus identifies how the transcendent power of the king could be integrated into an immanent field of micropower. The sovereign power of absolutism could be mobilized to impose itself on even the most intimate of social relationships, and at ordinary people's own request: "It often happened that the petitions for internment were lodged by illiterate or semiliterate persons of humble circumstance; they themselves, with their meager skills, or an underqualified scribe in their place, would compose as best they could the formulas or turns of phrase they believed to be required when one addressed the king or high officials, and they would stir in words that were awkward and violent, loutish expressions by which they hoped no doubt to give their petitions more force and truthfulness" (LIM, 170).

Here the exercise of sovereign power entailed that "the resources of an absolutist political power, beyond the traditional weapons of authority and submission, could be brought into play between subject and subject, sometimes the most humble of them, between family members and between neighbors" (LIM, 168). Notably, then, the king's power in such issues only struck down people who were already victims of marginalization by their own social group. The sovereign power would merely execute a marginalization that was secondary, as it were, to the first-degree exclusion from local social relations. As Foucault put it elsewhere: "It was as if the individual was told, 'Since you separated yourself from your group, we are going to separate you definitely or temporarily from society'" (TJF, 78).

In his description of this system of petitions Foucault shows that the king's power did not radiate downward as a symbol of his transcendent authority.

Perhaps Deleuze was right to suggest that this power was integrated into an immanent field of micropower relations; it could be solicited, he suggested, "like an immanent public service" for settling quarrels like family disputes (2006, 25). In this context Foucault's well-known dictum that the ruler—monarch or state—only governs on the basis of relations of micropower certainly takes on a quite sinister meaning. This text is not unique in Foucault's work. In his major books—*History of Madness* (2006, 47, 125, 420) and *Discipline and Punish* (1977, 214)—we find a parallel attention to how ordinary people act to eliminate "abnormals" and offenders of morality particularly through such everyday practices of denunciation.

The existence of practices of surveillance, control, and sanctioning arising from "below" in the social body was further extensively described by Foucault in his 1974 Rio lectures, "Truth and Juridical Forms" (TJF, 1–90). There, Foucault explored how in eighteenth-century England and France, a series of mechanisms for minuscule and continuous control of mostly ordinary individuals emerged "in an obscure fashion" (59–60). The obscurity of this emergence denotes the fact that, particularly in England, the control mechanisms arose locally and independently, outside the state-regulated judicial system: "There formed, at relatively low levels of the social scale, spontaneous groups of persons who assigned themselves, without any delegation from a higher authority, the task of maintaining order and of creating new instruments for ensuring order, for their own purposes" (60). In this context Foucault demonstrated that "panopticism" and disciplinarity, conventionally associated with state institutions (schools, barracks, prisons, hospitals), gradually emerged in religious communities, moral societies, and self-defense groups. These groups exerted petty moralism, minor prohibitions, and sanctioning of immoral conduct and hence established a kind of parajudicial surveillance and policing. In effect Foucault described how localized social domains, the *Gemeinshaft*, constituted the breeding ground for pioneers in policing mechanisms "from below" that would pave the way for the subsequent state-controlled apparatuses of order, hygiene, and discipline. Foucault's general narrative, which is repeated on many other occasions, tells us how techniques for intervening to modify and impose norms on human living were first invented in the context of local struggles and gradually taken up in state-administered biopolitics (e.g., Foucault 2003, 250; 2007b, 367). It is a narrative that explains power from below, with reference to contingencies, or intertwining passions, tactics, and accidents. Society becomes a breeding ground for *dispositifs* of legal and disciplinary power with an expansive reach.

In these studies of power mechanisms ascending from the interstices of the social body we begin to understand why constitutionalism was a problematic solution for Foucault. His uncovering of society as pervaded by relations of struggle and domination is at odds with theories of democratic politics and key tenets of representation and legitimate authority. Critical commentators have argued that Foucault's version of civil society is indeed a gloomy one. It is a site permeated with mutual surveillance where each is in virtual conflict with all. This turns on its head the notion of civil society as the privileged domain for democratic dialogue and instructive ethics, since it rather appears to be thoroughly imbued with microdisciplinary mechanisms, strategies of domination, and practices of social elimination of deviants. The classic cornerstones of democratic society, such as the autonomous individual capable of making voluntary commitments and forming associations, seem to be, for Foucault, merely utopian dreams of an escape from power. Emblematic of this critique are the critical theorists Jean Cohen and Andrew Arato, who give this characterization of Foucault's portrayal of civil society: "Autonomy is the illusion of the philosophy of the subject, voluntary consent is part of the deceptive juridical discourse, association (in our view, the truly modern dimension of sociality) is simply impossible in a society conceived of as a strategic field constituted . . . by disciplinary apparatuses" (1992, 295). Yet Foucault's suspicion of civil society actually goes deeper than this critique. It is not simply the composition of civil society through disciplinary mechanisms that is at stake; it is, at least in the example we have just cited, a view that civil society itself is riven with the petty jealousies, quarrels and vendettas, and social and familial exclusions that exist *prior* to being mobilized by the operation of sovereign power.

Foucault's excavation of regulatory mechanisms and laws in their inception resonates with his Nietzschean-inspired strategy of seeking the emergence of modern moralities not in lofty philosophy but in the "lowliest origins." These entail minuscule and infinite struggles for domination. Foucault discovers in Nietzsche a conception of genealogy as a resolute attack on any metaphysical idea of original and noble origins of what are merely messy historical accidents and incidents. In "Nietzsche, Genealogy, History" (NGH, 368–91) he emphasizes that genealogy must record the events in their singularity without reducing them to metahistorical principles, synthesizing logic, or the unfolding of a teleology. In place of complacent pursuit for the purity of origins that could reassure us of a continuous identity or permanent subject, genealogy locates events in the play of domination, secrecy, and deceit. In contrast to histories of the progress of humanism, functional integration of society, or natural evolution, the genealogist traces institutions, moralities, and laws to motley beginnings and hazardous and broken trajectories, pervaded by the will to dominate. It brings forth "a barbarous and shameful confusion" (381).

There is no doubt that Nietzsche's historicism left significant marks on Foucault's formulations on social morality, the political body, and constitutional institutions. But does the multiplicity of perpetually rivalrous forces ultimately mean that civil society can never transcend its unruly origins? Does it mean that the state can never make good its claim to universality and legitimacy by reference to the will of a people formed within this civil society? Or does it, on the contrary, prove the necessity of a law-governed constitutional state to bring order to such a space of confusion? Foucault's various meditations maintain striking ambiguities in respect to both civil society and the state.

CHAPTER 5

BLOOD-DRIED CODES

Michel Foucault addresses the key themes of conventional political philosophy most closely in his 1976 lecture series published later as *"Society Must Be Defended": Lectures at the Collège de France, 1975–76* (2003). In particular, he offers a rather blunt approach to the claims of universality of the modern state. This lecture series has been commented on by scholars from many different perspectives, from Blandine Kriegel (1995) and Pasquale Pasquino (1993) to Ann Laura Stoler (1995) and Alain Badiou (2012), resulting in quite diverse interpretations. It is certainly the locus of provocative, if not controversial, propositions in a way that contrasts with Foucault's more "prudent" governmentality lectures two years later. There is his renowned inversion of Clausewitz's dictum so that "politics is the continuation of war by other means" (Foucault 2003, 16). Crucially, this is a war between two parties, which brings him very close to the Schmittian version of the political as defined by the friend-enemy relationship. Then there is the account of genealogy as the union of scholarly erudition with the "insurrection" of local, disqualified, subjugated knowledges (7–9). Foucault tends to identify scientific, theoretical, and "totalizing" knowledge with a regime of power focused on the state. At its conclusion we find the claim that the murderous, suicidal, and genocidal "play between the sovereign right to kill and the mechanisms of biopower" that is taken by Nazism to a "paroxysmal point . . . is in fact inscribed in the workings of all States" (260). This is an astonishing claim and perhaps stands as the apotheosis of his antistatism. In a final coda he insists that "socialism was a racism from the outset" (260), particularly when it is conceived as an outcome or stake of the class struggle and its binary political logic.

Around the time of these lectures Foucault believed he was facing demands from critics who urged him to raise his previous institutional analysis to a more general level and to theorize the role of the state. In a roundtable published in 1977, he remarked in respect to historians' irritation with his methods: "How do you deal with the state? What theory do you offer us of the state? Some say I neglect its role, others that I see it everywhere" (QM, 237). In the introduction to the 1976 lectures he described his work in the previous years, with apparent dissatisfaction, as fragmented pieces of research that never formed themselves into a coherent body of work. He believed he had studied the rise of knowledge and power about insanity, psychiatry, and criminality without integrating his insights into an overall framework: "It's all repetitive, and doesn't add up" (Foucault 2003, 4).

Despite such self-criticism Foucault never fulfilled the demand for theorizing the role of the state. In fact, he rejected the idea of giving his previous "genealogical fragments" a "theoretical crown" (2003, 12). Instead, he spends considerable time during the first lectures explicating the problems of uniform and unifying theorizing, including state theory. He inverted the usual deductive theoretical approach by moving from genealogical singularities upward to theoretical unity, as Badiou (2012, 92) observes. Indeed, Foucault seemed to suggest a certain continuity in marginal forms of knowledge: between local knowledge of contemporary struggles against power such as in prisons and in psychiatry and the "buried scholarly knowledge" of the past (2003, 8). This continuity unexpectedly connects radical activists producing "counter-knowledge" at the social margins with the "counter-discourse" of the reactionary French nobility like Henri de Boulainvilliers who wrote to defend a privileged aristocracy against the "establishment of the great absolute-administrative monarchy" (Foucault 2003, 49).

Here, we foreground two central themes in the lectures. First, we examine Foucault's description of the transformation of the state from the perspective of "race wars," struggles between rival groups for capturing state power, to a modern state that wages war in the pursuit of internal purification. This transformation corresponds to a sovereign state power that will no longer be guaranteed by "magico-juridical rituals, but by medico-normalizing techniques" (Foucault 2003, 81). Two possible pathways emerge from this process. The first is of a state-centered, utopian, and totalizing biopolitics manifest at its worst by Soviet-style socialism and National Socialism; the second is of a medical normalization found in advanced, liberal welfare states.

Second, we will examine the *form* of Foucault's decentering of the state in these lectures. In Chapter 6 we suggest that Foucault will undertake a decentering of the state into a plurality of administrative rationalities and governmental apparatuses in his 1978 lectures. In 1976 he seeks to dissolve the unity of the state into a multiplicity of political forces. By aligning himself with a political historicism that approached state universality as a question of writing up victorious narratives of the nation, Foucault forges a link to the key themes of neo- and post-Marxist political theory, particularly its focus on the process of hegemony through the discursive construction of identities. By this move the transcendence of the political constituency, "the people," is rendered immanent. The binding of "the nation" or "the people" to the state is turned into a contingent and inherently dangerous accomplishment. These are indeed among the many stumbling blocks to reading Foucault as a proponent of the juridical state and the kind of sovereignty first manifest in absolutism.

Constitutionalism and the War of All Against All

For Foucault the model of sovereignty, largely identified with his idiosyncratic reading of Thomas Hobbes's *Leviathan*, established a break in political discourse that was both temporal and spatial. Implicit in this model was the relegation of war to either the premodern and the barbarian, which was symbolized by the state of nature and its war of all against all, or displaced to the outside of the civilized spaces of the modern territorial state. Throughout the Middle Ages and until the beginning of the modern era, he says, the practices of war underwent a fundamental change:

> The State acquired a monopoly on war. The immediate effects of the State monopoly was that what might be called day-to-day warfare, and what was actually called "private warfare," was eradicated from the social body, and from relations among men and relation among groups. Increasingly, wars, the practices of war, and the institutions of war tended to exist, so to speak, only on the frontiers, on the outer limits of the great State units, and only as a violent relationship between States. But gradually the entire social body was cleansed of the bellicose relations that had permeated it through and through during the Middle Ages. (2003, 48)

These spatiotemporal domains of war of all against all thus served as the negative other of a modern politics that promised to finally subsume power relations under an overarching, reconciliatory sovereignty. Foucault's conceptual provocations targeted precisely this juridical-political model of a transcendent, centralized, territorial power.

This is where Clausewitz's famous aphorism comes in: "war is the continuation of politics by other means." Foucault's citation of Clausewitz has often been presented as if Foucault inverted the principle to say that "politics is the continuation of war by other means," thus implying that war relations never actually disappeared from politics. But what Foucault actually did was to identify a forgotten discourse of "politics as war," which preceded Clausewitz and which Foucault reappropriated (Neal 2004, 379). Hence, Foucault tells his audience that it was Clausewitz who inverted an earlier political discourse that is the principal object of his interest: "Now I think that the problem is not so much who inverted Clausewitz's principle as it is the question of the principle Clausewitz inverted, or rather of who formulated the principle Clausewitz inverted when he said: 'But, after all, war is no more than a continuation of politics'" (2003, 48). Thus Clausewitz is in fact not at the center of Foucault's interest. That interest, rather, is for this longer-term conception of politics as a form of war.

Foucault is certainly not trying to establish a political-constitutional theory for himself. In the discourse of politics as war Foucault attempts to undermine the neat, dualistic schematic of premodern, barbarian, and external war of all against all and the modern subordination of war to juridical sovereignty under the carapace of the territorial state. His enthusiasm for perpetual war as a prism for understanding politics was an attempt to find a position to address critically the problems of state universality, legitimacy, and sovereignty without at the same time subscribing to conventional political theory, with its dualities of sovereign versus subjects and coercion versus consent.

This analytical testing, which Foucault admitted to be experimental, has been viewed as an attempt to arrive at a more adequate way of thinking about political power and the formation of statehood (Kelly 2009, 55–57). There is certainly some justification for such an interpretation. Hence, at the end of the first lecture of this series, Foucault states that he will study whether the schematic of war can be identified as "the basis of civil society" conceived as "the principle and motor of the exercise of political power." He poses the problem thus: "Are we really talking about war when we analyze the workings of power? Are the notions of 'tactics,' 'strategy,' and relations of force valid? To what extent are they valid? Is power quite simply a continuation of war by means other than weapons and battles?" (2003, 18).

We wish to underline that rather than adopting a certain model of analysis of state and politics, Foucault practices a kind of pragmatic perspectivism. As in other cases, he wants to test out the resources available in the war model for a critical description of political power struggles. Foucault's guiding question here might therefore be, "What will happen if I analyze political struggles and state formation through the vocabulary of war?" In the first instance this perspectivist strategy stems from the fact that Foucault himself did not claim to provide a more satisfying, or ultimately correct, theory of political power. Instead, he mobilized a preexisting discourse to "perform" the critique by recovering more or less marginal historical writers on race war and state sovereignty. The decisive issue for Foucault is not whether these historical writers represent social struggles, oppressed people, or historical events in a truthful manner, nor is it whether they can claim historical veracity. Rather, for Foucault, the historical writers of the nobility are important insofar as they provide an alternative "grid of intelligibility" for understanding politics, national identity, and state universality: "According to Boulainvilliers, it is war that makes society intelligible, and I think that the same can be said of all historical discourse. When I speak of a grid of intelligibility, I am obviously not saying that what Boulainvilliers said was true" (2003, 163).

What Foucault calls "the historical-political discourse" or "political historicism" develops in the sixteenth and seventeenth centuries as a counterdiscourse to the model of juridical sovereignty (2003, 111). He investigates its two variants: the first in England at the time of the bourgeois revolution, the second in France around the establishment of the absolute-administrative monarchy from the late seventeenth century (2003, 49). Political historicism hence emerges among the Puritans, the Levellers and the Diggers in England, and the writings of Edward Coke and John Lilburne in the seventeenth century; it is also found among French aristocrats, such as Henri Boulainvilliers and the count Buat-Nançay, who fought the absolute monarchy in the eighteenth century. After the discussion of the "Third Estate" by Emmanuel-Joseph Sieyès proclaimed the universality of the bourgeoisie to lead the nation, the same discourse was taken by up by late nineteenth-century historians, who associated it with class struggle, on the one hand, and biological conceptions of race, on the other. While Foucault is concerned to offer a subtle genealogy of political-historical writing, he emphasizes key points that unite these authors: they radically challenge the idea of a society at peace and a final reconciliatory order paradigmatically represented by the heroic law-bringer of the territorial state and its theoretical champion, Thomas Hobbes.

The Buried Discourse of Race Wars

When reading Foucault's lectures, one sometimes wonders about his evaluation of the political claims or the critical efficacy of the sources he reads. Yet in the case of the early writers on "race wars" we are left with no doubt about Foucault's sympathy: "Well, next time I would like to trace the history of this discourse of political historicism and praise it" (2003, 111). It should be noted that in this context *race* does not designate a specific biological entity but rather a historical-discursive strategy for narrating the perspective of one group against another engaged in conquests, usurpations, and ongoing power struggles. *Race* has a kind of heterogeneity in this discourse. The war of the races appeals to "ethnic differences, differences between languages, different degrees of force, vigor, and energy, and violence, the differences between savagery and barbarism, the conquest and subjugation of one race by another" (60).

A first reason for his praise is that Foucault finds in the discourse of race wars certain resonances with what he regards as urgent political problems in his own present, where the "capillary" mechanisms of domination were buried under the state's formal legality and apparently representative institutions. This discourse directs us to examine petty social struggles played out *beneath* the formal constitution, for instance, around police brutality, both in the prison system and in the treatment of illegal immigrants.

Conceptually, the historical-political discourse is praiseworthy for Foucault in that it breaks with the juridical-philosophical discourse centered on truth and justice that has characterized Western political thought since the first Greek philosophers. This latter discourse is about how a universal order can be legitimized that rises above partisan groups and subjects them all to a conciliatory sovereignty. By contrast, historical-political discourse is "historically rooted" and "politically decentered," insofar as it claims the truth for a specific group and from a specific perspective and demands rights for this group on the basis of historically contingent relationships among rival political forces.

The main point of Foucault's attention to texts about "race wars," however, is that he rediscovers a forgotten discourse beneath the claims of universalization by the state. More precisely, it is a discourse that seeks to demonstrate how social struggles, domination, and temporarily frozen conflicts are concealed beneath the apparent naturalness and functional necessity ascribed to the state, its institutions, and its laws. In these texts society is not governed by natural laws, inherited legitimate hierarchies, or functional mechanisms but by warring forces and their random, perpetual interplay throughout history: "And beneath the lapses of memory, the illusions, and the lies that would have us to believe that there is a ternary order, a pyramid of subordinations, beneath the lies that would have us believe that the social body is governed by either natural necessities or functional demands, we must rediscover the war that is still going on, war with all its accidents and incidents" (2003, 51). The ternary, pyramidal structure of the state covers over, and arises from, the binary structure of the division of society into two opposing camps.

In this regard the term *subjugated knowledge* should not be understood as if it were marginalized and underprivileged groups who used the historical-political discourse as weapons of social struggle. In fact, an example of subjugated knowledge in Foucault's sense would be the writing of history by members of the French nobility. Foucault examines how they used history as a means of struggle against the idea of the king as supreme and as constitutive of the whole nation, and how the king became a weapon for specific groups in their conflict with each other. The nobility redefined the concept of "nation" to show that "beneath the formal facade of the State, there were other forces and that they were precisely not forces of the State, but the forces of a particular group with its own history, its own relationship with the past, its own victories, its own blood, and its own relations of domination" (2003, 224). Thus, those engaged in historical-political discourse do not claim to take up the position of a universal legislator or stand as representative of eternal truth. Nor do they claim to be able to abolish social asymmetries. Rather, they admit that they try to use the truth as a weapon in a battle between conflicting interpretations in order to secure singular rights—namely, their own. Hence, Boulainvilliers wrote to interrupt the ritual reinforcement of the sovereignty of the monarch by means of counterdiscourse. The importance of this counterdiscourse for Foucault lies in the fact that it does not invoke fundamental and stable principles in history and does not claim that history has a final truth or terminus. It investigates the immanent plane of actual battles, struggles, and victories.

Foucault repeatedly emphasizes that any historiography is inevitably political, as it has tactical effects in its contemporary time and context. He is enthusiastic about the recognition by political historicism that it is, in itself, unavoidably political and an active player in contemporary struggles around the state and, later, around its claims to universality. For Foucault such a historian is aware that any history of the state partakes in a discursive battle, since it is a matter of narrating the state's history, accounting for a particular group's righteous victory, and thereby proving the legitimacy of the existing political order (52–54, 164). The historical-political writers take as their premise that history has no final goal, since they discover "beneath the stability of the law or the truth, the indefiniteness of history" (56). This indefiniteness is characterized by a series of contingencies: defeats, victories, passions, violence, envy, bitterness, courage, anxiety, forgetfulness, and all the coincidences and minor incidents that create victories and defeats. History is not merely about reporting struggle but functions as a weapon itself, both in times of contention and during peacetime. Hence, the scribe who writes the state's history inevitably becomes a warrior in the discursive struggles over power. The speaking subject is hence "a subject who is fighting a war" (54).

It is hard to ignore the resonance of Nietzsche in Foucault's reading of the political-historical discourse. This is evident in the basic premise of a "war between two races" and the idea that underneath respectable juridical theories we find a plane of emergence pervaded by the clash of forces. A comparison between Foucault's essay "Nietzsche, Genealogy, History" from 1971 and the 1976 lectures brings out evident parallels, especially around the distinction between the purity and continuity of origin (*Ursprung*) and the impurity, invasions, and takeovers found in descent or provenance (*Herkunft*) and emergence (*Entstehung*) (cf. Marks 2000, 130–33). In this sense Foucault reads the political-historical discourse as the ignoble paternity, rather than the pure source, of universal claims and values. Here, we merely wish to foreground the attack on political theory that comes from Foucault's rather explicit Nietzschean reading of the "race war" writers. The key parallel is Foucault's insistence that the universal values of freedom and justice do not reconcile opposing forces but arise from their rude and violent conflicts and, once established, continue to serve as tools in a permanent struggle for domination. In the essay on Nietzsche, Foucault had written: "Humanity does not gradually progress from combat to combat until it arrives at universal reciprocity, where the rule of law finally replaces warfare; humanity installs each of its violences in a system of rules and thus proceeds from domination to domination" (NGH, 378).

In Foucault's account of historical-political discourse, as far as politics and law are rooted in specific historical events and victories, there is by necessity talk of singular, temporarily forged rights, not universal rights (2003, 52). Boulainvilliers wrote that freedom can only be seized at the expense of others' freedom. Foucault reads Nietzsche as saying that "the concept of liberty is an 'invention of the ruling classes'" (NGH, 371). Linking the fundamental category of battle with historicism, Foucault says: "There is no escape from domination and there is therefore no escape from history" (2003, 111). Read through Nietzschean genealogy, the fundamental premise of political historicism becomes the insight that humankind moves from one state of domination to another and that all versions of the state are simply that, a state of domination. The difference between the two accounts is merely one of focus. In the essay on Nietzsche, Foucault was principally concerned with mobilizing "effective history" to undermine the European idea of a unified, constitutive identity. In his 1976 lectures the discovery of political historicism makes possible an undermining of the constitution of the state by rendering its universalism the outcome of contingent struggles and impossible totalizations. These lectures are very close to Nietzsche's genealogy. They argue that the universal claims of the liberal state to ensure freedom and protect rights were themselves the product of a mutation in historical discourse, having its roots in the resentments of the dispossessed aristocrat or the aims of popular struggles, and that it was these very claims that made possible the historical narratives of human emancipation or racial purity found in Marxism and fascism.

Viewing State-Formation as Hegemony

In *"Society Must Be Defended"* Foucault uses the writers on race wars to display an image of state formation as resulting from particular groups' more or less successful claims on the state. However, he regards Abbé Sieyès's famous and influential tract "What Is the Third Estate?"—written on the eve of the French Revolution—as an exemplar of the emergence of a new, if not modern, notion of universality (Foucault 2003, 217–26). For Foucault, Sieyès departs from the historians of the race wars in that he is no longer simply concerned to decompose the state into its warring factions and the multiple truths of their respective claims in the face of existing forms of domination. Instead of a fundamentally antagonistic relation between one group and another, Sieyès offers a historical account of the relation between nation and state in France. In it, Foucault recounts (2003, 219), the members of the Third Estate (that is, the people as opposed to the clergy and the aristocracy) already effectively occupy all the key "functions"—juridical, administrative, and military—within the state and make it possible for the state to exist by their "works," including crafts, commerce, and agriculture. Having achieved this, they are in a position to accede to the universality of a state (219). Foucault thus adds a layer of complexity to the history of race war. While Sieyès admits that they are one estate among others, this emergent "people" become the only group "capable of constituting a State, and the actual existence of the State itself" (Foucault 2003, 223).

Historical discourse, for Foucault, moves from an argument about the past, and a conception of right rooted in the distant past, to one about immediate future potentiality and a claim to universal right. Under this new, national discourse, he observes, what "defines a nation is not its archaism, its ancestral nature, or its relationship with the past; it is its relationship with something else, with the State" (Foucault 2003, 223). War begins to lose its centrality, and what is central is civil struggle. Now, military struggles will be no more than a moment within this civil struggle, perhaps even its exception or crisis (225). In sum, rather than the cycle of revolution and reconstitution, Foucault concludes, "the decisive moment is the transition from the virtual to the real, the transition from the national totality to the universality of the State" (224).

Historians, both of reactionary and liberal persuasion, will henceforth have to deal with the historical claim to universality. On the aristocratic right, according to Foucault (2003, 229–33), a figure like Montlosier will trace the coming to power of the popular classes as a long-term consequence of the king's appropriation of the nobility's economic and political power. Sovereign power, he claimed, created the people. "The people is therefore the heir, and the legitimate heir of the kings; it is simply completing the work of the sovereigns who preceded it," as Foucault puts it (229). In this sense the reactionary aristocrats tried to link the new bourgeois discourse on universality with the older historicism in their fight against monarchical despotism. Against them, liberal bourgeois historians, like Augustin Thierry, begin to view the present as a "moment of fullness," as Foucault cites him (233), in which the directionality of history is realized: "Universalization therefore began not with a relationship of domination that gradually swung completely in its favor, but with the fact that all the constituent elements of the State were born of it, were in its hands or had come into its hands" (235). In this liberal discourse a war sometimes continued, Foucault demonstrates, but it was not between two historically originary sides, such as the Franks and the Gauls, or between a Roman model and a Gaulish model, but "between right and freedom on one side, and debt and wealth on the other" (234). Foucault thus concludes that it is only with the bourgeoisie's appropriation of the historical discourses of race war that historical narrative is capable of superseding binary oppositions and achieves the possibility of a new kind of universality rooted not in the memory of a distant, authentic claim but in the direction of history itself. A kind of overlap occurs between history and philosophy, when both ask the same questions about the nature of the present as agent and truth of the universal: "What is it, in the present, that is the agent of the universal? What is it, in the present, that is the truth of the universal?" (237). Foucault draws a wry conclusion: "The dialectic is born" (237).

In this analysis of the transformation of political historicism into the philosophy of history Foucault addresses the well-known paradox of state universality—that any universalizing erection of the state's legal and constitutional order is inevitably based on a singular project originating from a particular group. This paradox is highlighted in the recognition that the codes that specify universal civil rights are necessarily rooted in specific social and historical conceptions. In other words, at least since the French Revolution the state has been rendered the contingent outcome of strategies that seek to universalize particular identities. Thereby Foucault moves close to theories that perceive state-formation as a perpetual struggle around identification in which hegemony becomes enshrined and reproduced in the state's institutional order. Reading the historical-political discourse leads Foucault to indicate the conditions by which it becomes possible to think about the interconnections between state sovereignty and social classes and the claims to be able to form both national identity and the institutions on which it rests.

By tracing the genealogy of political histories, Foucault thus discovers an insight similar to that found much later in neo-Marxist theory: political mobilization rests on a striving for unification and universalization of social identity. While political-historicist writers display a robust appreciation of the relationship between historical truth and partisanship, liberal bourgeois thinkers display basic discursive tactics that claim universality by means of a historical truth. This analysis of the way the bourgeois domination and liberal state is justified by its capacity for universality resonates with the premises of neo-Gramscian theorists such as Ernesto Laclau (1996, 2000).

The noble history of Boulainvilliers revealed that the king and his administration achieved domination through narratives of their rightful heritage and glorious past at the expense of the progressive marginalization of the aristocrats who had in fact unified and established the nation through war. The victors in a long internal battle thus use a rationality developed around historical justifications and mythical accounts of the past, which, as it develops, becomes more and more abstract and idealized. Foucault explains that this is "a fragile rationality, a transitory rationality which is always compromised and bound up with illusion and wickedness" (2003, 55). The group that benefits from the discursive and institutional victory that it has won hopes to silence any questioning of the contingent, blood-sealed, and transitory nature of this order: "This is, then, a rationality which, as we move upwards and as it develops, will basically be more and more abstract, more and more bound up with fragility and illusions, and also more closely bound up with the cunning and wickedness of those who have won a temporary victory. And given that the relationship of domination works to their advantage, it is certainly not in their interest to call any of this into question" (55). In Foucault's reading, then, the historical-political writers recognize that when one group succeeds in proclaiming the truth and silencing the imminent potential for discord, a conception of the nation will emerge that becomes increasingly illusionary, transitory, and fragile, based as it is on cruel exclusions and forgetfulness. What seems to be at stake here is the impossible representation of the particular in the universal. The act of championing the cause of the nobles against the king reveals the fundamental contingency and belligerence that the latter's claim to public right conceals.

According to the neo-Marxist discourse theory of Ernesto Laclau (1996), strategies for universalization require an abstract signifier to rally and unify diverse particular identities. In this context Foucault's analysis examines liberal bourgeois projects that seek to fix, or hegemonize, an idea of who constitutes "the nation." This idea was articulated in the shape of a signifier that had a rather indeterminate nature—such as "the rights of man and citizen"—made possible owing to the coming to power of the bourgeoisie and underlined by its historical potentiality.

For Laclau hegemony is construed through the elevation of a particular signifier, a "nodal point," through a process in which its specific signification and social origin are cancelled out: "The means of representation are . . . only the existing particularities. So, one of them has to assume the representation of the chain as a whole. This is a strictly hegemonic move: the body of one particularity assumes a function of universal representation" (Laclau 2000, 302–3). A hegemonic articulation, then, is one in which a particular signifier—the people, the nation, freedom, equality—articulates a series of elements into a unifying system of signifiers that may consolidate itself for a time. Any such attempt to manifest the universal must close itself off to remain hegemonic, and it must conceal its particularistic class origin and cynicism to prevent itself from being challenged. While the counterhistories of the nobles of the seventeenth and eighteenth centuries did not hide their perspectivism, Foucault shows how the liberal philosophy of history sought to cover the particularity of bourgeois accession to state power with the truth of a history revealed in the present.

Although the relationship between Foucault and neo-Gramscian political theory has been discussed before (Smart 1983; Clegg 2001; Bevir 2011), it has not been discussed specifically in relation to these lectures. The immediate parallels between Foucault's rendering of the development of political historicism and the neo-Gramscian problematic of hegemony are striking insofar as they both assume the nature of identity to be contingent on discursive practices. Indeed, Foucault's search for a political intelligibility that would be antinaturalistic, antieconomistic, and antijuridical is echoed by neo-Gramscian theory. They both also share a rejection of a class-foundational account. The implication would be that once class is dispelled as a fundamental category, hegemony is dislodged from class analysis and becomes identified with any discursive fixity or fixation of a chain of signification. Laclau thus radicalized Marxism in an "antifoundationalist" direction by rejecting the privilege of economic relations and social class over discursively constructed identities (cf. Bevir 2011, 85).

Foucault's genealogy of political historicism shares one fundamental move with post-Marxist discourse theory: the transcendent entity of "the nation" or "the people" is rendered immanent insofar as it becomes a set of fluctuating, antagonistic forces. Laclau's (1996, 89, 97) discourse theory conceives of identity formation, including state-making and nationalism, on the basis of his ontological claim of an inherent "structural undecidability" of the social. This claim paves the way for viewing the social as the unstable playground for hegemonic strategies that partially fix meaning. It becomes the field of ceaseless, discursive articulation, temporary fixation, and occasional sudden dislocations. Insofar as Foucault embraced the perspectivism of political historicism, he would adopt a view of the political field as similarly bereft of such foundations, including foundational social antagonisms. At the center would stand the construction of political identity viewed as resting on nothing more than ongoing, fragile, and always incomplete articulations of identities constructed in political struggle. The political historicism that Foucault identifies shares with Laclau's variant of theoretical neo-Marxism a conception of the body politic as a terrain of infinite competition between rival articulations. It also shares the implication that the domain of politics is one in which there exist no common interests that are not discursively constituted.

The price to be paid for the conceptual complexity of this antifoundational epistemology is the one taught by social theorists who still rely on some notion of social structure and material interest. Insofar as there are no structural or material positions constituted outside discursive practices, there can be no notion of identifiable objective interests. Moreover, in terms of the political effect of antifoundationalist analysis there is a risk of dissolving the possibility of any authority above and external to popular preferences. In Foucault's case this risk is aggravated by his Nietzschean historical ontology that refuses the question of the legitimacy of the legal-constitutional apparatus. For Foucault, as for Nietzsche, the very mechanism of safeguarding against the most extreme popular enthusiasms and strategies of domination is not only founded on the same partisan forces but also, hypocritically, claims to have overcome them.

Enemies Born in the State's Own Body

Foucault's analysis throughout *"Society Must Be Defended"* certainly foregrounds the perils of the modern universal state over its achievements. He demonstrates how, in the nineteenth century, the problem of sovereign power was gradually detached from the struggle between specific peoples and becomes instead a matter for the modern state. This happens along with the advent of modern biopolitics. From now on, says Foucault, sovereign power will no longer be exercised in the shape of "magico-juridical rituals" but rather by means of "medico-normalizing techniques" (2003, 81). Hence, fighting a "race war" fundamentally changes its meaning. It no longer entails using the state as a tool for the war waged by one "race" against another. Instead, we see the advent of a state racism, an "internal war," in which the state must defend society against elements internal to itself through continuous cleansing and normalization. The theme of "race war" is thus dislodged from the political-historical discourse and inserted into biological and medical discourse.

Foucault uses the term *biological* in a very broad sense. Discourses about the strength of the state do not need to be formulated in explicitly biological terms to be described as biologically racist. It is sufficient that the population is presented as a mass of forces threatened by external or internal elements and is assumed to grow stronger if these threats are eliminated (Kelly 2004, 61). Consequently, the race-war discourse mutates from designating disputes between rival social groups to the idea that society is "at war with itself," in the form of threatening enemies residing within it. Foucault paraphrases the voice of this emergent state-racist discourse: "It is no longer: 'We have to defend ourselves against society,' but 'We have to defend society against all the biological threats posed by the other race, the subrace, the counterrace that we are, despite ourselves, bringing into existence'" (2003, 61–62). In effect this war is less about coming to terms with external enemies or putting a lid on conflicts between internal groups or classes than about combating the threats that the state's population poses to itself. The modern state's juridical universality claims to overcome and contain social conflicts by extending civil, legal, and political rights to the members of its population (with historically varying but significant exclusions). Yet, at the same time, the formal legal subject is also a concrete living individual, fragmented into a multiplicity of deviations, pathologies, and behavioral dispositions that require analysis, expert intervention, and "normalization." The new biopolitical framework functions not through a mighty political sovereign but through various "experts," "managers," and "technicians." These carry out a normalization of society: "At this point, we have all those biological-racist discourses of degeneracy, but also all those institutions within the social body which make the discourse of race struggle function as a principle of exclusion and segregation and, ultimately, as a way of normalizing society" (61). Through these observations Foucault displays the modern welfare state's medical and correctional institutions as imbued with a genealogical lineage to state racism and the advent of biopolitical rationality. The modern strategy of medical cleansing and normalization can, of course, take many concrete forms and degrees of radicalization—from welfare-state planning and social engineering by governments to eugenics and Nazi extermination camps. Nonetheless, Foucault suggests that "state racism" is an intrinsic potential of the modern welfare state project: "we see the appearance of a State racism: a racism that society will direct against itself, against its own elements and its own products. This is the internal racism of permanent purification and it will become one of the basic dimensions of social normalization" (62).

In these lectures Foucault views all modern political rationalities as born with a seed of biopolitical state racism, articulated in National Socialism and fascism, and evident across variants of socialism and communism (2003, 258–63). Elsewhere, he refers to the two "pathological forms of power," fascism and Stalinism. Despite their historical specificity, however, they used many of the ideas and tools that characterize "our political rationality" (SP, 328). Thus universalist thinking seems indeed to be a double-edged sword for Foucault, and this ambiguity also pertains to the modern state as an institution. The moment when the state becomes universal, and is no longer a flexible instrument for one group's conflict with another, is the point at which the state's "warfare" against its internal enemies becomes more effective and finely meshed. At the same moment that the modern, universal state achieves a monopoly on violence and grants its citizens basic civil and social rights, there is the possibility of a war against the internal enemies of the body politic by a sovereign state power of hitherto unseen bureaucratic efficiency.

The Universal State as Virtuality

If we return from the "state-phobic" final pronouncements to the penultimate lecture in *"Society Must Be Defended,"* a more ambiguous understanding of state universality is revealed. Foucault uses a slightly different register for examining how war, as an analytical model for political processes, becomes replaced by the theme of national universality (2003, 215–19). Specifically, Foucault argues that the war metaphor began to disappear from the literature of the early nineteenth century, in the wake of the 1789 revolution in France. Hence, the advocates of the Third Estate did not proclaim the republic's legitimacy on the basis of a blood-sealed victory as did the nobility. The writers of the revolution changed the terms of the debate by a twofold assertion. First, they recognized that their state project was not rooted in a historically inherited right and that they, as a social group, were just one among many and therefore did not represent the totality of the social body. Second, however, they claimed that they were the best guarantors that state universality would be effectively established in a legitimate manner: "Perhaps we are not, in ourselves, the totality of the social body, but we are capable of guaranteeing the totalizing function of the State. We are capable of statist universality" (222). In this way they instituted a thus-far alien universalistic juridico-philosophical discourse.

With this discourse a transformed understanding of the character of the present emerges. In the old eighteenth-century historical-political discourse the present was always viewed as a moment of profound forgetfulness. More precisely, the present was understood to be permeated by a complex of shifts and alliances between rival forces that had rendered the fundamental and primitive state of war muddled (Foucault 2003, 227). The present was negatively valued because the objective was to awaken from or cure oneself of this forgetfulness. This would be a true violent reawakening. The political historicist notion of the truth of state universality, as revealed in the present, looks for inheritance, descent, and righteous victory in the past. It is a truth that points backward and identifies the social groups that have managed to forcibly establish themselves as representative of the universal in the contemporary state order (228). The aim was, in brief, to reawaken a consciousness of the past.

According to Foucault, however, in the new discourse of the first half of the nineteenth century the present was reinterpreted so that it came to positively define the moment at which the universal is instituted within concrete reality (2003, 227). Foucault discovers the beginning of this later problematic, the "striving toward the universality of the state" (225), in the French Revolution: "The demand will no longer be articulated in the name of a past right that was established by either a consensus, a victory, or an invasion. The demand can now be articulated in terms of a potentiality, a future, a future that is immediate" (222). We witness here the birth of the modern problematic of the universality of the state as a constant striving, an ideality that gives urgency to the present and future reality, not the past: "Once history is polarized around the nation/ State, virtuality/actuality, functional totality of the nation/real universality of the State, you can see clearly that the present becomes the fullest moment, the moment of the greatest intensity, the solemn moment when the universal makes its entry into the real" (227).

The theme of state universality as a virtuality to be actualized appears again in the 1979 lecture series The Birth of Biopolitics. At the beginning of these lectures Foucault emphasizes that modern reasoning about the state is characterized by its conception of the state as a permanently unfinished project, constantly in the process of realization: "The state is at once that which exists, but which does not yet exist enough" (2008, 4). In this perspective the state appears as a paradoxical object, since it is both the given structure within which one governs and the unreachable ideal-state always receding into the horizon. It is precisely both a present reality and a future ideality. Hence, modern state rationality is inherently transformative insofar as it seeks to realize the state's potentialities: "Raison d'État is precisely a practice, or rather the rationalization of a practice, which places itself between a state presented as given and a state presented as having to be constructed and built. The art of government must therefore fix its rules and rationalize its way of doing things by taking as its objective the bringing into being of what the state should be" (4). While the virtual is occupied by the nation in "Society Must Be Defended," however, in his governmentality lectures it will be preoccupied with different conceptions of the proper scope, objective, and form of government.

We will examine in greater detail the implications of this latter "reflexive prism" of the state's virtuality in Chapter 7. For the moment we note that while

Foucault shifts from a focus on the relation between nation and state to that of the relation between government and state, he continues to view the state less as a structure of institutions than as the more or less realized form of a virtual universality.

The State Must Be Defended?

Foucault does not draw out the possible progressive dimensions of the advent of the figure of the universalizing state. His pervasive reliance in 1976 on the category of battle impedes such a conclusion. Rather, he offers a twofold continuity based on the war lineage. On the one hand, there is the lineage between eighteenth-century political historicism's attack on sovereign right and the insurrection of subjugated knowledges and local struggles at the margins of the modern state. On the other hand, there is the continuum between the state racism of "pathological" regimes and the more mundane and less overtly bloody variants of a welfarist "normalizing society." This is a reading that does not allow an affirmative consideration of biopower in terms of the promotion of health, care, and protection. It is as if Foucault in 1976 has not fully discovered the positive, enabling dimension of biopolitics nor its sources in pastoral power. This biopolitical pastoral care for human life becomes visible, observes Sergei Prozorov (2007b, 55), when "the immanence of the life of the *population* is contrasted with the transcendent unity of the *people* as a collective sovereign" (emphasis in original). While it is in principle possible to establish such an affirmative investment in the concept of biopolitics from Foucault's 1976 lectures, his substantial analysis reads very differently.

This did not prevent Foucault's own student, Blandine Kriegel, from reading the textual archive and the 1976 lectures in a very different way. Kriegel's project was to confront what she viewed as the tendency of French academia to devalue law and state institutions. This project was initiated contemporaneously with Foucault's 1976 lectures and continued for some decades (Barret-Kriegel 1992). In her 1979 book, which would be translated into English nearly two decades later, Kriegel (1995, 12) lists Foucault among the few exceptions who have taken a positive approach in the history of political institutions, which "must still fight uphill battles against hostile attitudes." At the same time, however, she offers a novel understanding of key components of his analysis: sovereignty, law, biopolitics, and subjectification. In Kriegel's account juridical sovereignty is not a continuation of war, not even in its monarchical form. In fact, the advent of monarchical sovereignty in absolutism liberated individuals from the servitude and slavery of feudal Europe: "Feudalism is war, *jus vitae necisque*, conscription of human life; sovereign power is peace, security, and prohibition of the taking of human life" (24).

Kriegel also locates the advent of biopolitics somewhat earlier than Foucault with absolutism itself. She argues that modern sovereignty was already biopolitical at its inception. The sovereign power of the absolutist monarchies not only pacified their territories but also made the protection of the physical integrity and life of individuals their principal objective. Hence, absolute sovereignty "pacifies society, guarantees individual security, and makes life its chief aim. It is the product of a negotiation of rights rather than an expiation of arms" (Kriegel 1995, 40). This could almost be a direct response to Foucault: the sovereign state does not have blood dried in its constitutional codes but offers the protection of life itself. In an analytically similar (and political dissimilar) move to that of Giorgio Agamben's famous book *Homo Sacer* (1998), Kriegel perceived the origins of Foucault's biopolitics, or the power of life, in the emergence of sovereignty itself. But whereas Agamben critically mobilizes the "indistinction" between biopolitics and an ancient notion of sovereignty and its inclusion of "bare life" by its abandonment, Kriegel views absolutist sovereignty as the political innovation that offers the protection of individual corporeal or bare life. On this basis "early modern political philosophy gave birth to biopolitics by legitimating individual rights, security, and—at a later date—liberty, by subjecting the sovereign to the rule of law" (Kriegel 1995, 150). Sovereignty puts an end to the feudal "suzerainty," derived from the Roman *dominium*, which was in effect a "relation of subjection, in the manner of the relation between a master and a slave" (21). The absolutist state makes it possible to end this situation in which one individual's being, body and soul, can be owned or possessed by another.

Kriegel argued that the most ancient doctrine of individual right was not a child of the Revolution and the ensuing civic constitution but belonged to the absolutist state. She viewed this right as germane because it centered on personal security, emphasizing the protection of the body. Contra Foucault this power did not need to work through the constitution of subjectivities, through identities and their fabrication or "subjectification." Accordingly, the modern conception of rights does not rely on the philosophy of the subject that sprang from the modern techniques of discipline and biopolitical normalization and hence entailed a less invasive form of individualization. We see, then, that both Foucault and Kriegel would find the intellectual sources of modern state sovereignty around the time of the absolutist monarchy in France. If Foucault would use these sources to rescue counterdiscourses to juridical sovereignty in the territorial state and its claims to guarantee personal freedom, Kriegel would find the genuine roots of this protection in the very absolutism that Foucault's resurrected historians were writing fiercely against.

Kriegel's personal passage was one toward a republican statism that would appear to side with universalist political theory against Foucault's historical-political discourse. Foucault himself would soon move on from his admiration for such a discourse, although for a different passage. His detour through the problematic of war, political historicism, and the race war, indicates for Foucault one conclusion, almost diametrically opposite to Kriegel's. The modern territorial state and its claims to universality are particularly dangerous phenomena, not least when combined with modern, individualizing, and totalizing techniques of power. In 1976 such an observation throws the baby of political liberalism and democratic theory out with the statist bathwater. By 1979, however, Foucault had found a different kind of liberalism, this time economic, which would be more compatible with his radical antistatism and antihumanism.

CHAPTER 6

THE STATE OF IMMANENCE

In this and the following chapter we examine Foucault's well-known decentered approach to the state and institutions through the lens of his concept of the *dispositif*, which was further developed by Deleuze. By way of this development the concept was endowed with traces from Deleuze's neovitalist thought, principally foregrounding immanence over substance. Our question is, "What happens to state institutions when they become an unstable and contingent plane of immanence?" One answer is that the state and its institutions fail to appear as objects of analysis precisely because this perspective rejects the very possibility of supremacy within a particular domain, which is the defining feature of the concept of the state. Given Deleuze's influence on Hardt and Negri's and Rose's political thought, it is relevant to consider in detail the implications of it.

Scott Lash (2006, 324) observes that "contemporary neo-vitalism can in many respects be understood as Deleuzian." He situates Deleuze's seminal neovitalist philosophy within a broader intellectual stream of thought spanning philosophy, sociology, and the life sciences. What is distinctive for this stream of thought is the privilege granted to immanence over substance, multiplicity over unity, action over structure, contingency over necessity, and self-determination over external determination. Lash divides modern vitalism into two influential traditions that have distinct intellectual trajectories. On the one hand, there is a lineage from Gabriel Tarde to Henri Bergson and Deleuze; on the other hand, there is one running from Nietzsche through Georg Simmel to Foucault (Lash 2006, 324). The differences between these two intellectual trajectories are pertinent to our present concerns, especially with respect to their divergent conceptions of power and their different stances on the nature of ontological structure. The tradition of which Deleuze is representative foregrounds perception over ontology. It gives emphasis to power as relational capacity and disposition rather than a force of subjugation and the constraining of substance.

In this chapter we investigate what happens to political governance and institutions when they are relocated within this immanentist, relational, and productive framework of power. Our following analyses proceed as a reconstruction of the concept of the dispositif that has been developed from within the heritage of both Foucault and Deleuze. Hence, we read selected analysis by Foucault from the perspective of the dispositif. Our main concern is not to reestablish the precise connections and demarcations between Foucault and Deleuze; rather, we will consider what kind of approach to state governance and institutions emerges from the invigoration of Foucault's concepts by the Deleuzian vitalist epistemology. We do so by focusing on Foucault's thinking on institutions and dispositifs that is elaborated in different places during the mid-1970s and is most elaborated in the first three lectures of *Security, Territory, Population* in 1978 (2007b). We start with Foucault's "anti-institutional-centric" stance. We then examine how this stance emphasizes the "molecular" origins of institutions, privileges multiplicity over unity, and sees the ontology of objects of concern. During this examination we indicate how Foucault's decentered and anti-institutional position on the state resonates with characteristics of neovitalist epistemology. Finally, we explore how this stance locates social and political practices on what might be called a fractured plane of pure immanence.

While we have little doubt that Foucault's approach yields considerable local insights into regimes of government and their technologies and rationalities, there remains a question of whether these insights can substitute for the analysis of the history, concept, and institution of the state. Foucault famously wished to "cut off the king's head in political theory" and to produce an analysis outside the juridical-political framework of sovereignty. His work on the dispositifs is perhaps his most sophisticated attempt to do so and, as such, highlights the limitations as well as strengths of his approach to the state.

Anti-institutional Centrism

Foucault's pronouncement in a lecture in 1979 that he wished to do without a theory of the state as one "must forgo an indigestible meal" is well-known (2008, 77). We wonder, however, how digestible Foucault's smorgasbord of concepts and operations itself will prove to be. He also said that the state should not be viewed as a unified entity from which power radiates, principally by means of the law, sanctions, and prohibitions. For him the nature and functionality of the state should not be taken as a universal given, just as social practices should not be deduced from or referred back to the state as a centralized source of power. This is because the state has no defining interiority. "The state does not have an essence," said Foucault (77). "The state is not a universal nor in itself an autonomous source of power. . . . There is no question of deducing this set of practices from a supposed essence of the state in and for itself." By decentering the unity of the state, Foucault reapplied the anti-institutional position that he had pursued in *Security, Territory, Population*.

Here, Foucault states that he wishes to refrain from taking an institutional-centered approach in order to "go behind the institution" and situate it within a broader field of power relations, an overall "economy of power." This economy of power relations and its components are given various names by Foucault: *mechanisms, technologies*, and *dispositifs* are all used more or less interchangeably. They are broad-scale social strategies, "absolutely global projects" (Foucault 2007b, 117), such as public hygiene or correctional discipline, of which distinct institutions, such as the psychiatric hospital or the prison, are merely crystallizations. Foucault explains that he wishes to repeat his anti-institutional approach with regard to the state itself. Instead of conceiving of the state as a unified anchor point of power, or as composed of a set of distinct institutions, it should be decomposed into the multiple social strategies that gave birth to it and still saturate it. The state becomes, we will see, an immanent plane overridden by multiple, heterogeneous and often contradictory social propensities.

What unifies the range of "mechanisms," "technologies," or "dispositifs" that permeate the modern state and its institutions is that they tend to operate in a purely immanent domain. Foucault's genealogy of political power posits a major passage from the sovereign rule over a territory to a power that secures the vital capacities of the population. In the modern age political power and state institutions gradually lose their transcendent basis in hierarchical order and authority and enter the domain of immanence. They become fundamentally contestable and overdetermined, capable of bearing different and even incompatible rationalities.

Foucault never speaks at length about institutions, and his remarks express an ambiguous attitude to institutional analysis. On the one hand, institutions constitute privileged points of observation, since power relations crystalize there, being ordered and systematized to an extent that makes their rationality particularly intelligible. On the other hand, the origin of power relations cannot be explained by the existence of specific institutions or found in struggles played out between institutions. This is in line with the repeated dictum that power neither is located in nor emanates from particular places or centers in society. It is a matter of marking out the broad conditions of emergence for specific institutions rather than focusing strictly on the institution itself, as if it were a naturally given, distinctive, and uniform entity (Deleuze 1988, 116). Foucault makes explicit that institutions should be treated as sources neither of explanation nor of power. He writes that "one must analyze institutions from the standpoint of power relations, rather than vice versa" (SP, 343). This means that "the fundamental point of anchorage of the relationships, even if they are embodied and crystallized in an institution, is to be found outside the institution" (343). And at the beginning of his 1976 lecture series Society Must Be Defended he cautions starkly against restricting the analysis to formal institutions, particularly the juridical apparatus of the state, because they conceal or mask previous historical struggles on which they rest: "Historical contents alone allow us to see the dividing lines in the confrontations and struggles that functional arrangements or systematic organizations are designed to mask" (Foucault 2003, 7).

In place of the institution, Foucault asserts, one should focus on "technologies of power." This recommendation is made in the space of a few pages (and in footnotes) in the sixth lecture of 1978 (2007b, 116–20). There Foucault indicates a number of analytical pitfalls in the institutional-centric approach and suggests a triple displacement of the analysis (116). First, there is the tendency to explain the existence of a particular institution with reference to a given object, for instance those who are "mad." Second, there is a tendency to refer the effects of power back to the actions that the institution performs to reproduce itself. Third, there is the reduction of the institution to functions, or latent functions, that the institution may or may not fulfill. Instead of approaches that explain the institution with reference to its object, its striving for reproduction, or its functionality, Foucault wishes to embark on "the far more global, but also diffuse history of correlations and dominating systems, which cause a technology to be installed in a given society" (119). Rather than focusing narrowly on the institution itself, it is a matter of "going behind the institution and trying to discover in a wider and more overall perspective what we can broadly call a technology of power" (117).

Foucault argues that when studying institutionalized forms of power, one should begin with the more general and historically deep-seated strategies of power that gave birth to a particular institution: "We can proceed from the outside, that is to say, show how the psychiatric hospital can only be understood as an institution on the basis of something external and general, that is the psychiatric order, precisely in so far as the latter is connected to an absolutely global project, which we can broadly call public hygiene" (2007b, 117). Power, therefore, does not come from institutions; on the contrary, institutions are rather crystallizations of a particular set of power relations. Here Foucault clearly seeks to avoid conceiving of the institution as a powerful center, or a distinct and unified entity, in order to describe conditioning social processes of a much broader, historical nature, a "whole network of alliances, communications and points of support" (117).

Foucault's argument about "the technologies behind the institution" should not be mistaken for an underlying structure that would determine institutional forms. Rather, it is consistent with his general strategy of decentering what appear to be natural and unified objects—the subject, history, the state, and, here also, the institution. In his detailed historical accounts, such as *Discipline and Punish*, technologies rather emerge out of a series of problems, emergencies, and accidents, "a multiplicity of often minor processes, of different origin and scattered location" (Foucault 1977, 138). Hence, technologies arise from loosely assembled sets of solutions to local problems and practices and techniques that gradually proliferate and begin to appear in recurring configurations across diverse social and political spaces. This analysis of power configurations as arising from and shaped by a fractured plane of multiplicities echoes neovitalist thought and its emphasis on multiplicity over unity and contingency over necessity. It places into process and flux that which appeared to be solid, self-contained, and necessary. And it foregrounds the *interrelations* between different dispositifs as the source of perpetual transformation and social inventiveness. In this perspective the social body is a moving field of contingencies predicated on multiple relations of force.

Instead of addressing the state as such, Foucault seeks to deconstruct the idea of institutions, which, in turn, will inform his scattered comments on the state. This of course begs the question of whether the best way to approach the state in the first place is as a set of institutions, no matter how they are analyzed.

The Privilege of the Molecular

One way to conceive of Foucault's methodological orientation concerning the dispositif is by way of the concept of the "molecular," usually juxtaposed to "molar," found in Deleuze and Guattari. In *Discipline and Punish*, after noting the general rules that would guide his own study, and writing of a "political technology of the body," Foucault offers a nonspecific note: "I could give no notion by references or quotations what this book owes to Gilles Deleuze and the work he is undertaking with Félix Guattari" (1977, 309n2, 24). In the text, a couple of pages later, he begins to enunciate the approach he calls a "micro-physics of power" (26). The *molar* and the *molecular* are terms that come precisely from physics; thus, this project indicates the continued reference to Deleuze and Guattari's collaborative work. In his preface to the English edition of their *Anti-Oedipus* he delineates, at about the same time, a number of essential principles to guide everyday life that can be derived from their work. One of them is "Prefer what is positive and multiple, difference over uniformity, flows over unities, mobile arrangements over systems. Believe that what is productive is not sedentary but nomadic" (Foucault 1983, xiii). This seems almost a summary of the methodological injunctions he would make at this time and during the years in which he expounded, however briefly, on the dispositif.

While he does not use the term, Foucault's approach in these years resembles the particular privilege that Deleuze and Guattari give to the molecular over the molar. This distinction is used not only epistemologically but also politically in at least one significant place in the post-Foucauldian literature: the work of Nikolas Rose (1999, 5–6, 11). For Deleuze and Guattari (1983, 183–84) the distinction is, put crudely, between desire and the social. The molecular is the plane of unstable multiplicities, of flux, of formations and transformations; it is also one of plenitude and productivity and, in their language, of "desiring-machines." It is never separate from large molar aggregates ("social machines") such as the family, the political party, the trade union, the church, the institution, and of course the state; nonetheless, it animates them. In this sense Rose is correct to conclude that, from the perspective of "force relations at the molecular level," the state is a kind of secondary, molar formation. It "now appears simply as one element—whose functionality is historically specific and contextually variable—in multiple circuits of power, connecting a diversity of authorities and forces, within a whole variety of complex assemblages" (Rose 1999, 5). The opposition between the molar and the molecular is weighted to the "complex and subtle procedures" and "complex webs of affiliation" that link aspirations, habits, passions, gestures, individual bodies, and so forth, to the molar entities of economy and nation, and the political and social body (6). The primacy of the molecular disturbs the relation between microactors and macroactors (after Bruno Latour) and means that we must attend to shifts that "occur at the level of the molecular, the minor, the little and the mundane" (5, 11). The "minor," or "processes of minoring," is the location, as we saw in Chapter 3, where Rose locates an affirmative politics. Epistemologically, then, the molecular gives privilege to multiplicity, heterogeneity, and contingency; normatively, and therefore politically, to those flowerings of desire and resistance that arise outside, or in the interstices of, conventional politics and its characteristic organizations such as parties and trade unions.

This enables us to understand Foucault's genealogical decentering of technology into its multiple, constitutive components. The emergence of discipline, as a key example, demonstrates how mundane and dispersed practices of correction and training—the timetable, the examination, the military drill—at various sites link up and proliferate, gradually acquiring the shape of a generalizable technology. Singular, sometimes ad hoc, solutions to specific problems—of effective pedagogy, of efficient production—became routinized, interlinked, and rationalized into generally applicable models (Foucault 2003, 180). As for discipline "it was first to be introduced . . . at a local level, in intuitive, empirical, and fragmented forms, and in the restricted framework of institutions such as schools, hospitals, barracks, workshops, and so on" (250). Over time disciplinary technology is imbued with a distinct "strategic imperative," which is about preventing unruly and unproductive behavior by improving and correcting the human material (of the prisoner, the soldier, the pupil, and the industrial laborer) within the scheme of normality and deviance from the norm. The molecular provides us with the epistemic vantage point to understand the molar.

Foucault (1977, 257) describes the advent of discipline as "a technical mutation" in power relations at large, occurring in the nineteenth century. Specific techniques intensify, interconnect, and proliferate over time until they pass a certain threshold and begin to saturate social space. After this, "society" is no longer the same space, having passed a "tipping point" just like water that begins to boil (Nealon 2008, 39). This idea of a process of intensification and saturation comparable to the laws of thermodynamics is evident in the work of Deleuze and Guattari (1983, 286). Disciplinary technology crosses a threshold when a series of disciplinary institutional forms of knowledge and practice emerges, such as clinical medicine, criminal psychiatry, child psychology, and scientific management (Foucault 1977, 224).

For Foucault technologies of power have no single origin but heterogeneous sites of emergence. Accordingly, they never come to constitute a coherent, self-enclosed, and self-identical entity. In his account of "eventalization" in a round-table with historians he argues that it is thus necessary to start from "a sort of multiplication or pluralization of causes" (QM, 227). An event such as the birth of the prison should be analyzed "according to the multiple processes that constitute it" (227). We must construct a "polyhedron" (geometrical figure with many sides) of intelligibility, "the number of whose faces is not given in advance and can never properly be taken as finite" (227). There is a kind of progressive decomposition of the event that obliges the analyst to construct "external relations of intelligibility" (227). We start then from the prison, but we end up with schooling, the military, the timetable, the monastery, and so on. We must grasp, according to Foucault, several "polymorphisms": of what is brought into relation, of relations to be described, and domains of reference (228). The event of the prison is not born as a molar entity but emerges from a ragbag of things, including examinations, manuals on how to shoot guns, architectural diagrams, problems of banditry, ill-effects of public executions, changing theoretical models, the history of detail, strategies for the capitalist economy, and much more. Nonetheless, all this is formed into a "multiform instrumentation," an "epistemological-juridical complex," or a "political technology of the body," that arises in piecemeal fashion out of a multiplicity of social processes and technical innovations. These technologies, instruments, mechanisms, and finally, *dispositifs*, mark over time particular propensities for perceiving and organizing, gradually saturating social space.

The focus on technologies of power thus radically displaces institutional analysis: "If we want to avoid the circularity that refers the analysis of power from one institution to another, it is by grasping them [technologies] at the point where they constitute techniques with operative value in multiple processes" (Foucault 2007b, 119n). In brief, technologies are historically constituted systems of practices, entrenched social strategies that have given birth to the legal, disciplinary, and welfare institutions that make up the modern state. It is the molecular level that can explain the molar social formations and not vice versa, and it is the molecular that contains within it those relations of forces that will engender change. The molecular in this sense is of epistemological value in the insights it provides us not only of major social formations but also the level at which the most vital forces operate. As such, it is where we might find possibilities of political change.

Foucault does not stress the vitalist metaphysics underlying the dispositif in the same ways as his interpreters and followers. At times Deleuze and Guattari speak of social organization as directly comparable to biological organisms: "However, starting from this domain of chance or of real inorganization, large configurations are organized that necessarily reproduce a structure under the action of DNA and its segments, the genes, performing veritable lottery drawings, creating switching points as *lines of selection or evolution*—this, indeed, is what all the stages of the passage from the molecular to the molar demonstrate, such as this passage appears in the organic machines, but no less so in the social machines with other laws and other figures" (Deleuze and Guattari 1983, 289, emphasis in the original). Deleuze and Guattari thus imagine a passage from the unorganized, disparate multiplicity, the molecular, to the formation of selecting, structuring aggregations, which is "the molar." There is thus, first, molecular multiplicity, then, forms of selection and the performing of the selection, and, finally, molar or gregarious aggregates that result from this selection (343). These molar aggregates are "qualified forms" or "formations of sovereignty." They "play the role of totalizing, unifying, signifying objectivities that assign organizations, lacks, and goals" (343).The *molecular* is the diversified, the vital, the qualitative, and the nomadic, whereas *the molar* is the unifying, the quantitative, the statist, and the controlled.

This again links up with Rose's politics of life. Rose argues, together with Rabinow, as we recall, that a new biopolitics has emerged in which the object of the total population gives way to a conception of life as plasticity and contingency, grounded in ethopolitics. Rabinow and Rose (2006, 204) borrow here the "molecular" and the "molar" from Deleuze and Guattari's vocabulary, which they roughly equate with the micro and macro. While the latter was privileged in the era of the social state and eugenics policies, it is the molecular that comes to the fore in the biopolitics of advanced liberalism today. Now "we see the birth of new modes of individualization and conceptions of autonomy with their associated rights to health, life, liberty and the pursuit of a form of happiness that is increasingly understood in corporeal and vital terms" (Rabinow and Rose 2006, 204). Or, again, Rose's key argument is that the totalizing biopolitics of the population has been replaced by a diversified individuation: "The norm of individual health replaced that of the quality of the population" (Rose 2007, 13). Regardless of whether Rose and Rabinow misappropriate the notions of molecular and molar (Blencove 2012, 131), the result is a remarkably optimistic version of contemporary biopolitics. Freed from the horrors of race war and disciplinary rigidity, it opens up the world in a Deleuzian image—individuation as a process of bottomless differentiation.

The Dynamic Interplay of Forces

Foucault left ample space for indeterminacy and dynamic repercussions between different technologies or dispositifs. Recent contributions to Foucault scholarship emphasize the complex heterogeneity in his "topology of power" after the major books of the mid-1970s (Collier 2009). There Foucault presents us with a gamut of differing technologies, each with distinct rationalities. Foucault here departs from his analysis of "disciplinary society" and, later, "an era of biopolitics," and a diagnostic style marked by systematicity, functionalism, and epochal totalization. Instead, he begins to pursue a "topological" approach that leads to much more subtle descriptions of multiple and heterogeneous configurations of power, their correlations and structures of dominance.

The *loci classici* of this approach are the first three lectures in 1978, where Foucault introduced the three major dispositifs: law, discipline, and security (Foucault 2007b, 5–86). Foucault there demonstrated how these technologies produce particular problems and solutions from within their own rationality and frame of observation. In this context it is as if Foucault sought to carve out nascent rationalities of political regulation that still bear on our contemporary world and its political urgencies. The problems under deliberation include that of the penalty, the management of epidemics, urban space and the town, and scarcity and the regulation of grain.

In the case of crime, to take Foucault's most basic example, law, discipline, and security work with quite different objects as a result of their different ways of rendering unlawful acts intelligible. The sovereign law, or "the legal technology," makes possible a rigid and binary distinction. It isolates an action, which is viewed through "a binary division between the permitted and the prohibited, and [it then makes] a coupling, comprising the code, between a type of prohibited action and a type of punishment" (Foucault 2007b, 5). In contrast, within the framework of discipline "a series of adjacent, detective, medical, and psychological techniques appear which fall within the domain of surveillance, diagnosis, and the possible transformation of individuals" (5). The disciplinary technology perceives the criminal human material in a more preventive way, taking as its object not merely the criminal act and the culprit but the whole person behind the criminal act, with all his or her predispositions, deviant characteristics, and inherent potentials. Discipline revolves around an ideal of perfectibility, insofar as disciplinary interventions display the hope of reconstructing the human and social material to arrive at a point of perfection.

Finally, the technology of security starts from an observation of the actually given—for instance, the level of crime rates—and seeks to achieve what would be an acceptable level. Security calculations rest on the assumption that it is not possible to regulate things and processes down to the smallest detail and recognize that the level of crimes is interrelated to a whole series of factors. Security presupposes that human reality is not amenable to planning and regulation and that it is not possible to completely eliminate the undesired. Rather, security has the more limited ambition of facilitating and optimizing the processes already inhering in this reality. Thus, unlike discipline and its utopian desire, it starts from the given without aspirations to achieve a state of perfection: "It is simply a matter of maximizing the positive elements, for which one provides the best possible circulation, and of minimizing what is risky and inconvenient, like theft and disease, while knowing that they will never be completely suppressed" (Foucault 2007b, 19). Thus, security makes visible the object of government such as crime in relation to a series of likely events, and it reacts to crime by subjecting it to a calculation of costs, benefits, and probabilities: "Instead of a binary division between the permitted and the prohibited, one establishes an average considered as optimal on the one hand, and, on the other, a bandwidth of the acceptable that must not be exceeded" (6). It follows that the technology of security depends more radically on the objects of regulation than the two other technologies. Security works upon "series of probabilities" (19) insofar as it seeks to prepare for the future and account for future possibilities.

There are thus fundamental differences between the three dispositifs, or power technologies, regarding their degree of "sensitivity" or "immanence" in relation to the object of government. They differ in their readiness to modify and shape the exercise of power in relation to the object's inherent characteristics, processes, and reactions: "Discipline works in an empty, artificial space that is to be completely constructed. Security will rely on a number of material givens. It will, of course, work on site with the flows of water, islands, air, and so forth. Thus it works on a given. . . . This given will not be reconstructed to arrive at a point of perfection, as in a disciplinary town" (Foucault 2007b, 19). Foucault said that sovereignty's emblematic object is a territory, discipline targets bodies, and the privileged domain of security is the totality of a living population (2003, 253; 2007b, 11). Hence, fundamentally different objects ascribed with different inherent properties are foregrounded by what Foucault regards as the three major political technologies to appear in the modern West.

These topologies of power constitute in some sense Foucault's version of complexity theory. His 1970s genealogies (1977, 1979) were keen to trace the passages from transcendent forms of sovereignty to modern forms of power such as discipline and biopolitics. His lectures on the history of governmentality modify this metanarrative in two ways. Historically, it will be the ethos of liberalism that accomplishes the critique and limitation of sovereign power. Analytically, it is the dispositif that seeks to bring sovereignty down to earth by the technical vocabulary of mechanisms and apparatuses, correlations and multiplicities. Rather than the supreme power within a domain, or something founded on a divine law or authority, sovereignty becomes one immanent mode of organization among others and has complex relations with them. Suspending the framework of the linear movement between forms of power, which he nevertheless again employs a few lectures later, Foucault engages the metaphorics of complexity and fuzziness (2007b, 8–9, 109–10). It is the "system of correlations" between law and discipline that changes in the security dispositif rather than a succession of elements. The appeal to complexity allows Foucault to escape the axial and epochal bipolarity of much of his earlier work on power. But what are its implications for the state? Even if we leave to one side the vitalist metaphysics that have informed the dispositif, does not such a form of analysis act as a substitute for a concept of the state and its development? If so, then does it not risk becoming a form of the liberal reduction of politics to technology and technique?

Seeing and Being

Foucault's (1980a) approach to technology exhibits his debt to French historical epistemology. His interest in the historical-epistemic conditions of how phenomena could be rendered as objects of scientific classification helps us understand his idea that a dispositif has a particular "gaze."

Law, discipline, and security are epistemologically distinct, each rendering the world amenable to observation and calculation in particular and different ways. The imperative of a technology, then, pertains not only to the exercise of power but to the formation of knowledge. Foucault suggested that instead of separating the history of penal practice from the history of the human sciences, we should examine their intersection. The project was to discover "whether there is not some common matrix or whether they do not both derive from a single process of 'epistemologico-juridical' formation; in short, make the technology of power the very principle both of the humanization of the penal system and of the knowledge of man" (Foucault 1977, 23). Technologies are "patterns of linkages" between knowledge of human conduct and the practices and instruments that seek to shape that conduct. Put otherwise, technologies consist of practices where what can be known and what can be done interweave.

A technology, or dispositif, is hence instantiated both in modes of organizing and in practices of knowledge production. This is why the study of a dispositif requires us to study a "thoroughly heterogeneous ensemble" that includes institutions, architecture, practices, and instruments and procedures for uttering true statements (Foucault 1980b, 194). In line with his epistemic commitments, Foucault carves out what one might call "practical epistemological spaces." Dispositifs establish particular visibilities by "throwing light upon objects," making them shimmer and gleam in a particular way (Deleuze 1988, 52; 1992b 160). Notably, these visibilities are not the objects that would show up under light but rather forms of luminosity created by the light itself, which allows an object to exist only under a particular normativity. Consider a contemporary example: generalized auditing technology renders organizational settings, relations with "clients" and "customers," and professional practices amenable to a particular form of observation and evaluation, thus making the auditee visible to another governing agency or regulatory body (Miller 1992). The protected space constituted by the expertise of, for example, the professor, the school principal, and the doctor becomes open to continuous inspection and comparison. The university department may become visible as a space of research productivity, the classroom as one of student learning outcomes, and the hospital unit as one of efficient procedures and effective results.

Foucault's approach implies reverberations and frictions between multiple coexisting dispositifs in terms of the visualization of objects. The examples that Foucault gives in his 1978 lectures demonstrate how problems of theft, the layout of towns, or the regulation of grain production are visualized and reflected on from the perspective of fundamentally divergent optics (Foucault 2007b, 6–24). Problems like theft or fluctuating grain production oscillate at times between different technologies and thus become something entirely different, depending on the optical frame and calculative rationality. Dispositifs thus display a self-referring rationality akin to autopoietic systems that operate through recursive operations, continually coping with and integrating perturbations from the environment to which they are exposed. This characteristic resonates with Deleuze's assumption that technological systems are ontologically unstable, produced by processes of self-organization in complex relations with their environment (Kearnes 2006).

Different dispositifs may target the same problem, for instance, a specific crime, from within each of their limited optics, ascribing to it fundamentally divergent meanings, reasons, and effects. Among the several examples, Foucault noted that the practice of severe punishments, first belonging to the technology of sovereign law, would later additionally begin to function—by serving as example—as a corrective, disciplinary device. Similarly, a security calculation could make sense of strict punishments for specific offenses by inserting the offense within a series of probable events: "Just as, in the same system, when one severely punished domestic theft—with the death penalty for a theft of very, very minor importance if it was committed in a house by someone who was received there or who was employed as a servant—it was clear that what was targeted was basically a crime that was only important due to its probability, and we can say that here too something like a mechanism of security was deployed" (Foucault 2007b, 7). Foucault suggests, then, how a practice such as capital punishment can in some cases serve to mediate between the different power technologies, or dispositifs, while in other cases it may demonstrate their fundamental incompatibility. While a security dispositif can incorporate capital punishment to adjust the level of the production of crime, it would be difficult to imagine a system of discipline incorporating capital punishment, given that it eradicates the living forces of the body on which discipline depends.

We see that the problem of what is theft or shortage of grain becomes indeterminate, when the provisional fixation of an object may gradually lose its grip and be reconfigured. The problem-object escapes one fixation while being integrated into another dispositif. While dispositifs display a certain prescriptive tendency, making certain forms of organizing more likely than others, it becomes evident that they cannot determine social or institutional practices. The situation is rather one of "functional over-determination" (Foucault 1980b, 195) brought about by the emergence of various incongruent schemes for observing and acting on things. It is possible that Foucault was referring to Althusser's (1969) concept, but he restricted his use of "over-determination" to designate a situation of excessive causalities. This arises when the effects of a social arrangement enter "into resonance or contradiction with the others and thereby calls for a readjustment or a re-working of the heterogeneous elements" (Foucault

1980b, 195). It is possible, then, to speak of overdetermination arising from technologies in two senses. First, technological arrangements produce intended or unintended effects that inflict the system *from within*, necessitating perpetual readjustments. Second, there is overdetermination ensuing from the *interplay* between multiple, divergent technologies that overdetermine social space and create reverberations, disturbances, and reconfigurations.

It is relatively easy to develop these ideas in relation to the modern welfare state's institutional arrangements and governmental challenges. We can hence consider how initiatives based on a security logic that seek to relate to what actually occurs in a sensitive and flexible manner in order to optimize it will at times be at odds with a legal logic that operates in a binary, rigorous, and controlling manner. For example, a range of governmental problems in the welfare state could be said, after Foucault, to be about mediating between, on the one hand, a desire to act "holistically" vis-à-vis the living individual and, on the other hand, fitting the citizen into universal legal arrangements that operate "without respect for the person" (Villadsen 2011).

In this sense one might say that the living being, the normal individual, and the juridical subject are the objects that appear within the different optics of security, discipline, and law. Again, by emphasizing the creation of visibilities rather than substance, Foucault's thinking resonates with Deleuzian neovitalism and its foregrounding of perception over ontology. Indeed, Deleuze's reassessment of Foucault argues that Foucault was concerned with the visible as much as with the articulable (Deleuze 1988, 31). What is significant is not the object in and of itself, neither the eye as a sensory organ, but rather the particular kind of luminosity that allows us to perceive objects in a certain way. What becomes important, in brief, is not *what* one sees but *how* one sees. In this neovitalist view external production of knowledge of the object is annulled. Classification can no longer happen from above but enters into the domain of things themselves. In Deleuze's vitalist rendering of Foucault, knowledge is therefore not positivist or transcendental but immanent.

A Plane of Immanence

Commenting on his histories of technologies Foucault emphasized that the major dispositifs do not appear in any sort of sequential order: "There is not a series of successive elements, the appearance of the new causing the earlier ones to disappear" (2007b, 8). In this part of his work Foucault did not seek to outline overarching and irretrievable breaks from one epoch or system to another;

instead, he emphasized the continual interplay between multiple dispositifs: "We should not be looking for a sort of sovereignty from which powers spring, but showing how the various operators of domination support one another, relate to one another, at how they converge and reinforce one another in some cases, and negate or strive to annul one another in other cases" (Foucault 2003, 45). Foucault struggled to challenge the idea of a unified and centralized state by retracing the multiple points of genesis of major technologies of governmental regulation and their modalities of knowledge. This emphasis on multiple forms of governmental rationality in Foucault's approach echoes Nietzsche's conception of history as perpetual struggles between different forces (Bussolini 2010, 88). The plurality of dispositifs renders social space fractured by different imperatives, at times reinforcing and assimilating, at other times undermining and contradicting one another. In concrete terms components from existing dispositifs may be redeployed and recombined within a new dispositif, as, for instance, when "the old armatures of law and discipline function in addition to the specific mechanism of security" (Foucault 2007b, 10). Hence, when the dispositif of security emerged as a major technology, it began to redeploy some of the existing devices of law and discipline within new configurations, where they became linked to the new imperative of optimization of the population's inherent mechanisms. Although Foucault cautions against applying a model of historical succession and substitution, he still insists that the technology of security is gaining dominance at the expense of the more archaic forms of power, hence presaging our contemporary prevalent forms of political regulation and management.

New objects and problems may be born at the boundaries and from the unsettling interchanges among different technologies. One example is legal psychiatry, which was born out of the interchange between legal technology and biopolitical technology during the nineteenth century. Legal psychiatry arose from the increasing discord between the imperative of minimizing risks inherent to the population and the stipulations of formal legality (Tepper 2010, 61–62). The twin problem, then, was how to identify elements posing a biopolitical threat to the population, treating them not merely in accordance with medical knowledge but also inserting them into the juridical framework. From this urgency arose "a knowledge system able to measure the index of danger present in an individual; a knowledge system that might establish the protection necessary in the face of such a danger" (DI, 194). By foregrounding the contingent interplay between different technologies as a breeding ground for new innovations and, eventually, new technologies, Foucault could be said to imply that technologies arise from a "plane of immanence." At this immanent plane the dynamic *relations* between diverse forces take ontological priority over substance.

Dispositifs emerge, compete, and come to dominance within this immanent plane. While they might emerge in relation to a specific "urgent need" or an emergency of one kind or another such as the grain famine of the eighteenth century or the increase of vagabondage and vagrancy in the seventeenth (Foucault 1980b, 195), they themselves define the nature of the problems with which they are concerned through the way they cast their eye on them. Here we notice the similarities with the immanent focus of vitalism, which is unconcerned with the depth of ontological structure and starts from the relations between entities. From these, something like emergent forms are created that may attain powers of self-organization, yet they unfold in a tensional relationship to each other.

So the dispositif is the intellectual means by which Foucault sought to provide an immanent account of power and the exercise of political sovereignty. We have no doubt that the dispositif produces a much finer-grained analysis of issues of political and governmental regulation, and it temporarily frees that analysis from epochal totalization and functionalist explanation. These will produce new intelligibilities and local insights into the operation and optics of power formations.

Nevertheless, we do have doubts about whether Foucault succeeded in displacing the more conventional concerns of state-centered analysis by that of the multiple dispositifs. By seeking to decenter institutions into constitutive practices and technologies, by privileging the molecular over the molar, multiplicity over unity, and the optic over the problem, Foucault has placed the emergence and transformation of dispositifs within a kind of great Heraclitean flow and flux of immanence. The notion of sovereignty as a supreme entity within a domain, an entity that is separate (and thus not connected) and autonomous (and thus not dependent), that is, one that achieves the political form of transcendence, cannot become visible through such an analysis. But these are what define the very concept of a state as a form of political innovation. Some will of course say that this is right and proper and that it is time we rid ourselves of the mythology and monstrosity of the Leviathan. But even if we accept this, and downplay the vitalist presumptions of Foucault's followers and his interpreters, the political is in danger of being refigured as a mere play among diverse technical rationalities.

We return to the implications of this development in the next chapter. There Foucault's vitalist resonances become, if anything, even more pronounced when we examine Deleuze's reading of him on the dual composition of the dispositif, that of diagram and actualizations.

CHAPTER 7

VIRTUAL STATE-MAKING

Is the state a locus of a negative power that must be resisted? Did Foucault not essentially show us that the state impinges on our freedom in so many ways? His descriptions of the myriad authorities and experts—doctors, social workers, wardens, teachers, psychologists—who are all involved in molding and normalizing our behavior may certainly leave that impression. Or, is the state, by contrast, an agency of a positive power, one that generates and safeguards the basic conditions of freedom?

Foucault's work on governmentality and the state from the late 1970s cannot easily be assigned to either of these two alternatives and, indeed, seeks to avoid the antinomy they sketch. In these years Foucault struggled to find ways to avoid a unifying description of the state as a center of repressive power and ideology, often in a critical dialogue with contemporary Marxists. He also sought to move away from an epochal and univocal notion of a "generalized disciplinary society," and he is said to have worried about making an "extremist denunciation of power" (Pasquino 1993, 79). Yet these moves did not lead Foucault to any endorsement of the constitutional state or welfare institutions as safeguards of freedom.

Foucault's notion of the dispositif can be seen in the light of these contextualized attempts at navigating what state power means. In 1977 Deleuze wrote about the dispositif in a collection of notes intended to reach Foucault: "In itself and in relation to 'leftism': profound political novelty of this conception of power, in opposition to all theory of the State" (1977, 3). Some years later, governmentality writers could find much use in his concepts for developing a decentered approach to the state. While the dispositif was not part of the initial conceptual framework advanced by the emerging governmentality studies, it was later discovered with enthusiasm by Rabinow and Rose (2003, xv), who argue that it is "one of the most powerful conceptual tools introduced by Foucault." This was so, they asserted, because the concept cuts across inflexible categories such as institutions, classes, and cultures. The dispositif promised to move beyond conventional dualities like freedom and repression, including the opposition of negative and positive state power. Perhaps also the concept reflects—as we will see—key premises of that vitalism that Rose had been attracted to in Deleuze. As we noted in Chapter 6, the dispositif is characterized by radical immanence, relationality, transformability, autocreation, and indeterminacy.

In this chapter we explore how Foucault counters the idea of power as encompassing, centered, and univocal (repressive *or* liberating) by means of the concept of the dispositif. It is not simply that the idea of a uniform state power becomes unsustainable in light of the interrelated multiple dispositifs. We will now see that each dispositif itself is too unstable, modifiable, and incoherent to provide for any effective and univocal hold of the social body.

First, we explain the two sides of the dispositif, its diagram and its actual practices. Second, we suggest that the effects of the diagram are not of the order of constraint or determination but rather of animation and productivity. In regard to the state, we are deprived of the institutional-conceptual reality of the state; instead, there is a quest for fulfilling the state, a perpetual "state-making." Third, we develop this point by foregrounding the inherent contradictions and paradoxes that set dispositifs in ceaseless motion. We conclude by discussing the potentials and then the shortcomings of the concept, finding that integral to the concept are costs in terms of what cannot come into view and which questions cannot be considered.

A Concept with Two Sides

We have argued that for Foucault the notion of dispositif marks a specific imperative of power. Such imperatives are in turn perpetually embodied in practices and institutions. However, this instantiation is fragile, contingent, and diversified. This idea that Foucault's dispositifs are characterized by permanent actualization can be given a more precise vocabulary by observing that the concept has two sides: a side of strategy/imperative versus a side of practice/instantiation. This conceptual duality can be rendered variously as program/action, diagram/actualization, or strategic imperative/social apparatus. These notions all articulate technology as a system of perpetual operations that have recourse to, and are propelled forward by, a particular strategic imperative. Indeed, Foucault says that one may analyze a technology "as a dream, or better, as a utopia," which is the first form that it takes in its development, before it becomes a rule for real institutions or an academic discipline (PTI, 410). A technology or, more precisely, a dispositif, becomes an arrangement under constant enactment and hence characterized by instability, failures, and transformability.

Evident in Foucault's thinking is thus the effort to be able to speak, at one and the same time, of an idealized imperative and of actual, diversified instantiations of it. This conceptual duality is visible in Foucault's concrete analysis where, for instance, the imperative of discipline is actualized diversely in schooling, military organization, correctional punishment, hospitals, and factory production. Strategic imperatives are thus "actualized" in technological arrangements and variously shaped by the practices and institutions in which they find their concrete embodiment. A dispositif, in Foucault's words, is a "multiform instrumentation" that can never be ultimately localized in a particular institution or in the "state apparatus" (1977, 26). It is propelled forward by a strategic imperative, which is perceivable across organizational practices, but can be found nowhere materialized in its programmatic and idealized form. Deleuze (1988; 1992b) gives this idea a precise terminology by way of his distinction between virtual diagrams and their actualization that render institutions (of the state or otherwise) with a rather indeterminate character.

The diagram is a schematic that is abstracted and dislodged from any concrete functionality. The Panopticon should not be understood, said Foucault, as a "dream building"; instead "it is the diagram of a mechanism of power reduced to its ideal form; its functioning, abstracted from any obstacle, resistance or friction . . . detached from any specific use" (1977, 205). Foucault did not elaborate his notion of diagrams or how diagrams might relate to technologies or organizations. However, Deleuze attributed to Foucault the concept of the "diagram" as a virtuality that breathes life into specific practices and institutions (Deleuze 1988, 72). Again, the Panopticon is the exemplar of such a diagram. Its functionality is generalized to serve multifarious purposes, and it has a highly idealized and programmatic character, as if it were "abstracted from any obstacle . . . or friction," says Deleuze (34) while paraphrasing Foucault. Identifying a diagram means naming a particular configurational propensity in modes of organization and knowledge formation. There is thus no idealism here but rather a tracing of regularities across social practices, which are then abstracted to their purest functionality.

In elaborating the diagram, Deleuze offered an analytical remedy against the totalizing and deterministic style found in some interpretations of Foucault's work on power. Deleuze explained how it is possible to replace a deterministic conception of power with the idea of virtual diagrams that ramify through and are given shape in a multiplicity of instances and take multiple forms:

> Sometimes the assemblages are distributed in hard, compact segments which are sharply separated by partitions, watertight barriers, formal discontinuities (such as school, army, workshop, and ultimately prison, and as soon as you're in the army, they tell you "You're not at school any more"). Sometimes, on the other hand, they communicate within the abstract machine which confers on them a supple and diffuse microsegmentarity, so that they all resemble one another and prison extends throughout the rest, like the variables of the one continuous, formless function (school, barracks and the workshop are already prisons). If we continue to move from one extreme to the other, this is because each assemblage sets off the abstract machine, but in varying degrees. (1988, 40–41)

There is thus a twofold analytical strategy at play in Foucault. The first one gives emphasis to differentiation and discontinuities between institutions and their specific modes of ordering. The second traces resemblances, thereby marking out general configurational propensities. These can be subtracted from the different institutions to which they give shape, although "in varying degrees." This analytical move echoes Deleuze's general philosophical project insofar as it consists in "an effort to subtract the dynamics of creation from the mediation of the created" (Hallward 2006, 3). The diagram is shaped by the practices and institutions where it finds its concrete actualization, yet it is not reducible to them. This is because it is the locus of a virtuality, or an excess, that can never fully emerge in the actual. In this respect the diagram figures as a reminder of the nonactualized, of what could have been and what could become possible (Checchi 2014, 205).

An immanence perspective is evident in this reading. It clearly implies that in Foucault neither discipline nor other dispositifs can be captured within the scheme of underlying, invariant structure versus divergent surface manifestations. Rather, there are moments of irreducibility to practices and institutions, since they instrumentalize the diagram in diversified, localized, and indeterminate forms: "The institution has the capacity to integrate power-relations, by constituting various forms of knowledge which actualize, modify and *redis-tribute* these relations" (Deleuze 1988, 77; emphasis in original). Hence, there is an injunction to examine the diversified concrete instantiations, as well as to excavate the diagrammatic imperative: "There is a history of assemblages, just as there is development and change in the diagram" (42). The diagram is abstracted and purified analytically, but its development can only be traced by describing the institutional arrangements that continually animate it.

Deleuze's reading seeks to capture a twofold, unstable constitution of any institution, including schools, prisons, and other "social machines." Such institutions are "two-form" assemblages: "What is it that Foucault calls a machine, be it abstract or concrete (he speaks of the 'machine-prison,' but equally of the machine-school, the machine-hospital, and so on)? The concrete machines are the two-form assemblages or mechanisms, whereas the abstract machine is the informal diagram" (Deleuze 1988, 39). In this reading, Foucault's thinking conceives of institutions as produced by the double contingency of idealized diagrams and the ways in which these emerge and become operative in particular locales. This dual analytical perspective holds general value for grasping institutions as simultaneously imbued with specific professional codes and with more broad-seated social strategies.

One of the rare occasions where Foucault uses this dual institutional perspective is when he analyzes the advent of the modern hospital at the end of the eighteenth century (2007a). The text, entitled "The Incorporation of the Hospital into Modern Technology," describes how the medical hospital was a result of two parallel processes, "on the one hand, to the introduction of discipline into hospital space, and on the other hand, to the transformation that the practice of medicine in that period was undergoing" (148). The messy place of the general hospital, which had served the multiple purposes of exclusion, assistance, and spiritual reform of the sick, the mad, prostitutes, and the poor, now changed fundamentally. The emergence of disciplinarity entailed comparative observations and investigations of hospitals, combined with new divisions of individuals, means of inquiry, and the modification of architecture inside the hospital. At the same time, an inversion took place in the status hierarchy: religious authorities gave way to doctors, and medical interventions began focusing on "the environment which surrounds the patients," including the temperature, air, and drinking water (148). The institutional site of the hospital was thus pervaded by two configurational tendencies of different origin and became in this sense inherently overdetermined.

Dreams Suspended in Reality

The diagrams never take effect in the institutions in an integral way, which is further evident from Foucault's comments on institutional failures. For instance, the endurance of the correctional prison cannot be explained on the basis of its immediate results, since the failure of prisons to make lawbreakers self-disciplining has not at all eliminated the hope of disciplinarity. Rather than overthrowing discipline, failures provide disciplinary technology with targets against which to pit itself, and this involves a reutilization of unintended consequences and disappointments: "The real history of the prison is undoubtedly not governed by the successes and failures of its functionality, but is in fact inserted within strategies and tactics that find support even in these functional defects themselves" (Foucault 2007b, 117–18). Generally, then, the experience of failures at the level of institutions need not threaten the institution's existence, since these failures tend to animate a more deep-seated imperative of power—that is, the diagram (Deleuze 1988, 62, 67). It follows that diagrams will normally have a longer life span than specific institutions.

The history of diagrams, however, is not one that demonstrates their remarkable endurance and success; rather, it is a history of plans never realized. Foucault gives emphasis to the fundamentally unattainable nature of diagrams and their imperatives, comparing them to "a programming left in abeyance" (QM, 231). It is quite easy to extend Deleuze's idea of diagrams as abstract schematics in permanent quest of their instantiation to some of Foucault's most significant dispositifs of power: the panoptic dream of complete visibility and control; the confession's quest for an exhaustive account of the soul; and liberal government's fiction of perfect market-circulation. The disjuncture or mismatch between the diagrams and actual modes of organization animate social inventiveness and sets dispositifs in perpetual motion. The diagrammatic imperative always remains at a distance, as an inherently unattainable horizon, creating an impetus for social innovation or the redeployment of existent techniques. Hence, each dispositif is propelled by the inherent tension between diagram and practice.

Inherent Contradictions and Paradoxes

The permanent tension between diagrams and practices is not, however, the most fundamental cause of the constitutive instability in social arrangements. The principal difference and contradiction, explains Foucault, is "not one between the purity of the ideal and the disorderly impurity of the real" (QM, 231).

Instead, Foucault's dispositifs reveal built-in inconsistencies or intrinsic paradoxes that threaten the system and put it into contradiction with itself. Or to invoke Deleuze's notion of difference: what fundamentally differs it not so much one thing from another but the thing from itself (Žižek 2004, x). Although Foucault never theorized his discovery of inherent self-contradictions in dispositifs, it is fairly easy to reconstruct paradoxes inherent to each one.

Regarding the legal dispositif, Foucault spoke in "The Political Technology of Individuals" (PTI, 403–17) about the utopian idea of reconciling the law completely with the social order. At least since the seventeenth century, political thinkers have permanently debated the division between the state's negative tasks sustained by law and its positive tasks carried out via the biopolitical regulation of norms in the social order: "Law, by definition, is always referred to a juridical system, and order is referred to an administrative system, to a state's specific order" (417). The dream of reconciling this antinomy between law and order must, in Foucault's words, "remain a dream. It's impossible to reconcile law and order because when you try to do so it is only in the form of an integration of law into the state's order" (417). The remaining difficulty of separating the juridical, "negative" function from the norm-setting, positive one is the key intrinsic antinomy of the legal dispositif. And it is one that has continued to incite inventions in modern political rationalities.

The dispositif of discipline, for Foucault, is animated by the paradox of normality/deviance, which disallows a permanent fixation of either side of the binary. The relational diagram of disciplinary correction has infinite applicability, insofar as an individual who is first judged as normal may, on closer inspection, be found deviant. This can either occur when the individual is assessed vis-à-vis another standard of normality or when the original distinction is applied anew on the population of "normal" individuals. In the last case some members of the "normals" may again be identified as deviating sufficiently from the norm to be categorized as "abnormal." In this way the diagram of discipline constitutes a self-propelling, limitless mechanism, making possible a perpetual search for "the norm" and "normality" (Villadsen 2014, 656).

Considering the dispositif of security, we may observe that it is premised on the modern paradox of governing, which is constituted by the concomitant demands for regulation and autonomy. At the level of the state, this duality arises from the conception of "population as both the object and the subject of these mechanisms of security" (Foucault 2007b, 11). Hence, the population is at the same time conceived as the proprietor of inherent self-regulating mechanisms and in need of regulatory intervention to facilitate or foster this self-regulation. Likewise, the double conception of society as a natural given *and* cultural artifact is the fundamental paradox of security. Foucault explains that security calculations take as their point of departure "the naturalness of society" (349), which is precisely a composite of the natural and the cultural—that is, the regularities by which populations produce, consume, procreate, move, and so forth. This idea of the naturalness of society creates the need for regulations, which guarantees that the natural mechanisms of regulation inherent in the population operate freely. The problem becomes one of establishing regulations that replicate the natural regulations that, however, are not fully intelligible.

In this way Foucault's dispositifs are imbued with self-contradictions and constitutive instabilities. These intrinsic contradictions drive them forward, but they do not constitute some kind of hidden logic that secretly animates institutions and agents. Rather, dispositifs are pervaded by inherent paradoxes as a result of their fragmented, heterogeneous origins in diverse strategies and at dispersed sites. Crucially, diagrams convey to institutional practices a particular reflexivity that can be reduced neither to determination nor to an underlying system or rationality, untouched by concrete acts. They instead mark out configurational tendencies that arise from efforts in the social body to respond to diverse urgent events, emergencies, and mundane problems. To sum up, institutions are shaped by both diagrammatic imperatives and by specific events, localized power relations, and accidental happenings. Translated into an analysis of the state, this dual-composite approach renders the state as a plane saturated by institutional instabilities, contradictory rationalities, and permanent frictions. Accordingly, then, the Foucauldian framework renders state institutions as arrangements under perpetual enactment. Diagrams do not determine institutional practices but merely imbue them with injunctions to see and act—they convey to institutions programmatic ideals, persistent contradictions, and the experience of recurrent failures. They are ideals ever in quest of their political and institutional context where they find their effective, concrete embodiment. In this view the institutional structure of the state is not merely "decentered" into a plurality of social strategies; it becomes a virtual structure, a permanent becoming state.

The dispositifs that pervade the modern state reiterate the impetus of a continual *state-making*, the constant striving for the fulfillment of the state, which Foucault had discovered in *raison d'État*. Commenting on the emergence of modern state reason, Foucault (2008, 4) observed that the state "plays the role both of a given" and "at the same time, as an object to be constructed." The calculations of governmental practices should be "modeled on something called the state" and thus took place in the gap between the state that was already there and the state that was to be constructed, rendering the state as a permanently unfinished project. It seems, indeed, that in Foucault's analysis, and more strongly in Deleuze, the major dispositifs of state-making (law, discipline, and security) imbue the social field with diagrammatic ideals (the rightful verdict, perfect discipline, and unconstrained circulation) that propel governmental practices forward. Hence, one of the meanings of governmentalization is that of a state that always remains a reality to be achieved. Or, in Foucault's words, "the state is at once that which exists, but which does not yet exist enough" (4). The state is constantly in the making and hence becomes a kind of phantom or phantasm.

Deleuze's reading of Foucault effectively discards the idea of a state that is a particular historically formed political and jurisprudential innovation that puts an end to confessional and other conflicts and establishes public order and civil peace within a given territory. In this reading "the State itself appears as the overall effect or result of a series of interacting wheels or structures which are located at a completely different level" (Deleuze 1988, 25). We get the image of a state that is not anchored or embodied in institutional and legal orders. The state does not gain legitimacy through legality because the law can only act as a norm, a tactic, or a technology. Nor can its claim to a monopoly of violence be anything but an authoritarian gesture because power has become productive and sovereignty merely interdicts, forbids, and represses. Furthermore, the state's claim to a "transcendent" supremacy over a particular domain or territory is dissolved into multiple technologies, dispositifs, and virtual diagrams on a plane of immanence. As a result power seems to be dislodged from the conventional institutional locus of the state apparatus. It becomes a stream of forces that is shaped by the polymorphous points that it traverses: "Power is not homogeneous but can be defined only by the particular points through which it passes" (25). This assertion reflects the differential universe and the privilege of becoming over substance, which is emblematic of vitalism.

Indeed, the coexistence of multiple dispositifs renders the state a perpetually dynamic field where practices and institutions are overdetermined by different rationalities. Here, Foucault would appear to bear the mark of Deleuze's attempt at establishing a thinking of difference as such, which required that "substance must itself be said *of* the modes and only *of* the modes" (Deleuze

1994, 40–41; emphasis in the original). The imaginary solidity of the state is dissolved into a purely modal or differential universe. Put another way, the concept and the institution of the state can no longer be distinguished from the general regimes of governing that traverse it. The state becomes nothing but the fragile effect of multiple governmentalities.

Analytical Potentials

The analytical approach that can be reconstructed from Foucault's thinking on institutions, dispositifs, and diagrams has a number of possibilities for analyzing the contemporary welfare state, its potentials, and its challenges.

One possibility would be to look for inflection points where the institution's immediate self-description and its virtuality meet, intersect, or conflict and thus open up routes of contestation, innovation, and escape (Badiou 2000, 192). In Deleuzian terms what counters and threatens the power of the actual is, by definition, the nonactualized that constitutes lines of flight, a reservoir of potential means of contesting the existing order. To take a key problem: what does it imply to discover the technology of pastoral power animating the modern welfare state? As we know, Foucault indicated pastoral power as one of the constitutive technologies in the formation of the modern welfare state (SP). Pastoral power became a concrete political technology that gave rise to both the protection of the population's welfare and a pastoral guidance of individual consciousness. The merging of political power wielded over a population and an individualizing power directed at the subject within the welfare state structure was, in Foucault's words, a "tricky combination" and a "double bind" (336, 332). By integrating the old technology of pastoral power, the political subject of rights was dispersed into a series of subjective experiences and dispositions to be treated by experts of health and welfare: "instead of a pastoral power and a political power, more or less linked to each other, more or less in rivalry, there was an individualizing 'tactic' which characterized a series of powers: those of the family, medicine, psychiatry, education and employers" (335). Whereas subsequent scholars have foregrounded Foucault's comments on this individualizing side of pastoral power in critically studying welfare expertise, almost no attention has been given to the other side of pastoral power—namely, its universal imperative of compassion and care. One could, for instance, consider the counterintuitive assertion that "the 'hidden' foundation of bio-politics is love" (Ojakangas 2005, 5). Indeed, one potential for studying welfare institutions could be to interrogate points where the notion of divine grace and the

universal appeal for justice, healing, and caring irrespective of the person intersect with, challenges, or irrupts within welfare institutions and their individualizing and disciplinary practices.

A second potential consists in foregrounding the *interrelations* between
different dispositifs as the source of perpetual transformation and social inventiveness. In this perspective the social body is a moving field of contingencies predicated on multiple relations of force. We have noted the possibility
of interrogating how the interaction of multiple dispositifs—their mutual support, interpenetration, friction, and confrontation—induces movement in the
social field. At a given time the balance of forces may produce indeterminate
problems, governmental urgencies, or even new dispositifs. Recall Foucault's
analysis of how, in the nineteenth century, legal psychiatry emerged from the
urgency of minimizing risks internal to the population, while integrating measures to do so within the juridical system. There was, as we noticed in the previous chapter, a productive interchange between the legal technology and the
biopolitical technology (DI, 194).

In respect to the present day one might, for instance, explore the kind of
problems that have recently emerged at the intersection between different
dispositifs. For instance, problems within the European Union regarding the
control of national budgets as a requirement for a common economic policy
and monetary union could be elucidated as overdetermined by the dispositifs
of sovereign law, discipline, and security. Should the national governments of
the southern countries of the EU be subjected to sovereign intervention in the
shape of indisputable limits and sanctions imposed by the EU? Is it better to
discipline national administrations and banks by seeking to align them with
certain standards of financial responsibility? Or could market forces be relied on
to cure the sick economies by securing the freer circulation of capital and goods
across the member states? In other words is this an occasion for turning to regulatory practices organized as sovereign, disciplinary, or security dispositifs?

The anti-austerity struggles during recent years, especially in Greece and
Spain, reflect the paradox that inheres in twenty-first-century European welfare states that were born as at once capitalist and national-territorial entities.
On the one hand, member states' financial policies and public budgets must
be aligned and kept within certain levels to secure the effective functioning of
the internal market of the EU and membership of the Eurozone. On the other
hand, the inhabitants of EU countries are still granted social rights on the basis
of a political inclusion logic that is in essence territorially delineated within

national states (Lessenich 2011, 307). In Foucauldian terms the EU deploys a security dispositif to regulate the provision of rights granted under a sovereignty dispositif. Hence, we have seen mass protests against cutbacks on national social budgets, which are directed not only at governments in southern Europe but also at the EU, the European Central Bank, and the International Monetary Fund. The tension between formal equality and the production of substantive inequality characteristic of industrial capitalism *within* the national state now becomes a tension *between* national states with their democratic legitimation and the governmental-economic logics of the EU.

The recurring, thorny questions of immigration are other instances of the fundamental contradiction between the security imperative of facilitating free circulations, on the one hand, and the national sovereign rationality of political inclusion and access to rights premised on citizenship, on the other hand. Here, the conflict between the rationality of security and that of sovereignty helps elucidate why immigrant workers can now be conceived as a threat to the welfare state rationality, based on the maintenance of national boundaries and restricted access to rights and residence within the territory (Lessenich 2011). Novel governmental measures and techniques have been invented to "shield," control, isolate, survey, and distribute the threats allegedly posed against the national welfare state by immigrants, refugees, and other groups "on the move." Applying the optics of the dispositifs of law, discipline, and security and their mobile interplay could help analyze the rapid inventions taking place in this domain.

Limitations and Blind Spots

Deleuze saw vitalism as an enduring ontological premise in Foucault. It could be argued that this Deleuzian reading incorrectly turns Foucault's thinking into a "philosophy of immanence and becoming," an indigestible smorgasbord. Yet our examination of Foucault's elaborations of dispositifs and diagrams demonstrates many points of convergence with basic tenets in Deleuze's philosophy. We must also remember that neither the concept of the dispositif nor the diagram can be ascribed exclusively to Deleuze. Today these are rather "hybrid concepts" that have been developed from within a research stream that includes both Foucault and Deleuze (Checchi 2014, 203). In this light, seeking to establish precise demarcations between the two thinkers becomes less pertinent to present concerns, or at least more of a limited, biographical interest. For the key purpose of this book we are more concerned with marking the intellectual landscape that has arisen from, and is in dialogue with, the Foucauldian heritage.

In the present context we have witnessed the rise of intellectual streams that display fundamental similarities with the key sources of neovitalism: perspectivism and a focus on immanence, contingency, and the empirical. A number of converging interpretations have gained salience, associating Foucault with theories of social complexity (Collier 2009), autogenerative power (Pottage 1998), organizational polyphony (Kornberger, Clegg, and Carter 2006), or a nonfoundational approach to "the state as practice" (Bevir and Rhodes 2010). Stephen Collier (2009, 80) suggests that Foucault's analysis of dispositifs marks out "the broad configurational principles" through which formations of new practices take place. In Jeffrey Nealon's (2008) reinterpretation of Foucault's concept of power, the key category is "intensity" insofar as Nealon suggests that different forms of power are merely different in terms of their degree of intensity. Alain Pottage's (1998) comparative reading of Deleuze, Foucault, and Niklas Luhmann recasts power from "substance" to "emergence," rendering power as the momentary outcome of the repetition of systemic actions. In organizational studies Richard Weiskopf and Iain Munro (2012) interpret Foucault's views of neoliberal government as the regulation of "controlled circulation" and a framework for understanding postdisciplinary Human Resources Management. This regime is constituted by managerial strategies that strive to become immanent to "work relations"; it generates flexible organizational forms that contain both the possibility of increased control and more freedom and autonomy. Common to these different intellectual streams is that they view organizing as involving ever-changing movements and becomings rather than as arrangements of substances, entities, and constraints. If we consider these tendencies within governance theory, process philosophy, management studies, and more, Foucault's prediction in "Theatrum Philosphicum" (TPH, 343) that "perhaps one day, this century will be known as Deleuzian" was not completely misplaced. Deleuze and, it must also be said, Foucault have arrived and been welcomed at business school disciplines such as entrepreneurship, innovation management, and organizational aesthetics.

The evacuation of all static and institutional frameworks of analysis has a number of costs. Serious limitations weigh on this Foucauldian intelligibility. Law, for example is not simply a binary code of allowing and forbidding, or an expression of omnicompetent sovereignty. It can be approached through its practices of lawmaking, implementing, and administering its rules and procedures, such as those of criminal and civil proof, the adversary system, pleas, appeals and penalties, and various institutional spaces (from the court to the parliament), personages (lawyers, judges, jury, legislators, police officers), forms of judgment, and kinds of training. Law can be just as facilitative as it is prohibitive. Importantly, law facilitates the modern state, which is not only a lawmaking and law-governed entity but a law-organized, law-regulated, and law-coordinated one, as Gianfranco Poggi argues (1990, 29). Foucault's multiple *topoi* of power at times begin to look like caricatures of this relationship. There is no doubt that they allow us to understand the interplay between modern administrative rationalities that structure the space of state regulation. And they may facilitate studying diverse *regimes* of government (welfarism, neoliberalism, and their related technical means) that seek to appropriate the state, but they do not begin to approach the long-standing key questions of the constitutional state itself and its defining features. Where Raymond Aron made the distinction between "regime" and "state," Foucault would try to reduce the latter to the former.

On the one hand, the immanentist rendering of Foucault's framework harbors an analytical openness to complex social processes. It enables us to track the unpredictable, nonlinear emergence of self-propelling imperatives of power and their difficult materialization. On the other hand, this analytical landscape bears the traces of Deleuze's philosophical conception of immanent creativity. This concept entails, as Hallward (2006, 7) argues, an orientation "towards a contemplative and immaterial abstraction" that rather than engaging with this world seeks to escape it. This is so because Deleuze's philosophy is concerned with affirming an immanent creative force running through all events and creatures allowing their differentiation and counteractualization. Hallward emphasizes this philosophy's quasi-transcendent tendency: "the affirmation of an expressive or creative immanence does not so much eliminate the question of transcendence as distribute it throughout creation as a whole" (6). Considering the political implications of Deleuze's philosophy, Hallward concludes that his "philosophy of creation without limits" ironically "inhibits any consequential engagement with the constraints of our actual world" (160–61), including how to empower its inhabitants.

It may be argued that the rendering of the state as a virtual structure does not merely have effects in terms of what is left out of view, such as legality and legitimacy, the organization and coordination of the state and its agencies through law, the state and sovereign capacities, and coercive instruments and social conditions. According to Žižek, there is a particular performativity in postmodern representations of the world as a "permanent becoming," as deeply heterogeneous, fragmented, and intersected by webs of micropower whose effects and social value cannot be decided. This "extremely suspect rhetoric of complexity," championed by Foucault and his followers, portrays power as an "intricate network of lateral links, left and right, up and down . . . a clear case of patching up, since one can never arrive at Power this way" (Žižek 1999, 66). The rhetoric of complexity—itself mirroring the use of complexity theory by those such as Friedrich Hayek (1967)—separates the microprocedures of power from any overall system or structure. The concrete effect renders it impossible to point out someone as power-holder, to perceive some structures as primary to others, or to conceive of some form of cultural, social, political, or economic dominance. Taking aim at institutional analysis, it can be argued that to introduce an ontology of becoming, productive differences, and free-flowing process easily conveys the image of a withdrawal of power and control. Thus the play of differences is set free to unfold in its natural and creative form. No structural measures of equalization and no major dispositif of power are needed for such virtuality to thrive and unfold on the newfound planes of immanence.

We wonder whether, by such means, this immanence perspective has not systematically occluded key problems inherent to the analysis of the state, that is, of a historically specific set of institutions separate from rulers and ruled, organized through law, and claiming a centralization of power and supremacy or transcendence within a given domain or territory. This figure disappears in the optics of dispositifs, diagrams and practices, multiplicity and immanence. Not only does the possibility of the use of sovereign violence recede, but other sovereign rights and capacities do so as well: the monopoly of the final decision, of taxation, of lawmaking and law enforcement, to declare war, to make treaties with other states, and so on. One may speculate, what civil chaos would ensue, were the state and its agents to take seriously this field of virtuality and plane of immanence?

CHAPTER 8

WHEN SOCIETY PREVAILS

The many parallels between Foucault's general statements on politics and his statements advocating the virtue and vitality of civil society suggest, as Ian Hunter (1998, 260–61) maintained, that Foucault approached civil society as the "social delimitation of the state." But in his most extended discussion of civil society Foucault adopts an approach that is neither the social delimitation of the state nor quite an artifact of "political improvisation and juridical decision" (261). Civil society, in this rendering, is indeed an artifact, but it is one of a particular form of knowledge and governmental innovation. In this discussion it becomes an entirely constructed entity or kind of imaginary domain internal to liberal governmentality and a key site of "veridiction." That is, it is a form of truth-telling required to make operable a liberal art of government.

As an epistemic-governmental innovation, however, civil society for Foucault does not quite amount to a "political neutralization of confessional society" (Hunter 1998, 260). Its main function for Foucault is to mark a key event in the becoming-immanent of governmental rationality so that it is no longer tied to the transcendent figures of God, natural law, the sovereign, the prince, the father, or even the state and so that the "rationality of the governed must serve as the regulating principle for the rationality of government" (Foucault 2008, 312). Foucault's account, nevertheless, cannot quite escape confessional or theological elements. They keep reentering his genealogy. In the case of civil society, its logic creates the possibility of a kind of countermovement, or counterpractice, based on an antigovernmental and antistatist eschatology. It is precisely this paradox of Foucault's genealogy of the arts of government that we now address, first by an exposition of his discussion of the eighteenth-century concept of civil society and its relation to what he calls political eschatology.

Civil Society

The most extended discussion of civil society appears near the end of *The Birth of Biopolitics* (2008) and is focused on Adam Ferguson's (1819) *Essay on the History of Civil Society*, first published in 1767. Foucault proposes that the notion of civil society has key consequences for how we may think about government and, in particular, the government of the state. In a related interview he suggests that the moment when government seeks a principle of its limitation in an outside that is not completely penetrable by its own mechanisms is the moment when government has to deal not only "with a territory, with a domain, and with its subjects, but . . . with a complex and independent reality that has its own laws and mechanisms of disturbance. This new reality is society" (Foucault 1989, 261). The approach to civil society here is not first of all a normative or political one but a genealogical one that seeks the conditions of emergence of such an object of knowledge in the liberal arts of government.

In a number of very different contexts Foucault brings up the difficult and complex relationship and treatment of different pairs of subjects. These pairs include juridical-political subjects with rights and governmental ones with needs, those presupposed by the shepherd-flock game and city-citizen games, those placed in forms of totalization and individualization, those subjected to sovereignty and the living beings of biopower, and those formed by techniques of government and by techniques of the self. Giorgio Agamben (1998, 6) has observed that Foucault never succeeds in resolving their relationship since they trace a series of nearly parallel lines toward a kind of vanishing point. In the case of the emergence of thinking about civil society, the existence of two kinds of subjects is presented as the problem to which civil society is the solution. Here the problem is the fundamental incompatibility between two different domains of governing and the subjects who are to be governed within them, that of political economy with *homo œconomicus*, on the one hand, and that of jurisprudence, with the juridical subject of rights crucial to the composition of a political order, on the other. Civil society emerges, in Foucault's words, as a "transactional reality" that allows for balancing or integrating two divergent images of the governed subject—the juridical subject and the economic subject (2008, 296).

For Foucault *homo œconomicus* is, in the eighteenth century, a kind of ideal point inserted into the field of governing: "With regard to *homo œconomicus*, one must *laisser-faire*; he is the subject or object of *laissez-faire*" (2008, 270). He then proceeds to show that in British empiricism the choices or interests of the subject are irreducible because, like David Hume's case of the preference for health over sickness, they cannot be broken down any further. Moreover, they are nontransferable. This principle is demonstrated by Hume's argument that, despite the obvious difference in order of significance, we would prefer not to cut off our little finger even if doing so meant the prevention of the death of someone else (Foucault 2008, 272–74). By contrast the juridical subject undergoes, in the jurisprudence of William Blackstone, a series of reductions and recompositions of its interest. The subject of natural rights agrees to give them up and accept their limitation under the law. In the social contract the interested individual is transformed into the subject of rights and obligations. The latter, having exercised an initial interest in entering the contract, now has an interest in the continuation of the contract and accepts it as a kind of transcendent source of obligation. Hume, in an imaginary dialogue, answers that there is no transcendence of interest by right. Subjects continue to be bound by the contract only insofar as it is in their interest to do so; when it ceases to be in their interest, they will abandon it.

Foucault (2008, 276) argues that these types of subject are "absolutely heterogeneous and cannot be superimposed on each other." The economic subject has a "multiplying and beneficial value through the intensification of interest"; this simply does not match the transition from natural right to civil subordination of the legal subject. The involuntary harmonization of interests by *homo œconomicus* engaged in exchange is pitted against the voluntary renunciation and composition of right in a totalized and transcendent law. Foucault concludes: "Liberalism acquired its modern shape precisely with the formulation of this essential incompatibility between the non-totalizable multiplicity of economic subjects of interest and the totalizing unity of the juridical sovereign" (282). In this setup *homo œconomicus* becomes the "island of rationality possible within an economic process" that points to the "impossibility of a sovereign point of view over the totality of the state he has to govern."

For Foucault two impossible solutions are presented to this problem of the sovereign finding this rational island, which must be let alone, within its juridical domain. The first is the excising of political economy from the sphere of sovereignty. This is the role Adam Smith's "invisible hand" is assigned in the scenario. It is possible to imagine that the sovereign exercises a kind of "reason of state" over the entire domain of rule with the economic domain occupied by *homo œconomicus* as a space of exception. "The market will be, if you like, a sort of free port or free space in the general space of sovereignty" (Foucault 2008, 293). Then there is the more baroque solution of the physiocrats, who maintain the authority of the sovereign over the entire domain of rule but construct a table of all the economic exchanges within the state so that the sovereign can recognize the "evidence" that places them in a position of theoretical passivity in relation to the economy (284–86).

In reality neither of these can be applied, argues Foucault; rather, "a complete reorganization of government reason was carried out on the basis of this problem" (2008, 294). A new "plane of reference" is needed, which is more than a collection of atomic economic subjects or merchants and more than a subject of rights from which is constituted a political order. This plane will answer three questions: how do we preserve the global character of governing? how do we ensure governing is not subject to economic reason? and how do we ensure that it is not split into a juridical government and an economic government? More positively, the unity, generality, and specificity of the art of government must be given by reference to this new plane of reference: "civil society" (295).

Thinking about civil society ("which is very quickly called society" [Foucault 2008, 296]) comes about, then, as a correlate of an art and technology of government. This new style of thinking is distinguished from the juridical discourse of sovereignty that posits a state of nature prior to the consent that establishes or accedes to civil government. It is also distinguished from *Polizeiwissenschaften* or police sciences, mercantilism, and *raison d'État* in that all of these assumed a fundamental transparency and effectiveness, of knowledge and will, between the governors and the governed. None of these proposes an opaque domain outside the political order, with its own history, its own forces and struggles, its own groups and hierarchies, and its own voice. In all these ways "civil society" is a kind of third term that places sovereignty and economic governance, and their respective subjects, as relative moments within a specific and concrete milieu.

We wish to underline that this historical-natural plane of civil society from which government organically emerges is not merely a new truth discovered by the Scottish Enlightenment. It is a new way of organizing the art of government of the state; and from this perspective "civil society" is anything but a natural, extrastate, domain. Notably, Foucault does not ascribe any substantial qualities to civil society but inserts the concept into a genealogy that describes the various functions attributed to it by Enlightenment political thinkers, Ferguson in particular. Foucault thereby counsels a form of prudence "regarding the degree of reality we accord to this civil society. It is not an historical-natural given which functions in some way as both the foundation of and source of opposition to the state or political institutions. Civil society is not a primary and immediate reality" (2008, 297). Here Foucault opposes the idea of civil society as representing a source of inherently progressive resistance against the state. "Civil society" for Foucault remains an epistemic-governmental innovation that emerged historically as a solution to specific difficulties and concerns. There is nothing universal about it. Civil society appeared, then, not as a substantial social domain but rather as the key imaginary object *internal* to liberal governmental rationality.

Foucault undertakes four analytical displacements of the concept. First, he performs a denaturalization and desubstantialization of civil society and thereby avoids naturalism and ideology critique. This means that civil society is not a naturally given object but one that cannot be reduced to an illusion or an ideological effect. Foucault thus applies his particular variant of historical nominalism to civil society, like he did to madness, delinquency, sexuality, and the state. For him civil society does not exist as a concrete reality. It is not a universal that appears in different historical guises. However, certain practices have recourse to it, invoke it, and organize themselves in relation to it, in particular, with regard to questions of true and false ways of governing.

Second, as mentioned above, civil society emerged as a "transactional reality." This means it served to balance or arbitrate the "transaction" between two forms of knowledge of the subject—as legal subject and as the subject of interest. It is a register that allows the integration into the administrative rationality of political rule of another figure: the culturally embedded subject about which the sovereign can never achieve exhaustive knowledge. Civil society was an important governmental innovation since it established an immanent domain that dispensed with the assumption of an all-knowing sovereign.

Third, civil society is also a transactional reality in another sense that concerns the relations of power between the governors and the governed. Foucault says that transactional realities are born "at the interface . . . of governors and governed" (Foucault 2008, 297). This transactional reality is an unstable surface of engagement between government and governed, an "interplay of relations of power and everything which constantly eludes them" (297). Civil society thus opens government to the governed in a more flexible and mobile fashion.

Foucault comments that this implies that a "limitation is not exactly imposed by either one side or the other, or at any rate not globally, definitively, and totally, but by, I would say, transaction, in the very broad sense of the word, that is to say, 'action between,' that is to say, by a series of conflicts, agreements, discussions, and reciprocal concessions" (12).

Finally, civil society has in Foucault's analysis an open-ended, multivalent, and almost virtual character. The operation of power will no longer be founded on an original contract but on the specific practices, constraints, and capacities existing at the interface between governors and governed. Civil society can be mobilized by very different political forces, which invoke divergent images of it. As we will soon see, Foucault is particularly observant in regard to religious or quasi-religious articulations of civil society that promise unification, final reconciliation of all conflicts, and a fusion of state and society.

This analysis thus stands in stark contrast to Foucault's earlier and indeed ongoing "enthusiasms" for local struggles and subjugated knowledges, for a form of power and resistance that arises from the bottom, and for a warm vitalism against the cold monster of the state. It is also different from his view of the social body under the *ancien régime* as one of petty squabbles, denunciations, and collusions with sovereign power. Here we have a measured, analytical Foucault who brackets his own and others' enthusiasms and passionate identifications for a rather cooler analysis of the way civil society features in and makes possible liberalism, considered not as a political philosophy but as an art of government. And when we consider this is a rationality of state governing, then Foucault's analysis would seem to question the very opposition between state and civil society.

Teleology and Eschatology

Civil society and a law-governed state are, as Dominique Colas will later conclude (1997, 346–53), the interrelated parts of one set of political arrangements. They are properly opposed neither to each other nor to a state despotism but to the "fanaticism" of those who call for unmediated authority and reject representation and "the 'interval' between the City of God and the Earthly City" (354–55). Fanaticism, in this sense, forms around passionate enthusiasms for civil society and manifests itself in what Foucault characterized as an antigovernmental "eschatology" (2007b, 356).

The eschatological tradition lends to political movements claims of directionality and purpose in human history, promises of salvation, and the idea of a final time of fulfillment. It is an idiom that involves unifying theories of human nature and justifies political intervention for the fulfillment of ultimate purposes of human existence. But while Foucault notes that modern political eschatologies emerged alongside and as a response to the process of governmentalization, he ignores the theological elements in Scottish Enlightenment thinkers such as Adam Smith and Adam Ferguson.

In contrast, the intellectual historian Lisa Hill (2006, 43) has argued "it is extremely important to understand Ferguson's attempt to build a social science in the context of his prior theological and moral commitments." We can see these clearly in an early passage from his *Essay*: "We forget that physical powers, employed in succession or together, and combined to a salutary purpose, constitute the very proofs of design from which we infer the existence of God. . . . We can only collect the laws which the Author of nature has established; and in our latest as well as our earliest discoveries, only perceive a mode of creation or providence before unknown" (Ferguson 1819, 10–11). In straightforward terms, since "Ferguson's God is a distant, non-interventionist 'General Providence,' the world requires laws to maintain an 'order of things, which in a state of counteraction and apparent disturbance, mutually regulate and balance one another'" (Hill 2006, 43). This God is one of design and providence, a first cause that works through the operation of efficient causes, including that of the free will of individuals, which, apparently blindly operating amid conflict, result in equilibrium and harmony. It is such a God who is behind Ferguson's spontaneous-order thinking. And while Ferguson's history is not explicitly eschatological, it is, as Hill points out, "theologically conventional in terms of its perfectibilist and teleological aspects" (55). Civil society results from God's design, and its development serves his ends.

Foucault highlights Ferguson's assumptions about the spontaneous, self-generating nature of the social-economic order and the necessary self-limitation of government. Ferguson figures in his analysis as an early proponent of the postulate of an autonomous domain, civil society, which is independent of the artificial constructions of government. Located in a transition, Ferguson represents the modern idea that the principles of governing are intrinsic to the social order and should not be derived from a divine, preordained plan or even from the reality of the state itself. Nevertheless, contra Foucault, Ferguson's thought displays a significant theological dimension, insofar as he asserts the existence of a "providential order" that secures an inherent directionality of human history. Like Foucault, Hill views Ferguson's work as located in a transitional phase of social science, but she emphasizes that Ferguson, as a moral philosopher, sought to "persuade a sophisticated, enlightenment readership of the enduring relevance of the agency of the 'Divine Architect' to modern social theory" (Hill 1998, 58). The transitional element that Hill finds in Ferguson is his synthesis of classical teleology with a modern conception of progress.

Ferguson's dual claim of self-creation of the human species and the existence of a preordained order is predicated on a distinction between "efficient causes" and "final causes" (Hill 1998, 52). The first defines the immediate, individual motivations that drive people in their daily acts, while the latter designates the divine plan that is realized by way of these acts in their accumulation. Hill concludes that Ferguson's thought meets the "minimal requirement of teleology" insofar as "any teleological formulation must, by definition, refer to God as unrealized perfection" (54).

The theological dimension in Ferguson inscribes a continuity in the genealogy of government that problematizes Foucault's historical narrative of a rupture between medieval theology and the atheistic modern political rationalities such as the reason of state and liberalism. Foucault consistently sidelines the theological and teleological dimension in Ferguson and deliberately rejects providentialist elements in the "hidden hand" of Adam Smith. The presence of notions of preordained order and divine plan in early liberal thinkers complicates Foucault's view that political economy fundamentally confirms the secularism of modern political reasoning inaugurated by reason of state. The idea of a purely empirical reality, "an open seriality," becomes difficult to sustain. Similarly, to depict the object of liberal governing as an immanent domain of unfolding transactions in time and space is to tell only one side of the story. On the other side lie notions of the ontological scarcity discovered by Malthus, which teaches humans proper political and moral conduct and the existence of a transcendent domain of territorial sovereignty that restricts movements, bars entry, and disqualifies categories of the governed.

There is, however, one exception to Foucault's occlusion of the theological in modern political thought. At the very end of *Security, Territory, Population* he seeks to forge a link between the notion of civil society and eschatology, not as an intrinsic feature of the notion of civil society but as a kind of counterconduct to the "indefinite time" of governmentality (Foucault 2007b, 355). After leaving out the providential elements of the emergence of the concept of civil society, he suggests the concept may function as a condition of possibility of an eschatological counterconduct. Foucault's argument is this: the indefinite time of modern governmentality, presupposed by reason of state doctrines, had "excluded the Empire of the last days" and "the kingdom of eschatology" (355–56). However, "counter-conducts develop that make it a principle to assert the coming of a time when time will end, and to posit the possibility of an eschatology, of a final time, of a suspension or completion of historical and political time when, if you like, the indefinite governmentality of the state will be brought to an end and halted" (356).

These countermovements do this by means of the notion of civil society itself that allows them to conceive of a time when civil society can free itself of the state or absorb the state into itself. Accompanying the advent of modern governmentality were utopian movements that adhered to beliefs in the coming of a human community not regulated by the state. These movements shared the hope for a day when the state would dissolve into a unified, organic community. This vision extended from utopian experiments with ideal socialist colonies to the scientific Marxist postulate of the withering away of the state to aspects of the 1960s counterculture. In some respects fascism and National Socialism promise a similar replacement of state authority with that of the movement, the people, the nation, or the *Volk*, grounded in the organic realities of blood and soil and as articulated by the Leader. Libertarian liberalisms exhibit an antistate eschatology in the name of a community of free individuals interacting around the market. All these movements rest in some degree on the promise to bring the indefinite existence of the state to a halt by invoking the coming of a final, noncontradictory, and predestined people, nation, society, or population (Foucault 2007b, 356–57).

We might think that Foucault's use of the term *political eschatology* is a way of denoting strong Left and Right political positions such as the Marxist "withering away of the state" or fascist nationalism. There is certainly an element of that in his view. However, its linkage to civil society is here telling and resonates very strongly with a suggestion at the end of *The Birth of Biopolitics*. There he cites the English-American revolutionary republican views of Thomas Paine at the beginning of his famous 1776 pamphlet *Common Sense*, which Foucault interprets as asking, "Could not society exist without government, or at any rate, without a government other than the government it has created spontaneously and without need of institutions which take charge of civil society, as it were, and impose constraints which it does not accept?" (2008, 310). Paine's polemic, we might note, on the goodness of society and the wickedness that gives rise to government is germane not simply to English political thought but also to the entire American republican tradition, over which Paine was influential at the time of the American Revolution, and the milieu in which the founding documents of the United States were composed. With Paine, and his political mobilization of the notion of civil society, we find the possibility, following Foucault, of a kind of eschatological reading of the notion of civil society that remains to our time an enduring presence within American politics and makes more intelligible the rejection of government by the recent Tea Party faction of the Republican Party and in American libertarianism broadly.

There are two further notable exemplars within Foucault's genealogy of eschatological themes in politics. The first is eschatology as one of the five examples of the "counter-conducts" to the Christian pastorate in the Middle Ages (Foucault 2007b, 214, 225–26n72). Here eschatology is a way of disqualifying the pastor's role by invoking the imminent return of the true pastor, God. Foucault provides us with the example of the twelfth-century Cistercian monk Joachim de Fiore of Calabria. It is worth dwelling on the form of this eschatology with the help of Norman Cohn's *The Pursuit of the Millennium* (1970) and Karl Löwith's *Meaning in History* (1949). Writing of Joachim's eschatology, Cohn suggests that it was the most influential one known in Europe until Marxism (108). What was novel about it was that Joachim had discerned in the scriptures the organization of history into three ages, which became a way of understanding and forecasting mundane human history. He had discovered the Age of the Father, which was an age of law and fear and servitude, in the Old Testament, commencing with Abraham. This was followed by the Age of the Son, an age of the Gospel, faith, and filial submission or "learning and discipline" (Löwith 1949, 148), commencing with Christ. He now forecast the imminent Age of the Spirit, an age of love, joy, and freedom in which God directly resides in the hearts of all men. This would initiate a Kingdom of the Saints that would last until the Last Judgment, which itself would be preceded by the years of the Antichrist and a *novus dux* (Cohn 1970, 109). (Later, Franciscan Joachites would find the Antichrist in the emperor of the Holy Roman Empire, Frederick II, in whom others found the new king.) Each of these ages corresponded not only to a Person of the Trinity but also to the figure of the Prophet, the Messiah, and the Holy Spirit, and to the seasons of winter, early spring, and high summer. Foucault therefore finds something of the virtue and vitality that is sometimes attributed today to the realm of civil society: "Now the Holy Spirit is not incarnated in a prophet, and he is not incarnated in a person; he is spread over the entire world. . . . There will be a particle, a fragment, a spark of the Holy Spirit in each of the faithful and so they will no longer need a shepherd" (2007b, 214). One of the interesting features of Joachim's stages is that they are overlapping and coexist at different levels and meaning (Löwith 1949, 148).

The second example of eschatology concerns reason of state (*raison d'État*) itself and its critique of the absolute eschatology of the waiting for the kingdom of the final days (Foucault 2007b, 300). In doing so, it opens the possibility of a kind of "relative eschatology" of a perpetual peace that is "expected from a plurality without major unitary effects of domination." The plurality, of course, is a world of different but formally equal sovereign states. In the following year's lectures Foucault (2008, 57–58) will make reference to Immanuel Kant's narrative of perpetual peace, which is, again, like Joachim's history, tripartite: the human propensity to exchange leads to the civil law of the separate states, the separate states in turn to international law, and the movement of exchange across borders to cosmopolitan law. As Foucault suggests, "the guarantee of perpetual peace is therefore actually commercial globalization." Liberal economic government initiates, in other words, the possibility of a kind of commercial eschatology.

On the one hand, then, Foucault's genealogy of the arts of government wants to emphasize, against the evidence as it were, the secular and even atheistic elements of the emergence of these critical governmental rationalities, such as Enlightenment protosociology and economic liberalism. He finds in civil society the milieu in which the relative claims of the juridical subject of rights and the economic subject of interests can be managed and resolved. Civil society emerges as the prism through which the subject can be conceived as no longer subordinated to the prince within a theological-cosmological order but as an empirical being who stands in a complex relationship to the worldly order of men and things. On the other hand, Foucault is keen to remind us of the eschatological possibilities entailed in these governmental rationalities, especially those based on civil society.

CHAPTER 9

POLITICAL AND ECONOMIC THEOLOGY

Foucault's genealogy of political sovereignty in the West is marked by a curious ambivalence. On the one hand, it resembles something like a story of secularization. This narrative links the emergence of modern governmentality to Christian confessional practice through the Judeo-Christian heritage of the pastorate. It then designates a series of secular breaks—reason of state, liberalism—with the theological-cosmological continuum he finds in the Middle Ages, particularly in Thomist thought. In this sense he postulates a progressive movement toward more secular forms of governmental thought and reason. On the other hand, as we have just seen, theological and eschatological themes recur in his narrative, not least in his discussion of the eschatological potentials of civil society and population and in the multiplication of forms of pastoral expertise.

How can we understand this component of his political thought and its implications for the state? To answer this question, we here situate Foucault in relation to the important debates that have occurred in relation to political theology and secularization and the theme of economic theology.

Political Theology and Secularization

In his brief meditations on the way the concept of civil society makes possible a political eschatology that dreams of an end of the state or a wholly self-governing society, Foucault stumbles backward onto the terrain of two key and related debates that framed important discussion in German political thought throughout the twentieth century. They concern political theology and secularization.

The debate on secularization achieved some degree of prominence in Germany during the 1960s. The key combatants at that time were Hans Blumenberg and Carl Schmitt. In *The Legitimacy of the Modern Age* (1985) Blumenberg sought to maintain the "self-assertion" of modernity in a radical caesura with its cosmological and theological origins. Blumenberg does not deny the theological and eschatological elements in many ideas that express this self-assertion. But they are contingent, not necessary, features of modern rationality, which is characterized by a "reoccupation" of the Christian medieval schema. "The idea of 'reoccupation' says nothing about the derivation of the newly installed element, only about the dedication it receives at its installation" (Blumenberg 1985, 49).

Schmitt (2008), in his response, would identify a kind of aggressiveness in such a position in which the new, the present, and the secular attacked the old, the past, and the religious. In this respect Schmitt found himself aligned with Löwith (1949), who had detected an eschatology in Western philosophy of history. For Schmitt, Blumenberg's stance is a nihilism of the utmost aggression: "This is the opposite of creation *out* of nothing, because it is the creation *of* nothingness as the condition of the possibility of the self-creation of an ever-new worldliness" (Schmitt 2008, 129; emphasis in original).

The alternative positions within this debate would consider secularization, through a series of qualifications, clarifications, and restatements, in terms of either the continued eminence of the theological in the present or a definite rupture with theology. What was at stake was the founding of political modernity, its thought and practice, either from theological concepts or out of itself.

Foucault's political thought cannot be definitively situated in relation to this debate. There are his well-known precepts against teleological and totalizing historical narratives, both in respect to archaeology (1972) and genealogy (NGH, 369–91). But the general tenor and directionality of his genealogy of the arts of government would appear to place him in the first camp. Thus, he characterizes medieval political thought as positing a "theological-cosmological continuum" that is punctured by the secular rationalities of "reason of state" and, later, liberalism (Foucault 2007b, 234–37; 2008, 282). Indeed, Foucault is at pains to emphasize the atheistic character of these secular rationalities of rule.

For Foucault reason of state is denounced as the "devil's reason" by Pope Pius V because it transfers political authority and its legitimacy to the domain of earthly rule (2007b, 242). It shatters the eschatology of medieval political cosmology that situates mundane government between Christ's appearance on earth as the Messiah and his Second Coming. And it places the worldly sovereign on a continuum between God and the father by way of nature and the pastor—a kind of Great Chain of Being of authority (234). In consequence politics is now no longer expected to reach a closure with the definite end at the Apocalypse. Instead it recognizes the plurality of states in international law and the relationship between and among states as a "balance of forces." Politics will henceforth be conducted in an "open time and a multiple spatiality" of conflict and history (291). While medieval thought dreamed of the reconstitution of the Roman Empire to await the Second Coming, reason of state now accepts the plurality of more or less equal states and sovereigns.

The impression of a historical trajectory that breaks with a theological cosmology is confirmed by Foucault's characterization of classical political economy, the critical form of knowledge in dialogue with the liberal art of government, as an atheistic one without God or totality (2008, 282). Basing his position on Adam Smith and the invisible hand metaphor, Foucault argues that such a form of knowledge knows neither a sovereign point of view nor totality and cannot therefore have a place for a God within it (278). Foucault wants to emphasize the element of invisibility in the metaphor, thus stressing the idea that knowledge is denied economic actors in the market or any political agent. To emphasize "hand," by contrast, would mean Smith's view is something like that of "a providential god who would occupy the economic process a bit like Malebranche's God occupies the entire world" (278). This reference to providentialism is extremely telling because, as Hill (2001) has extensively shown, providence is fundamental to both Smith and Ferguson in that "far from being an aberrant 'trinket' Smith's notion of a Providential invisible hand is, not only the centrepiece, but the unifying principle or 'metaphysical core' . . . of his entire *oeuvre* without which much of his thought makes little sense" (2). Foucault's characterization of the "invisible hand" perhaps willfully ignores the scholarly treatment of Smith's conscious use of it on three separate occasions (Macfie 1971), its location in his broader moral and political philosophy, including in *The Theory of Moral Sentiments*, and the theological genealogy of the hand metaphor in theology (Agamben 2011, 284). All stand as evidence of the existence of a divine presence, manifest in first and final causes, in establishing the natural and providential order of market and society. The mention of Father Malebranche, the author of a seminal tract on theodicy, *The Treatise on Nature and Grace*, is also interesting here, as we will see in revisiting Foucault's discussion of Rousseau.

Using the "invisible hand" as a kind of warning signal about Foucault's historical narrative of the arts of government, we might ask how he could have

made what on the face of it seems an elementary error? The answer is that Foucault wants Smith and, with him, Adam Ferguson to stand as crucial markers
within a more general movement from transcendental foundations of rule in
divine, natural, or human law toward immanent forms of government in which
governing will come to be founded, as Foucault puts it, on "the rationality of
the governed." This would seem to indicate a strong secularization thesis in the
manner of Blumenberg.

Given that Foucault reads Ferguson and Smith in such a secular way, it
is strange that he rediscovers the eschatological impulse in notions such as
civil society and in the kind of settlement between states imagined in reason of state, as we have noted. But there is a second side of Foucault's genealogy of government, one that falls in the camp of those who maintain the
eminence of the theological in the political practices of the present. Thus, in
his lectures on governmentality from 1978, Foucault devotes the major part
of five lectures to the genealogy of the government of conduct in pastoral
practices inherited from Judaism by way of Christianity (2007b, 115–253). The
point of all this is not especially clear, although he suggests toward the end
of the fourth of these lectures on the pastorate, that it was "to find the inner
depth and background of the governmentality that begins to develop in the
sixteenth century" (215). But the passage from ecclesiastical government to
secular government remains obscure in Foucault and appears to be explained
by the development of "counterconducts" that will finally explode in the Reformation and the Counter-Reformation. There is, however, something unsettling in the way he cannot leave the problem of the pastorate and, even after
promising not to speak about it further at the end of this fourth lecture on
it (216), he returns to it the following week with equally unsatisfying results.
In a related text, "The Subject and Power," however, Foucault distinguishes
between the lost "ecclesiastical institutionalization" of the pastorate and "its
function, which spread and multiplied outside the ecclesiastical institution"
(SP, 333). It would thus seem that Foucault's thesis is that it is the loss of the
monopoly of the Catholic Church at the time of the Reformation that releases
the pastoral function from its purely religious locus onto multiple institutional sites and personages in contemporary society. He appears to want to
maintain a view of secularization as the changing institutional forms of the
function of pastoral care.

One way to address this equivocation at the heart of Foucault's narrative of
the development of modern governmentality would be to consider the theme

of political theology, a theme not particularly well understood by social theorists. Political theology refers us back to Carl Schmitt and the two books of the same title first published in 1922 and in 1970 (2005, 2008), particularly the earlier one. There the term famously referred to the structural analogies that could be drawn between theological and political concepts, such as between God and the sovereign, or, as he famously noted, the miracle and the exception (Schmitt 2005, 36). In his analysis of those thinkers who be believes presided over the birth of the liberal art of government, Smith and Ferguson, Foucault actively suppresses the theological element and thus the possibility of a kind of structural analogy between theological and political concepts. At almost the same time in *Roman Catholicism and Political Form* (1996), however, Schmitt offered another way of thinking about political theology. In a kind of point-by-point complement to Max Weber's thesis of the elective affinity between capitalist economic acquisition and the ascetic Protestant Ethic, Schmitt argued for a relationship between the form of the modern state and the juridical rationalism embodied in the Roman Catholic Church and its canon law.

There are, then, not one, but two, axes of political theology in Schmitt. Along one we find a synchronic sociology of juristic and political concepts that establishes a systematic structural analogy between theological-metaphysical and political concepts. Along the other there is a diachronic genealogy of political form, which follows the secular modifications and adaptations of the institutional practices of the church, including its canon law and its notions of vicarious representation and office.

Foucault offers us a political theology in something like this second sense. It is the very function of the pastorate that has entered into modern expertise and officialdom in the modern arts of government. If elsewhere Schmitt (2010) talks of a political *neutralization* of theological conflict that leads to the establishment of the secular state, we could say that Foucault offers us a liberal economic neutralization that releases the function of the pastorate onto modern experts and officials in private and public organizations, bureaucratic hierarchies, contractual market relations, and institutions of social care.

Foucault also adds the dynamic relation between religious authority and diverse countermovements. Again, however, we note that Foucault's claim about the nature of the relationship is rather vague. He muses: "And I wonder whether we could not establish some, I don't say analogies exactly, but correspondences, as it were" (2007b, 355). He follows this with a long list of possible relations and examples of these correspondences between the counterconducts of the Middle

Ages and resistance to *raison d'État* of modern liberal governmentality without, it must be said, reaching any definite conclusion.

Economic Theology

The focus on the genealogy of the pastorate in Foucault could thus be understood as a concern with the theological sources of the political form of the government of conduct and thus closer to Schmitt's genealogy of political form, what Ernst-Wolfgang Böckenförde during this debate on secularization called an "institutional political theology" (Müller 2003, 166–68). However, this leaves aside the discovery of the eschatological dimension of the notion of civil society. It is interesting that for Foucault civil society is discovered as a "plane of reality" in which human subjects can be governed as something more than either *homo œconomicus* or juridical subjects of right, that is, as social subjects with bonds of association, communal ties, customs, conflicts, and so on. It is therefore not strictly fashioned as a political concept but as a governmental or even managerial one. Here we can invoke the key distinction made by Giorgio Agamben (2011, 1) between the paradigms of political theology and economic theology. Whereas the former concerns the terrain of the political narrowly conceived as that of sovereignty and the traditional concepts of political philosophy, the latter addresses the theological genealogy of the concepts and practices through which social existence and life more broadly are regulated and thus brings into play concepts around governing and the management of the economy. In *The Kingdom and the Glory* (2011, xi), which he immediately "locates in the wake of Michel Foucault's investigations into the genealogy of governmentality," Agamben traces a theological genealogy of government and economy from ancient thought, and the early and medieval Christian theology of the *oikonomia*, which would be called on to explain the mystery of the Trinity and of notions of providence and order. One of Agamben's theses here is that although reflection on secular government is a relatively recent phenomenon, the vocabulary and logics by which we think about problems of governing the economy, and the management of social life, have a long inheritance from theology and ancient philosophy.

The possibility of an economic theology reopens the relationship between the genealogy of the arts of government and, first of all, the genealogy of the term *oikonomia*. This relationship, however, had been closed by Foucault when, after citing the Greek Father Gregory of Nazianus's phrase, *oikonomia psychōn* (which might be translated as "economy of souls"), he quickly rendered the term *oikonomia* as "conduct" (2007b, 192–93). In this way *oikonomia* appears at the start of Foucault's genealogy of the arts of government in the fourth century only to disappear and mysteriously reappear with the physiocrats and Adam Smith some fourteen centuries later. Foucault thereby cuts himself off from the theological inheritance of the vocabulary and sources of the major terms by which the governing of mundane life is rendered thinkable. An exemplar of this is Foucault's casting of eighteenth-century political economy in the following terms: "Economics is an atheistic discipline, economics is a discipline without God . . . without totality . . . that begins to demonstrate not only the pointlessness, but also the impossibility of a sovereign point of view over the totality of the state that he has to govern" (2008, 282). Such a position is not only naive and counter to the explicit formulations of Smith's invisible hand and, as we have seen, recent scholarship; it also runs counter to the views of the twentieth-century neoliberals and Ordoliberals Foucault himself analyzes. In a theological-metaphysical tour de force, for example, Alexander von Rüstow (1942, 269–70) surveyed the multiple sources of the idea of "invisible harmony" and discovered a pagan and pantheistic economic theology in laissez-faire capitalism. Even Friedrich Hayek (1976, 73, 179n) dated the development of the market order to sixteenth-century Jesuit thought on the "just price."

Foucault also cuts himself off from the theological sources of reflection on the arts of government by referring only to the writings by theologians on secular or, at best, ecclesiastical government, rather than examining the fundamental conception of the divine government of the world. Thus, Agamben notes that Foucault cites Aquinas's *De regno*, in which he finds the figure of the "theological-cosmological continuum" (Agamben 2011, 111; Foucault 2007b, 232–49). Nevertheless, he fails to address that part of the *Summa theologica* that deals with the divine government of the world, *De gubernatione mundi*. Here, Agamben argues, Foucault would have found, in a discussion of God's government of the world, "the basic elements of a theory of government as distinct from reign" (2011, 111; translation modified). Chief among those elements are the key notions of providence and order.

One of the consequences of this is that the shadow of the binary opposition between sovereign reign and economic government falls over Foucault's entire conceptual apparatus, even when he seeks to escape it. Thus, while Foucault views Rousseau as articulating a terminology of nature, contract, and the general will that allows both "the judicial principle of sovereignty and the elements through which an art of government can be defined and described" (2007b,

107), he neglects the way Rousseau borrows these terms quite directly from Malebranche's theological model of providence. As in Malebranche's concept of "occasional causes" as nothing more than the actualization of God's "general will," for Rousseau "the government, or executive power, claims to coincide with the sovereignty of law from which it nevertheless distinguishes itself as its particular emanation and actualization" (Agamben 2011, 275).

Foucault's genealogy of the arts of government is incomplete. We need to remind ourselves that it is presented in his lectures of 1978 and 1979 and in related minor texts but that it never received a book-length treatment. It is a project that is not quite abandoned, however, and the vocabulary and even analytical frameworks of governmentality remain present during his later work on ancient ethics and ascetics (e.g., Foucault 2005, 252; 2010, 5; 2011, 8–9; 2014, 15–17). Nevertheless, Foucault's indications on power and government in these lectures do remain a kind of proxy for an analysis, if not quite a theory, of the state within poststructural thought, and they are enormously influential in the discussion of what has today become known as governance. In this sense it is fair to try to understand the narrative Foucault offers us and its implications for our thought on state, power, and governance.

In this respect we are concerned to find that Foucault's own genealogy of political sovereignty starts to reproduce elements of the theologies that he analyzes. We suggest that Foucault's genealogy of the arts of government is, contrary to his own self-description, a dialectical and teleological philosophy of history and itself a kind of economic theology. Löwith (1949, 18) gives us an excellent briefing on the term *eschaton*. It combines two meanings of the notion of an "end": one as the finishing of a process, as *finis*; the other as the completion of a goal, as *telos*. "Not only does the *eschaton* delimit the process of history by an end, it also articulates and fulfills it by a definite goal." If a compass gives orientation in space, he continues, "the eschatological compass gives orientation in time by pointing to the Kingdom of God as the ultimate end and purpose" (18). Such an account is very useful for thinking about the genealogy of the arts of government.

Foucault's overall narrative of the arts of government is a strong secularization one from ecclesiastical institutions to modern expertise, from forms of power such as sovereignty to ones of modern governmental management, from the safety of the prince to the security of the population, from governing as a part of a theological-cosmological continuum with God at its top to liberal governing based on the rationality of the governed. It is a story of the becoming immanent of formerly transcendent forms of power, such as sovereignty and reign. But this overall narrative has a dialectical character in which each of its elements stands in relations of tension to its opposite. There is both a process of becoming immanent and the retention or production of quasi-transcendental elements that act as obstacles to the same process. Consider the dialectical opposition and tension between the following: secularization and the quasi-religious retention of the authority and hierarchy of pastoral expertise; the immanent rationality of reason of state and the attachment of this rationality to the "transcendent" figure of the state itself; political economy and its attempt to break with the model of the household, the family, and the father as "head of household"; liberal arts of governing through civil society and the eschatologies of civil society, population, and nation. The drivers of the movement from transcendence to immanence, then, are the successive rationalities of government that offer critiques of transcendental forms, some of which are the result or by-product of the previous critiques. And drivers in the opposite direction, from immanence to new forms of transcendence, are the counterconducts made possible by the new eschatologies of civil society, nation, and the population. In other words ideas about how to govern act as a series of successive breaks with theological and transcendental forms of thought and figures of power, rule, and authority that, nonetheless, reproduce transcendental and quasi-theological forms and counterconducts that act as further targets of critique.

Foucault offers us a complex, incomplete, and not entirely convincing account of the transition from ecclesiastical pastorate to the secular pastorate. He also offers us a dialectic between immanent and atheistic rationalities of government such as reason of state and liberalism and a series of transcendent obstacles to the realization of the telos of governing in a manner consistent with the rationality of the governed and with self-governing. These obstacles include the theological-cosmological continuum, sovereignty and the juridico-political theory focused on it, the omnipotent state, the model of the family, and political eschatology. As each immanent rationality accomplishes its critique, it realizes another transcendental or theological obstacle that must be overcome to move ever closer to the goal of an immanent form of governing— that is, a governing that is a self-governing or a governmental rationality that is at one with the rationality of the governed.

There are certainly other ways of deploying Foucault, such as extracting the "economic" figure of the *dispositif* from this narrative, that give emphasis to the nonlinear, complex, and empirical dimensions of his analytical thought (as we explored in Chapters 6 and 7). Viewed as a whole, however, Foucault's genealogy of governmentality partakes of elements of a metaphysical and dialectical philosophy of history that is driven by this critical ethos—most manifest in liberalism—toward an end, an *eschaton*, that might be called governing through self-governing or the idea of a rationality of governing based on the rationality of the governed. But this end is not a clear *finis* or finality, in Löwith's sense, in that it resonates with the thesis of the constant contestability of the political. What we have, to use Foucault's expression (2007b, 300), is not an *absolute* eschatology, such as of the coming of the last days, but a *relative* eschatology, not of perpetual peace but of perpetual contestation or "agonism." What emerges through this dialectic of transcendence and its permanent critique is a teleology of governing through self-governing, a becoming immanent of governing, that is further and further refined through the critical overcoming of the obstacles it itself produces or, at the least, makes possible. The question of the suppression of providentialism in thinkers such as Smith and Ferguson, in the physiocrats and Rousseau, and the whole problematic of economic theology, is not so much an empirical oversight on the part of Foucault as it is an indication of his own teleological and dialectical metaphysics. He has negated economic theology only to produce a version of it.

We would further substantiate this claim by noting that economic theology, resting on the *oikonomia* or economy of the Trinity, invests history with a meaning, narrative, and goal in the form that God creates humanity and then sends his Son to lead its members to salvation. It invests history with a specific directionality. In this sense the movement from transcendent to immanent forms and rationalities of governing is, in Foucault, already an economic theology. But we could go further and examine Foucault's tripartite classification of power and government into sovereignty, based on the law and command; discipline, based on submission to the pastoral expert or official; and a form of governmentality that constructs and acts on the freedom of the governed and the intrinsic virtue in all members of a civil society. In his suppression of the theological roots of the physiocrats, Rousseau, Smith, and Ferguson, we could ask, has he not given us a typology of power that takes a distinctly Trinitarian form and that, moreover, resembles the three ages of Joachim di Fiore in the twelfth century? For like Joachim, Foucault offers a tripartite schema that can be described in terms of definite periodizations. There is "the state of justice" of the Middle Ages, the "administrative state" of the fifteenth and sixteenth centuries, and the "state of government" of modern times (Foucault

2007b, 110). Just like Joachim's ages, Foucault's forms of governing and power, approached from their "economic" or dispositif side, can have a much more "fuzzy history of the correlations and systems of the dominant feature" (8). And like the movement from the heavenly Father, to his worldly incarnation in the Son, and thence to the generalized Spirit in each and all, the movement that Foucault traces from the authority invested in the transcendent Sovereign and Law, to its incarnation in worldly pastors, experts, and officials, and then to the self-governing of each and all in a civil society, is a movement of progressively becoming immanent.

It would be a mistake, too, to think the notion of the dispositif escapes this economic theology. For the idea of an immanent and heterogeneous ensemble of distinct yet interconnected elements is nothing if not a more recent thought-figure of the ancient *oikonomia* that Cicero, in respect to rhetoric, translated as *dispositio* (Agamben 2011, 19). It is this notion of *oikonomia* that would be used to explain the mystery of the Holy Trinity ("the mystery of the economy") by the early church fathers and that Foucault would discover and then repress in his reading of Gregory of Nazianus. The dispositif, then, reproduces a thought-figure that has been most clearly developed in relation to a divine unity of three distinct but interrelated personages.

Giorgio Agamben (2011, 5)—relying on Löwith (1949, 209–10)—traces the entry of economic theology into modern philosophical schemas of history to Hegel and Schelling. "The eschatology of salvation of which . . . German idealism was a conscious resumption," he suggests, "was nothing but an aspect of a vaster theological paradigm, which is precisely the divine *oikonomia*." Yet there is more to it than this. Löwith (208) himself singles out Lessing and his fragment on *The Education of the Human Race* as an explicit assimilation of the Joachite doctrine. Lessing conceived of the idea of the three periods as leading to "the coming reign of reason and human self-realization and yet as the fulfillment of the Christian revelation." Now we know that Foucault explicitly rejected the totalizations and teleologies of German idealism and is much closer to the French positivist tradition of the history of science and reason. It is here that Löwith (208) articulates a connection that could provide valuable further research: "Lessing's influence was extraordinarily deep and far reaching. It affected the Saint-Simonian socialists in France; and even Comte's law of three stages was probably influenced by it, since Lessing's essay was translated by a Saint-Simonian when Comte was still a member of that group." Remarkably then, this scriptural hermeneutics of a twelfth-century monk found a medium in Lessing to influence two major nineteenth-century approaches to history: the one idealist, German, and philosophical; the other materialist, French, and positivist. If Foucault has explicitly located himself in respect to the second one and its descent from Comte (Foucault 1980a, 53–54; Descombes 1980, 110–11; Gutting 1989, 9) and the canonical figures of Gaston Bachelard, Jean Cavaillès, Alexandre Koyré, and Georges Canguilhem, this does not mean that he was able to avoid the economic-theological inheritance made most explicit in the first.

There are, of course, many ways to read Foucault's genealogy of governmentality. Nevertheless, this is an unexpected and astonishing conclusion to our investigations of Foucault's understanding of a form of liberal governing through civil society, but, subject to further investigation and the bringing to light of contrary evidence, it is one we find completely compelling.

CHAPTER 10

FOUCAULT'S APOLOGIA OF NEOLIBERALISM

The question of neoliberalism *must* be posed. Why? On the one hand, neoliberalism is at its base a position on the state, which is our central concern here, and it has had considerable influence and impact on governments and international organizations over at least the last five decades. Indeed, it is not only a position on the state; it is *action* toward the state. It is a form of "politically oriented action," as Max Weber (1978, 54) put it—that is, an action that "aims to exert influence on the government of a political organization; especially at the appropriation, redistribution or allocation of the powers of government." Neoliberalism, then, is a form of political action aimed at the appropriation of the powers of government of the state and other organizations but with the apparently paradoxical intention of limiting, dismantling, and restructuring the state to give greater scope to markets and market-like forms of organization. On the other hand, Foucault devoted almost an entire lecture course to the topic, *The Birth of Biopolitics* (2008), and his followers have mobilized his work more broadly to address the themes of liberalism and neoliberalism, and advanced or contemporary liberalism (e.g., Rose 1993; Barry, Osborne, and Rose 1996; Hindess 1998). In this respect the problem is a *critical-intellectual* one: how to mobilize Foucault and those who employ his work as a framework to diagnose and analyze neoliberalism.

Neoliberalism has also become an urgent *political* problem for Foucault and his followers, which retrospectively casts its shadow over his lectures on the topic. There is the example of François Ewald, Foucault's student and assistant, whose biography would follow a trajectory from Maoism to receiving France's highest award for his work of advocacy of neoliberal reform on behalf of the French employers' association. Ewald, as conservator and editor of Foucault's lectures, writings, and interviews, is arguably the most influential and loyal Foucauldian today. Indeed, Ewald himself has opened the question of Foucault's relationship to neoliberalism. He had recently suggested that Foucault's works offer an "apology of neoliberalism," particularly of the Chicago School economist Gary Becker. We cannot therefore raise the question of neoliberalism without raising the question of the relationship to it of not only perhaps Foucault's closest follower but also of Foucault himself.

After decades of his American reception as a kind of political radical, a Saint Foucault invested in radical struggles in different locales in civil society, who simultaneously shifted the paradigms of power, knowledge, and subjectivity, things have begun to change. The case of Ewald and the publication of the extent of Foucault's engagement with neoliberalism raise questions about Foucault's own intellectual and political trajectory in the minds of a new generation of American scholars such as Michael Behrent (2009, 2010) and Andrew Dilts (2011). For the former, Foucault represents a "strategic endorsement" of economic liberalism (Behrent 2009, 567). For the latter, Foucault's engagement with human capital theory and its "thin" conception of the subject was crucial to his later interest in the "care of the self." Addressing Behrent specifically, Dilts parses Foucault's position carefully in a footnote as "one of sympathetic critique and indebtedness" (2011, 133n11).

There is undoubtedly a relationship between Foucault and neoliberalism that is irreducible to a knee-jerk *gauchiste* critique or a simple improvement of a Marxist ideology critique. But is it possible to imagine the more far-reaching learning from or fascination with neoliberalism that is being proposed by recent scholarship? At the end of his deliberations on power, had Foucault found something attractive in neoliberalism? And what impact did he have on the future political trajectory of those followers who would adopt explicitly neoliberal paths—those, such as Ewald, who first heard about neoliberalism in his lectures? Is there an attempt to enroll Foucault, even retrospectively, as a member of the neoliberal "thought collective" he set out to study, as Philip Mirowski (2009) calls it? Would this really be "an absurd counterfactual," as the same author later says (Mirowski 2013, 97)?

We begin by locating the critical-intellectual function of Foucault's analysis within different approaches to neoliberalism and then move to the case of Ewald and its implications for our understanding of Foucault's political trajectory.

Approaching Neoliberalism

Among certain Foucauldian scholars one influential reading of Foucault's analysis of neoliberalism is that it opens up another way of approaching it outside the standard gestures of "ideology critique" and of Marxism, which, in the final analysis, reduces neoliberalism to the logic of capitalism or capital accumulation (Dardot and Laval 2013). Marxism unmasks neoliberalism's claim to foster liberty by rolling back the state in favor of the market as a cover for material relations and interests of capitalism, or of financial capitalism, or of the crisis of capital accumulation. This means there is little need to distinguish neoliberalism from other forms of "free-market" ideology. Foucault himself is the source of such a view on Marxism. As he put it, the reduction of neoliberalism to "a way of establishing strictly market relations in society" is a way for it "to be turned into practically nothing at all" and for us to avoid the need "to try to grasp it in its singularity" (Foucault 2008, 130). In contrast, he proposes to take seriously neoliberalism as a rationality of government with a number of distinct strands (German, French, American), which themselves can be differentiated from the classical economic liberalism of those such as Adam Smith. In contradistinction to the latter, "it is not a question of freeing an empty space but of taking the formal principles of the market and referring and relating them to, of projecting them on to a general art of government" (Foucault 2008, 131).

For his followers Foucault promises a better, thicker, and more sensitive description of neoliberalism, which permits us to view its variations, its limitations, and its potential points of engagement and is thus a condition for more serious evaluations and even critique. Moreover, this approach connects us to the shaping of individual and collective conduct and subjectivities. As Pierre Dardot and Christian Laval have argued, his approach is far more radical than Marxism in that it regards neoliberalism as a "rationality" that "employs unprecedented techniques of power over conduct and subjectivities" (2013, 7). Foucault thus produces a more sharply lit critique of the new relations of domination and exploitation characteristic of the neoliberal transformations of capitalism and the way they are intimately connected with the kinds of freedom and social identities that they seek to construct and foster.

There is little doubt that Foucault offered a distinctive analytical framework for analyzing neoliberalism that shifts attention from its ideological contents to its political methodology or capacity to critique and test the forms and extent of government. He does this in three ways. First, Foucault presents neoliberalism, like liberalism more generally, as an art and rationality of government.

He focuses on the plural forms of neoliberalism and their differences, particularly German Ordoliberalism in the post–Second World War period and the American neoliberalism of the Chicago School of Economics. He regards these as different ways of thinking about and reflecting on the government of the state and problematizing previous forms of state. In his attempt to summarize this approach, Foucault states that he regards liberalism and neoliberalism "as a practice, that is to say, a 'way of doing things' directed towards objectives and regulating itself by continuous reflection . . . a principle and method of the rationalization of the exercise of government . . . which obeys . . . the internal rule of maximum economy" (2008, 318). Foucault thus regards neoliberalism primarily as neither philosophy nor ideology but as an art of government—that is, a *technē* or practical rationality oriented to specific objectives.

Second, Foucault directs us to the technical character of neoliberal governing and moves beyond regarding it as merely a set of general principles. Instead, it becomes a specific set of programs linked to diverse intellectual and governmental technologies pursuing diverse goals. The art or *technē* of government concerns, above all, techniques for the shaping of conduct and the formation of subjectivities. Foucault's followers, particularly in the governmentality school, have extended this focus from rationalities of government to the diverse material, intellectual, and representational techniques and technologies through which neoliberal goals and agendas are to be achieved.

Third, we should note that Foucault's approach shares with Marxism the idea that neoliberalism is oriented toward an enemy. That enemy comprises policies such as state planning, economic protectionism, and, after the Second World War, the Keynesian welfare state. Thus, the Ordoliberals identify a range of policies that fail to implement a market regime: the notion of national economy, Bismarckian socialism, the planned war economy and Keynesianism (Foucault 2008, 107–9). The Chicago School has as its targets the New Deal, war planning, and the social and economic programs of postwar Democratic administrations (323). But Foucault goes further than Marxism in raising this critical function to the defining, if not essential, feature of liberalism and neoliberalism. Thus the content of liberalism and neoliberalism is less important than their critical ethos, and the focus on the latter moves toward stripping neoliberalism of its content. In this sense neoliberalism should not be judged by its ideological contents and substantive goals but by its status as a kind of open, flexible, process of constant critique and self-critique. As Colin Gordon (1991, 18) observes, for Foucault the "theoretical closure of the world, the con-

ception of reality as the scene of a potentially total effectuation of political doctrine, is the very essence of what liberalism, in contradistinction both to the
science of police and to scientific socialism, denounces and abjures." The third
characteristic move of Foucault's approach is this focus on the critical ethos of
neoliberalism. The Foucauldian approach rejects what it sees as the denunciatory mode of Marxism toward neoliberalism and brackets assumptions about
the relation between neoliberalism and class interests, forms, fractions, and
crises of capital and so forth. The distinctiveness of Foucault's approach to neoliberalism can thus be summed up as how the theory of ideology is displaced
by the notion of governmental rationality, the falsification of subjectivity by an
art of government that fosters and shapes forms of conduct, and the critique of
liberalism by the critical ethos of liberalism.

As a consequence the Foucauldian or governmentality approach has
stressed the way neoliberalism took local and contingent forms and developed quite differently in particular contexts—national, transnational, local,
and translocal (Ong 2006). It has shown that rule in advanced liberalism is
composed from elements, alliances, and collisions of forces across the political spectrum, from politics conducted within and outside the state, and from
not only top-down policies but also bottom-up local movements (Rose 1996b).
While these have been broadly accepted as fruitful methodological starting
points, including by Marxist urban sociologists and geographers, the latter
have replied that no amount of insistence on contingency, irreducibility, and
multiplicity precludes the possibility that neoliberalism can become both a pat-
terning and patterned form of regulation with identifiable "path dependencies"
(Brenner, Peck, and Theodore 2010). They argue that Foucauldians have raised
a methodological precept into an ontological given, and thus a kind of dogmatism. Others would suggest it is symptomatic of the Foucauldian approach that
it has failed to link neoliberalism to changes in the nature of the contemporary economy, and forms of capital and to connect the emergence of a concept
such as "human capital," for example, to the composition and recomposition of
capital and its circuits (Lazzarato 2009). We consider that there is something to
these charges, which leads some neo-Foucauldians to systematically downplay
the whole issue of neoliberalism, contra Foucault himself. Thus Nikolas Rose
(1996b, 61, 53) argued that political rationality in advanced liberal democracy
is irreducible to "the brief flowering of neoliberal rhetorics," and "it would be
misleading to imagine that the neo-conservative political regimes that were
elected in Britain and in the United States in the late 1970s were underpinned

by a coherent and elaborated political rationality." While it is deeply problematic to ascribe everything that is wrong in contemporary societies and public policy to the presence of neoliberalism, and thus make it a kind of synonym for political evil, Rose's view seriously underestimates the efficacy and impact of neoliberalism considered as an organized form of political action deploying intellectual means. Such a position would seem to ignore the fundamental Foucauldian precepts such as the tactical polyvalence and reversibility of discourse, and the paradox-driven character of neoliberalism that Foucauldians and others have identified. In our view, moreover, the field of dispersion that constitutes the paradoxical character of neoliberalism cannot be formulated in purely epistemic or discursive terms.

This observation brings us to a third way of addressing neoliberalism (after ideology and art of government) and that is as a definite "thought collective" (Mirowski and Plehwe 2009). This kind of analysis recognizes the contingent historical emergence of a political and intellectual movement with definite aims and limited, but identifiable, impacts and traces as an empirical matter and the multiple projects, programs, and impacts of this movement in many different countries and within international organizations. Philip Mirowski (2009, 428) has appropriated Ludwik Fleck's definition of *thought collective* as "a community of persons mutually exchanging ideas or maintaining intellectual interaction," and he has employed the criterion for membership in that thought collective to groups or individuals with direct links to, or at one remove from, the Mont Pèlerin Society, founded in the late 1940s by Friedrich Hayek.. Faced with the inevitable incoherence of a movement that claims to be antistatist and pro–individual freedom but was hell-bent on appropriating state power to institute particular forms of life, Marxism would appeal to its old dialectical chestnut of "contradiction," and Foucauldian studies would look to the way neoliberal forms were combined with neoconservative and authoritarian rationalities and techniques. But if neoliberalism is neither first of all a more or less coherent philosophy or ideology, but a form of political action engaged by a definite group, then the a priori assumption of *intellectual* coherence disappears. While we have no doubt that the epistemic paradox of an object that is at once natural and constructed proves a fecund thought figure, to view neoliberalism as a thought collective is to indicate that its ultimate unity is given by its political aims, variously expressed as the renewal of liberalism or the implementation of particular policies, not by the various forms of truth it promotes to itself and to particular publics.

On this account neoliberalism has a range of constitutive aporias between constructivist and naturalistic conceptions of the market, between democracy and the demand for constraints on it, between deregulation and reregulation, between a claim concerning the limits of knowledge and a program for unfettered growth and welfare, between free trade and the need for international regulation by international organizations, and ultimately between the ideal of a free market and the requirement of a strong state to enforce the conditions of that market (Mirowski 2009, 434–40). In this respect, at least, such accounts find common ground with the findings of governmentality studies and their interpretation of Foucault. Such studies find that the objects of government— the market, civil society—are at the same time conceived as natural and cultivated, and it is this, as Gordon remarks, that makes liberalism a "prodigiously fertile problematic, a continuing vector of political invention" (1991, 18). Oddly enough, then, Foucault's lectures can also be approached as contributing to precisely this third model in that they trace the history, biographies, exchanges, colloquia, and networks that constitute the neoliberal thought collective. They focus on the now recognizably fundamental strands of the neoliberal thought collective: German Ordoliberalism, American neoliberalism of the Chicago School, and the Austrian neoliberalism of von Mises and especially of Hayek himself. Given that this is the only time he formally addresses contemporary politics, it is interesting to note that Foucault admits to departing from his usual methods: "I will break a bit from my habits and give a few biographical details" (Foucault 2008, 102). This is precisely the approach the historian Michael Behrent (2010) has adopted in regard to François Ewald.

A Case Study

The intellectual and political biography of François Ewald, the general editor of Foucault's lectures and shorter writings, is of signal importance in the discussion of Foucault and neoliberalism. Antonio Negri (2001) has called Ewald a "right Foucauldian" who "considered that the law of the market could function without the guarantee of the state." For Maurizio Lazzarato (2009, 110) Ewald is "one of the promoters of the policies and mechanisms for intervening [in] . . . and reconstructing society according to neoliberal principles" revealed to him in Foucault's lectures and in the posthumous works he edited. And for his fellow Foucauldian Jacques Donzelot, in conversation with Colin Gordon, Ewald was "a classic case of counter-transference where the analyst falls blindly in love with his object" (Donzelot and Gordon 2008, 55).

Ewald begins to constitute something of a case study in the relationship between Foucauldian thought and neoliberalism. Most of these commentators, however, would believe that Ewald has fundamentally departed from his intellectual master and place Foucault as a leftist critic of neoliberalism. Thus Negri speaks of a "true Foucault" who follows Marx in the view that the "free market has never existed, it has always been a mystification" (2001). And Colin Gordon has long positioned Foucault on the independent or "free Left," and others have placed him in relation to the "Second Left" in France during the 1970s (Gordon 1986, 74; 1991, 7; Behrent 2009, 552–55), a theme that we will explore further shortly. In brief, for his sympathetic commentators Foucault offers us a far more intellectually nuanced and politically nimble account of neoliberalism than does Marxism, one that firmly originates, even if somewhat vaguely, on the Left.

The intellectual, political, and personal trajectory that traces Ewald's development from a young bourgeois Maoist radical to the driving intellectual voice of "social restructuring" (*fondation sociale*) on behalf of the French employers' association MEDEF (Mouvement des entreprises de France) is without doubt fascinating. Michael Behrent (2010) has provided us with a discussion of this trajectory in a piece of exemplary contemporary intellectual history. Whether this trajectory makes Ewald a "right Foucauldian" is another matter. It certainly places him on the Right of politics and close to, if not a member of, the neoliberal thought collective. As Behrent (2010, 585–86) points out, Ewald received the Légion d'honneur not for his considerable labors in the conservation and editorship of Foucault's works but for his contribution to the insurance industry and employers' association. While working for the latter, Ewald had been the leading intellectual voice within MEDEF for a break with the established corporatist processes between employers' organizations and workers' unions, overseen by the state, and for the direct renegotiation of the terms of the social contract, a kind of self-styled "coup of civil society against the state" (Behrent 2010, 619). While such a vision would appear to be a right-wing version of the pro–civil society position others found in Foucault, it was consistent with Ewald's own position on the welfare state. For him, *L'État providence*, to use the title of his book based on the doctoral thesis largely completed under Foucault, had marked the rise of society, not the state. The MEDEF move, then, was nothing more than the claim that the properly social dimension of the French welfare state had to be revivified. As Ewald explained at the time, the problem with the old way of doing things was that "politics had believed that it could legislate for the social";

in contrast, the *fondation sociale* would "depoliticize the economy" through an "ethos of contract" and thereby be "a last chance for the organizations of employers and employees to be the organizers of civil society" (Ewald, cited in Behrent 2010, 620–21). As we have seen, Foucault's position on society and civil society is rather more ambiguous than this. Fortunately, we now have other documents at hand to help us follow what Ewald believed he had found in Foucault.

Among these have been two seminars held at the University of Chicago in 2012 and 2013 that entailed the reading of Foucault's relevant lectures by both Ewald and Foucault's principal Chicago School protagonist, Gary Becker, moderated by the political scientist Bernard Harcourt (Becker, Ewald, and Harcourt 2012, 2013). Becker and his colleagues have some two and a half lectures devoted to them by Foucault.

In the first seminar, held in 2012, Ewald draws the context of Foucault's lectures on Becker and proceeds to say what he thinks fascinated Foucault about Becker's work on human capital and its application to crime and punishment. Ewald strikingly describes these lectures as the place "where he [Foucault] would make the apology of neoliberalism—especially the apology of Gary Becker, who is referred to in the book, *The Birth of Biopolitics*, as the most radical representative of American neoliberalism" (Ewald in Becker, Ewald, and Harcourt 2012, 4). Ewald seems to interpret Foucault here not as offering an apology *for* neoliberalism but an "apologia" *of* it and of Becker, that is, a form of public defense of it, and of Becker, against critics and accusers. After discussing the post-1968 situation, to which he believes Deleuze and Guattari's theory of desire and Foucault's theory of micropowers were responses, Ewald suggests Foucault answered the demand for a theory of the state with the notion of governmentality within which economists would act as "truth-tellers" in relation to government. Foucault, he suggests, was searching for nonmoral and nonjuridical theory, and he found it in the economists. "That is the celebration of the economists' work, of your [i.e., Becker's] work" (5). According to Ewald, what Foucault found in Becker was the "possibility of thinking about power without discipline. . . . Your [i.e., Becker's] theory of regulation makes it possible to conduct the behavior of the other without coercion, by incitation" (6). And there is no doubt that Ewald means all of this in an extremely complimentary way when he concludes with respect to Foucault's view of Becker: "Certain kinds of truth-telling are death for liberty, other kinds of truth-telling give new possibilities for liberty. And he sees your work, your kind of analyses as creating the possibility to promote, to envision new kinds of liberty" (6).

This is striking. But how should we read it, or hear it, as it was a spoken rather than written word? Is Ewald merely using terms like *liberty* and *truth* in nonnormative, value-neutral ways consistent with a general Foucauldian orientation? Or is he actively appreciative of the possibilities of Becker's approach to power and truth for forms of liberty? Doesn't the opposition between "death for liberty" and "new kinds of liberty" clearly indicate an evaluative criterion at work here? And if he is saying that Foucault endorsed Becker's theory, then is this merely the reminiscence of one who projects his own current values and commitments retrospectively onto his former supervisor's words? Or is this a more or less accurate, more or less astute, interpretation of those words by one who was not only close to Foucault but knew from direct experience the context in which these analyses were made and who, in his editorial role, continues to work closely with them?

At the end of this preliminary presentation of Foucault's interest in Becker, Ewald refers to Foucault's interest in the model of the economic agent contained in Becker's theory, and he goes further than the proposition that Foucault actively admired the latter's accomplishments. He claims that the idea of *homo œconomicus* contained in Becker's theory "was very close to what Foucault searched for with his theory of the subject and of subjectivity. . . . And for Foucault, with his theory of power, it was very difficult to think how the subject decides: he is decided by power relations . . . . But Foucault could find in your work a solution and maybe we can see the reading of your work by Foucault like a step between his earlier theory of power and the later Foucault lectures about subjectivity and so on" (Ewald in Becker, Ewald, and Harcourt 2012, 7). For Ewald, Becker, "the most radical of the American neoliberals," as Foucault (2008, 269) called him, was decisive in the transformation not only of Foucault's theory itself but also of the very movement of his thought from the analytics of modern forms of power to the analysis of ancient ethics and ascetics.

We leave aside most of Bernard Harcourt's critical comments as moderator, not because they are without interest but because we are concerned here with the relation to neoliberalism of Foucault and those closest to him. We do note that Harcourt attempted to construct a critique of Becker's human capital theory by finding implied references to the dangers of a new kind of eugenics in Foucault's lectures. This has received an explicit and, we would add, proper rejection by Colin Gordon (2013, 5–6) on the grounds of its lack of textual support. We also will put aside most of Becker's extremely pleased response to

Ewald's statement of "Foucault's apology." However, there is something rather telling in this early exchange between Harcourt and Becker:

> BERNARD HARCOURT. As a teaser for this seminar I will tell you that in a glorious email that Professor Becker sent to me the day before yesterday, Gary Becker wrote (referring to Michel Foucault's work), "I like most of it, and I don't agree with much . . . "
>
> GARY BECKER. I don't *disagree* with much.
>
> BERNARD HARCOURT. "I don't *disagree* with much." Did I just say that? Is that Freudian perhaps? I will slow down and repeat that! "I like most of it, and I do *not disagree* with much. I also cannot tell whether Foucault is disagreeing with me." That truly sets the tone for this historic conversation. (Becker, Ewald, and Harcourt 2012, 3)

We wonder what indeed "sets the tone." Is it Becker's surprising endorsement of Foucault's view of his work? Or is it Harcourt's slip? Perhaps we should not read too much into a slip of the tongue, for fear of being accused of deep hermeneutics or psychoanalysis. Yet there is something symptomatic in a Foucauldian academic's desire to find a fundamental disagreement between Foucault and the exemplary neoliberal economist. Harcourt in this sense makes a slip for all who would want to maintain the critical nature of Foucault's engagement with neoliberalism when even the most attentive reader would be hard-pressed to find the grounds for such a critique and when the closest English follower of these lectures (Gordon) finds little evidence of such critique. And we think, in this regard at least, that Becker is right.

At the end of this first conversation Ewald does venture what amounts to a kind of criticism of the notion of human capital when he suggests that it is vulnerable to the charge that it is liable "to produce a vision of man that is very impoverished" (Becker, Ewald, and Harcourt 2012, 17). That vision is a "poor behaviorism" in which individual behavior can be modified by different kinds of stimuli. This simply gives Becker the chances to proclaim the richness of a vision of man based on choice (18). Nevertheless this does start to map out some of the ground for future discussion.

The second seminar focuses on Becker's theory of crime and punishment and the corresponding lecture by Foucault of March 21, 1979. Again it commences with Ewald's lauding of Becker's theory on a number of points he ascribes to Foucault: as a critique of governmentality, which is a new kind of truth-telling outside of moral consideration; as a liberation from past criminological and anthropological models of *homo criminalis*; and, finally, as an economic approach that creates limits to power and the state (Ewald in Becker Ewald, and Harcourt 2013, 2–3). Again Becker fails to find a critique of his work in Foucault (9). In the course of the discussion the issue of Becker and behaviorism is raised again, now by Harcourt, and reference is made to Foucault's mention of the techniques of the behavioral psychology of B. F. Skinner (Foucault 2008, 270). Ewald for the most part is silent and only weighs in to contradict Becker's supposition that Foucault was a socialist:

> FRANÇOIS EWALD. Socialist, no! On the Left.
>
> GARY BECKER. But well, what does Left mean? In terms of the role of government, let's say that Left usually means bigger government.
>
> FRANÇOIS EWALD. At this time, Foucault was in search of a new kind of governmentality. It was the research for new possibility in politics that motivated his work on governmentality. (Becker, Ewald, and Harcourt 2013, 19)

If Becker is somewhat puzzled by what Foucault's critique of his work is meant to be by this stage, he now seems rightly bewildered at the use of the very term *Left*. Ewald does not help matters when he answers a question about political orientation by incanting the word *governmentality*. The discussion has moved into the frame of a polite conversation between friends, at least as far as Ewald and Becker are concerned. Ewald concludes that Becker made possible a "positivist" and immanent "critique of governmentality that is internal to a system" but raises what he regards as a Kantian normative question (Becker, Ewald, and Harcourt 2013, 21). This concerns both the use of deterrence as a tactic of punishment that uses human beings as means to another end and the impossibility in Becker's terms of gaining the information necessary to make the calculus that such deterrence will be effective.

There is another important document by Ewald in this case study: his description of the contemporary relevance or the "actuality" (*l'actualité*) of Foucault dated from the mid-1990s. In it he describes Foucault as a "philosopher entirely dedicated to the truth," including truth in its strongest sense: "the truth is the possibility to produce as a rupture, as an interruption of the present, an other form of being" (Ewald 1999, 83). Such truth is the province of philosophy rather than the human sciences, although it can be produced within specific disciplines (such as by Freud, Russell, and Saussure in psychoanalysis, logic, and linguistics). It concerns philosophical acts: "philosophy has an important role in human history to the extent that it is capable of

producing events which have the value of acts concerning being" (84). If we
return to Ewald's discussion of Becker, we recall his suggestion that Becker has
produced a form of truth that makes new forms of liberty (i.e., other forms
of being) possible. Becker has thus produced, in Ewald's estimation, a philosophical act. We also learn that Foucault had a "clear commitment" to make
each word such a philosophical act.

After introducing this bizarre and somewhat elite view of Foucault and
philosophy, Ewald specifies four main points of Foucault's contemporary relevance, at least from his perspective at around 1997 or somewhat before. The
first of these is particularly germane to understanding Ewald's own trajectory
from revolutionary Maoist to neoliberal policy advocate.

In an amazing prolepsis Ewald makes Foucault foresee events that would
occur only in the years and decade after his death: he "described, ten years in
advance, the world that would be our own" (Ewald 1999, 85). Ewald argues that
as early as the 1970s, "Foucault posited that our current situation (*actualité*)
is very fundamentally post-revolutionary: if there was an event in the 1970s,
it was the disappearance of the revolution" (85). Foucault thus discerned an
event that would be finally realized in the fall of the Berlin Wall. In an explicit
reference to the great Franco-Russian Hegelian and high bureaucrat Alexandre
Kojève (and a nod to Francis Fukuyama) Ewald suggests that it "is clear that
the end of revolution and the end of History represent the same event: it is
an event in our consciousness of time" (85). What is left only belongs to "the
order of administration, of management," and owing to this we are left with
the "impossibility to be able to do something." But this does not mean that the
state assumes a central importance; quite the contrary, for the end of revolution brings about the end of the philosophical relevance of the state: "Foucault
explained that there are not any events to be anticipated with respect to the
state: the state, in a certain manner, is no longer a philosophical concern. . . .
The stakes are with respect to power, and this is a totally different location, a
totally different zone, a totally different type of reality" (86–87). In Ewald's view
the fact that everything has come to a standstill does not mean that nothing
more can happen but that it is possible that everything can emerge out of it. It
is this possibility that makes the philosophical act so important and relates it
to decision, responsibility, and care (90). What would a philosophical act look
like, then, in the realm of a politics without revolution and with an irrelevant
state, which has been reduced to the order of management and administration?
We think Ewald found an exemplar in Becker's theory.

Within a few years of these statements, and guided by his understanding of Foucault's actuality for the present, Ewald would be able to join in relations of power on the side of the neoliberalizing fraction of capital in France and seek fundamental social restructuring to the corporatist welfare state. For the disillusioned Maoist Foucault was less the theorist who extended politics to the domain of multiple local struggles and more one who diagnosed the vacuity of a politics around the couple revolution/state. The events of 1968 gave way to a melancholy awakening from the grand dream of cultural, political, and social revolution. To make something more than an analogy, this was a kind of rarefied French philosophical version of the cultural hangover reported in the 1970s by a myriad of maudlin singer-songwriters after they awakened from their extended "acid trips" in California and London. Some of the latter would no doubt cure their melancholia by joining the personal experimentation in parties, clubs, and discos of the "Me Generation" at a time when "yuppies" would displace hippies. Some of those French philosophers would come to realize that they had entered the temporality of individualism and identity politics, or of subjectivity and the aesthetics of the self, in which, for a time at least, neoliberalism presented far from the worst political response.

Foucault and Neoliberalism

In a significant paper written several years before the actual publication of *The Birth of Biopolitics*, Thomas Lemke (2001, 203) concludes that in these lectures "the theoretical strength of the concept of governmentality consists of the fact that it construes neo-liberalism not just as ideological rhetoric or as a political-economic reality, but above all as a political project that endeavors to create a social reality that it suggests already exists." This political project "tries to render the social domain economic" and reduces welfare expenditure as it promotes self-responsibility and care. Lemke concludes, "This enables us to shed sharper light on the effects neo-liberal governmentality has in terms of (self-)regulation and domination. These effects . . . are the product of a re-coding of social mechanisms of exploitation and domination on the basis of a new topography of the social domain" (203). Lemke is absolutely sure that Foucault's rendering of neoliberalism as a form of governmentality is a critical one, and, in this regard he is at one with much received opinion on the matter. Yet the difficulty that Becker and Ewald have of finding this critical reading in the lectures on American neoliberalism, and the failure of Harcourt to establish his case for it, at least according to Gordon, should give us pause. On rereading, perhaps the closest to a critical point raised by Foucault comes in the final lecture and indeed concerns the possibility of a relationship between neoliberalism and behavioral psychological techniques of manipulation through adjusting stimuli in the environment. This seems to be a point that Ewald hints at in the conversations with Becker, and it is one that Gordon (2013, 3–5) reiterates in his comments on the first conversation. Reviewing Becker's conception of intelligible individual conduct as answering to the "single clause that the conduct in question reacts to reality in a nonrandom way," which Foucault (2008, 269) calls a "colossal definition," Foucault then moves to pinpoint the "paradox" of *homo œconomicus*. On the one hand, starting in the eighteenth century, "from the point of view of a theory of government, *homo œconomicus* is the person who must be let alone. . . . And now, in Becker's definition which I have just given, *homo œconomicus*, that is to say, the person who accepts reality or who responds systematically to modifications in the variables of the environment, appears precisely as someone manageable, someone who responds systematically to systematic modifications artificially introduced into the environment. *Homo œconomicus* is someone who is eminently governable. From being the intangible partner of *laissez-faire*, *homo œconomicus* now becomes the correlate of a governmentality which will act on the environment and systematically modify its variables" (Foucault 2008, 270–71). This is a perspicacious understanding of neoliberalism; however, it hardly amounts to a particularly critical position in any sense of that word. In fact, the observation fails to ruffle Becker, and when it is put to him, he in fact concedes that this is indeed the point: "I mean, yes, if you have things under certainty, there's a certain deterministic aspect of behavior you can modify a lot. But within that broad spectrum, people have a variety of choices they can take" (Becker, Ewald, and Harcourt 2012, 18). Choice, for the neoliberal, would seem to be the caveat that dissolves the critical point of this observation. As Gordon (1991, 43) noted in his introductory essay on governmentality, while choice is a "principle which empowers economic calculation effectively to sweep aside the anthropological categories and frameworks of the human and social sciences," for Becker "*homo economicus* is *manipulable man*, man who is perpetually responsive to modifications in his environment."

In fact, we would say a keener appreciation of the significance of Foucault's reading of American neoliberalism is given at the end of the previous lecture, after his long discussion of the theory of crime and punishment in Becker and other neoliberals. Because of his supposition that power is omnipresent, Foucault's problematic is not one that seeks a freedom from *all* sorts of power but rather an alternative to *particular kinds* of power and regulation. Foucault finds in American neoliberalism a precisely defined alternative to the other new kinds of power and regulation he had analyzed: "you can see that what appears on the horizon of this kind of analysis is not at all the idea or project of an exhaustively disciplinary society in which the legal network hemming in individuals is taken over and extended internally by, let's say, normative mechanisms. Nor is it a society in which a mechanism of general normalization and the exclusion of those who cannot be normalized is needed" (2008, 259). This statement directly addresses the governing of crime but not *just* that. It can be read in terms of the movement of Foucault's thought through forms of power. What is envisaged by American neoliberalism, then, is a form of regulation that is not one of a sovereign power exercised through law, or of disciplinary society with its norms, or even of the general normalization of a biopolitics of the population. It is not one of the major forms of regulation discussed by Foucault prior to these lectures on governmentality in 1978 and 1979, nor is it the framework of biopolitics still attributed to the 1979 lecture course (no doubt due to its rather misleading title). Rather it is a new program and vision: "On the horizon of this analysis we see instead the image, idea, or theme-program of a society in which there is an optimization of systems of difference, in which the field is left open to fluctuating processes, in which minority individuals and practices are tolerated, in which action is brought to bear on the rules of the game rather than on the players, and finally in which there is an environmental type of intervention instead of the internal subjugation of individuals (*de l'assujettissement interne des individus*)" (Foucault 2008, 259–60; 2004a, 265). We have seen that Foucault expresses reservations about the project of the manipulation of choice through environmental interventions of the behavioral type, but these would seem simply to be the costs—in his language, the "dangers"—of a form of neoliberal regulation that he finds has many benefits—or at least much political potential. Chief among these is that regulation is no longer the internal "subjectification" (*assujettissement*) of the individual. We draw attention to the French phrase translated as "of the internal subjugation of individuals." *Assujettissement* has a specific dual meaning in Foucault's thought: it is not only subjection in the sense of "submission to" or "subjugation" but also entails the fabrication or production of subjectivity, a process he links to knowledge (Harrer 2005, 79). This dual meaning is underlined by the adjective *internal* that emphasizes not the mere external forms of subjugation (as the equivalent of domination) but the internal forms of subjugation as "subjectification," as the fabrication of subjectivity. Thus Foucault here distinguishes the neoliberal program from those forms of regulation and power such as discipline that subjugate individuals through the production of subjectivity, that is through tying individuals to the truth of their identity—for example, the occasional criminal, the recidivist, the invert, the homosexual, and so forth. For Foucault in this passage neoliberalism does not subjectify in this sense. Rather, it opens up the space for tolerating minority individuals and practices and optimizing systems of differences. As Foucault himself might have said, this appears to offer, from his own perspective, a "colossal" endorsement of neoliberalism.

Some commentators have not been surprised by these statements of Foucault. While he too readily places him in the liberal tradition, Alain Beaulieu (2010, 812–13) draws our attention to Foucault's discussion, which prefaces his excursus on American neoliberalism, of Hayek and the liberal utopia: "Some years ago Hayek said: We need a liberalism that is a living thought. Liberalism has always left it to the socialists to produce utopias, and socialism owes much of its vigor and historical dynamism to this utopian or utopia-creating activity. Well, liberalism also needs utopia. It is up to us to create liberal utopias, to think in a liberal mode, rather than presenting liberalism as a technical alternative for government" (Foucault 2008, 218–19). It is difficult to interpret this passage, but it seems reasonably clear that Foucault is citing Hayek and speaking in Hayek's voice rather than his own. What is interesting here is not that Foucault implausibly endorses Hayek but that he found in the environmental interventions by which the American liberals sought to shape choice a liberal way of governing that was not only technical but also utopian.

This does not mean that Foucault was or became a neoliberal. But it does show that the normative import of Foucault's approach to the state remains resolutely antistatist, just as his excursus on war and his views on diagrams and dispositifs were theoretically and analytically antistatist. There is no doubt that he found neoliberalism extremely relevant to his normative suggestion that one should play games of power with "as little domination as possible" (ECS, 298). And while we have not explored it fully, there is a sense in which economic liberalism could be attractive in that it allowed Foucault to maintain his distance from the humanism of political liberalism, as Behrent (2009) has shown. In this chapter we have followed his own *theoretical* pathway to this position and that of one of his key followers. But there is also a more practical political pathway that is worth at least our brief attention.

While Foucault was careful not to specify a political position in his writings and lectures, this did not mean that he was immune to displaying overt political preferences. Behrent (2009, 552–55) details Foucault's relations with the "Second Left" in the late 1970s. The Second Left was an "important minority current in French socialism, closely associated with the Parti socialiste unifié (PSU), a small party led by Michel Rocard, and the Confédération française démocratique du travail (CFDT), a major trade union" (552). The major target of the Second Left was the "first Left's" fixation with the state, and, in response, it sought to decompose and distribute the state into a voluntary institution. The central concept in this regard was "self-management" (*autogestion*). The Second Left emerged during a long period of frustration with the failure of the Socialist Party under François Mitterrand to achieve electoral victory amid the extended economic crisis that followed the postwar Long Boom or the *trente glorieuses* (thirty glorious years). It sought to free the Socialist Party from "social statism." The major intellectual of this movement was Pierre Rosanvallon, who would later attend Foucault's seminars (and today occupies a chair at the Collège de France). Having sent a copy of *Pour une nouvelle culture politique* (For a new political culture), a book he had coauthored with Patrick Viveret, to Foucault, Rosanvallon received an effusive reply, "praising the authors for their 'remarkable perception' of the present and for proposing an analysis that was trenchant without being 'immobilizing'" (Behrent 2009, 553–54).

Foucault would also, we think quite tellingly, disclose Rosanvallon's influence on his view of liberalism in the Course Summary of *The Birth of Biopolitics* (2008, 320). There Rosanvallon's 1979 work, *Le capitalisme utopique*, is said to confirm that "the market's role in the liberal critique has been that of a 'test,' of a privileged site of experiment in which one can pinpoint the effects of excessive governmentality and take their measure" (320). Rosanvallon had indicated that the aim of liberal analysis of the eighteenth-century grain trade was "to show the point at which governing was always governing too much."

Foucault expressly approved of the Second Left's grassroots politics as evidence of what he called the "disappearance of terrorism, of theoretical monopolies, and of the monarchy of accepted thinking" (quoted in Behrent 2009, 554). He also contributed an interview entitled "A Finite Social Security System Confronting an Infinite Demand" to one of its collections published in 1983 (translated into English in 1988). In this interview, conducted by Robert Bono, the then general secretary of the CFDT, Foucault (1988, 160) approaches the contemporary problems of social security as ones of facing "economic obstacles that are only too familiar," as being deficient in terms of the "political, economic and social rationality of modern societies," and leading to the "perverse effects" of "an increasing rigidity of certain mechanisms" and "a growth of dependence." It is, however, not marginalization but "integration" in the social security system that leads to dependency (162). Foucault then seeks a "security that opens the way to richer, more numerous, more diverse, and more flexible relations with oneself and with one's environment" that guarantees a "real autonomy," and he casts his indications in the language of "lifestyles" and new ways of life (161, 164–65). Welfare dependency can only be combatted, Foucault argues, through "a process of decentralization," which would close the distance between users of services and "decision-making centers" (165). Foucault thus turns to new forms of subjectivity and the decomposition of the state to meet what others would regard as structural problems manifest in the fiscal crisis of the welfare state. He concludes that the social security system should become a "vast experimental field" (165), and the "whole institutional complex, at present very fragile, will probably have to undergo a restructuring from top to bottom" (166). These few remarks, consonant with the orientation of the Second Left, give us a clue to what the book on the art of government and socialist politics might look like. Taking this into account, we could say that Foucault's interest in neoliberalism stemmed from a particular conjuncture of French politics on the Left and not from any great admiration of the emergent politics of neoliberalism in the United Kingdom, United States, or France. Yet the attack on social statism and the position of the Second Left on economic liberalism was often indistinguishable from the position of those advocating a resurgent liberalism in France and was recognized as such by advocates of that resurgence (Behrent 2009, 553).

It is true that Foucault never completed a proposed book or report on the art of government and socialist politics (Foucault 2008, 100n53). But even allowing for the Gallic intellectual idiom, it is highly unlikely such a book would have ever functioned in the manner of Hayek's *The Road to Serfdom* or Milton Friedman's *Capitalism and Freedom*—that is, as a militant statement of a neoliberal philosophy intended for a large public. The closest example in the Anglophone world we can think of is perhaps that of Anthony Giddens's book *The Third Way*, published in 1998. Here a prominent thinker, social theorist, and intellectual tried to cast a general policy framework for a newly elected moderate-Left government, in this case, the British Labour Party, that would learn from market-oriented philosophies and developments. But whereas the

English thinker would deliberately move to elucidate a centrist position, Foucault continued to draw on the radical practice of self-management advocated first by militants.

It should not surprise us that even stripped of its immediate political context, Foucault's understanding of neoliberalism has received favorable responses by both major schools of the neoliberal thought collective he analyzed: the Ordoliberals, still residing at the Walter Eucken Institute in Freiburg (Goldschmidt and Rauchenschwandtner 2007), and Gary Becker at the University of Chicago in the discussions of 2012 and 2013. Considering its own very specific *political* context makes Behrent's understanding of his relationship to neoliberalism as one of "strategic endorsement" much more plausible, if we allow that the strategic direction of this endorsement was one coming from the Left and seeking to enlarge its policy and intellectual repertoire. In any case, and while this is outside the scope of the current book, Andrew Dilts (2011) has provided the textual support for Ewald's view, which we have already noted, that Foucault's relatively brief engagement with neoliberalism, and in particular the theory of human capital, proved to be the pathway to his later themes concerning the care of the self. That would seem to suggest an affinity much more fundamental than this limited, politically conditioned, strategic endorsement.

CONCLUSION

This book began with some key examples of a pervasive tendency in the contemporary social and political sciences: the claim that the state has or should be deconstructed or dissolved, whether analytically, normatively, or politically. One small but no doubt influential strand of this dissolution has been inspired by the political thought of Michel Foucault. In doing so, this strand continues the theoretical and analytical antistatism that we have found in Foucault's writings. Often this line of argument takes the form less of the state phobia that Foucault diagnosed than the claim that there are sufficient analytical resources within his work to replace the analysis of the state and sovereignty. Politically, it inclines toward an extrastate politics founded in the struggles of what others would call civil society but that we have found in a number of guises at different scales—from the "molecular" scale of "minor" ethico- and ethopolitics to the "molar" politics of the multitude. However, this positive valorization of diverse versions of civil society takes place at the same time that Foucault's inheritors have excluded the classic question of the emergence of state authority as a way of containing the destructive potential inherent in the confessional and other conflicts within civil society. It has also rendered it incapable of analyzing the forms, institutions, and bases of legitimacy of the state.

We have investigated the claim made in much of the poststructuralist analysis of power, as well as governmentality and Foucault studies, that we need to abandon analysis in terms of the state and the binary language of state and civil society. We have tried to probe and give nuance to the question of state and civil society by closely examining the key inspirations for that claim, particularly Foucault's lectures on race wars, biopolitics, governmentality, and neoliberalism (2003, 2007b, 2008), and by drawing out their analytical and substantive implications. In doing so, we have placed particular emphasis on the context of Foucault's statements and the specific role that the question of state phobia plays in these lectures. We have thus argued that Foucault's statements should be understood in terms of the context of the 1970s and a number of key interlocutors.

When we started this book, we imagined that context in quite general terms. Then we viewed Foucault's concern to decenter the analysis of the state outside the terms of juridical-political discourse as addressed to the Marxist theory of the state. It was also addressed, we thought, to the institutional versions of state socialism either abroad (the Soviet Union and the revelations of its gulags) or at home (the French Communist Party). We also imagined the context in terms of events such as the Croissant Affair or the Iranian Revolution, which have been clearly documented by his biographers and editors. But we have also come to consider his context in a much more concrete way, as an address to Foucault's most direct interlocutors, starting with his assistants and students, his immediate colleagues, and those present at his seminars. While historians such as Michael Behrent have now begun the task of a proper intellectual history of Foucault's political thought, it is strange that the voluminous reception of Foucault in English has rarely tried to tackle this question. Foucault's political thought was initially positioned on the Left by many of his interlocutors, some of whom had had serious affiliation with Maoism in the late 1960s. Yet his thought on power and politics would become a bridge to help these disenchanted militants find their way to other, ultimately more mainstream and antirevolutionary, positions, from versions of social democracy to republican statism and, in the most famous case, to neoliberalism. Only his Italian interlocutors maintained the view that Foucault was a radical thinker compatible with *marxisant*, radical theory, as in the case of Negri and, more recently, Lazzarato and Agamben. One can read echoes of these different receptions, and perhaps even echoes of some of these rarely documented debates and disputes, between various currents of post-Marxist thought, both "conservatizing" and radicalizing, in the acrimony of liberal, Anglo-American Foucauldians when faced with post-Marxist Italian thought around sovereignty and biopolitics (e.g., Rabinow and Rose 2006).

In contrast to much of the poststructuralist lionizing of Foucault as a radical of local movements and critic of power relations, however, the "Foucault effect," at least in France, can be located as a "conservatizing" movement for ultra-Left militants in a state of disenchantment after the 1960s. For his own part Foucault would be attracted to, and would significantly engage with, those factions of the institutional Left in France who were willing to experiment with the introduction of neoliberal techniques and policies into a revamped social-democratic politics—the Second Left. This is how his critique of socialism, first as inherently racist and second as lacking an art of government, can be understood.

We are sympathetic to those who would point out that Foucault's thought is more elusive than one that can be captured in a particular political position. We agree that it takes the form of repeated experimentation, that its concepts are in perpetual metamorphosis, and that its methods are but provisional and often post hoc discussions. But at least as far as his status as a "political thinker" is concerned, we would suggest he can be characterized best not by any one event in this continuous experimentation but by the movement of his thought. This experiment reached and was unfortunately and contingently concluded in part by his death but also in part by a certain, highly contextualized terminus of his own political thought. His main, but of course not exclusive, focus after the "governmentality lectures" of 1978 and 1979 would not be politics but ethics, not power but the self and the arts of existence. This, too, might be read in terms of the movement and trajectories of his thought, but for present purposes we can say that following the tumult of the late 1960s, and the efflorescence of a radical extraparty and extraparliamentary Marxism with which he engaged, Foucault's political thought came to rest where many later radicals and social scientists would find themselves: trying to find a new path that somehow introduces greater creativity and innovation into an older socialist or social-democratic tradition. Foucault was not exactly an Anthony Giddens, theorizing a Third Way for New Labour in Britain in the 1990s. While there were no doubt similar realignments occurring in France twenty years earlier, Foucault's thought was concluded before the massive experimentation with neoliberalism in advanced countries, as well as on the peripheries of capitalism and in its emergent territories. In any case, and this would distinguish him from Giddens's more direct political-intellectual interventions, Foucault would never fulfill his express wish to write a book on socialist politics and the art of government.

What, then, of our own context? Intellectually, we fear it is or at least has been dominated by antistatism on many fronts. First, there are the themes associated with globalization by which social science has already acceded far too easily to the claim that the national state has lost its ability to manage the economy in the face of unbounded flows of capital and finance. This in turn easily opens the space for a blurred analytical and normative boosterism of all that falls outside the national state: a global or transnational civil society populated mainly by international nongovernment agencies, "democratizing" social and political movements, and so forth. It is *de rigueur* for liberal political journalism to be surprised when the activities of those movements against authoritarian forms of state from Yugoslavia to Egypt presage heightened ethnic and confessional civil war, *coup d'État*, and counterrevolution. At higher levels of abstraction the state is said to have been displaced in various ways: in a "governance without government," in the "hollowed-out state," and in a "stateless state." Power is a concept said to be deprived of any analytical capacity, and analysis should be focused on any number of its much more leveled-out surrogates such as networks and assemblages. Contingency, locality, differentiation, and heterogeneity are the order of the day, and "theory" is treated with suspicion. As the social and political sciences descend into the minutiae of vital and vibrant materialities and the performativity of markets, they seem to have so detached themselves from critical analysis of social and political structure as to be unable to speak to key challenges of our times.

We may thus wonder if the context of today has not changed rather dramatically compared to the time and place of Foucault's considerations on state and power in the 1970s. We have witnessed prolonged economic crisis in Europe and growing inequality in the Anglo-Saxon world, particularly the United States, continued global poverty, civil unrest and bloody conflicts, and the now trenchant effects of climate change. Recently, there have been popular uprisings against cutbacks in state services, especially in southern Europe, where national governments have been forced to dramatically reduce expenditures on health and social security. The direct addressees of these protests are, ironically but perhaps understandably, the national governments; but in Greece and Spain the protests also address the "troika" of the European Union, the International Monetary Fund, and the European Central Bank. We have witnessed the reemergence of widespread poverty in terms of escalating numbers of heavily indebted families and homeless people and massive youth unemployment within the borders of major developed nations. In both cases "the social question" and thus the welfare state is put at center stage. The far Right, not only in Greece but across Europe, has turned to a kind of "race war" giving questions of national unity and identity a new urgency and reminding us of the recent past in the former Yugoslavia. In these struggles, claims rooted in religious or ethnic identity, or a fusion of both, are fiercely directed at the universality of the modern state.

In this setting the ongoing publication of Foucault's lectures is of course to be welcomed. But they have given rise to a veritable industry of interpretation and mobilization. Whereas one could say his work represented a massive challenge to orthodoxies in the 1970s and 1980s, today it feeds into many of the antistatist intellectual currents we have mentioned and finds them hospitable academic environments in which to prosper. Again, however, these lectures and other writings are largely extracted from their context and turned paradoxically into generalities that can be applied in any situation. This canonization of Saint Foucault devoid of the earlier ironies is a strange destiny for a form of thought so experimental and ready to change.

Many of these insights and theoretical and analytical limitations are demonstrated by the two examples with which we started the book. Hardt and Negri, we have argued, diagnose a blurring between poststructural concepts of difference, singular identity, nonfoundational critique, and self-creation, on the one hand, and the operations of contemporary capitalism, on the other. This marks a key task for current intellectual work and directs our attention to an important analytical challenge. Contemporary reforms and forms of governing often speak in terms of respect for cultural diversity, facilitation of individuals' self-determination, and recognizing plural values. Here, contemporary critical diagnostic political thought should be aware that "differences" and "plurality" do not exist naturally prior to their discursive mobilization within strategies of power and counterpower. While "culturally sensitive" programs should be defended against the race wars of the extreme Right, we should also be careful that they do not solidify and naturalize differences of economic inequality and social and ethnic segregation. The politics of difference leads easily to a naturalization or, better, a "culturalization" of difference. Diversity can begin to function as a substitute for both formal and more substantive equality when people are imagined to exercise their freedom within the predicates of particular identities and social positions.

Hardt and Negri make acute observations regarding the compatibility between the politics of difference and postmodern, globalized capitalism. Yet there are problems in their totalizing, abstract, and metahistorical approach. On the one hand, they overcome the state by insisting that the forms of power of Empire are omnipresent and inscribed in all kinds of social relations and thus, like theorists of globalization, displace the national state as a key locus of politics. On the other hand, while arguing that civil society has withered away, they produce a nonstate externality, the multitude, which, although constituted in relation to biopolitical production, fulfills the same antistate eschatological role that Foucault discerned in the mobilization of the notion of civil society in republican, national, and classical Marxist overcomings of the state.

Diagnostics such as those offered by Rose can help us demonstrate that there is never one civil society but many "fictions" of it produced by various experts, including those of a poststructural persuasion. By this route we can avoid a unified and substantialized image of civil society and instead investigate how particular "communities" emerge in strategies for crime prevention, urban renewal, health promotion, the integration of immigrants, and other domains. On the one hand, these communities are shaped through forms of expertise and multiple relations of government and power, as much as through the demands and aspirations of grassroots movements. On the other hand, insofar as they are systematically construed as a new locus of politics beyond and often opposed to the state, they fail to escape the classical position taken by the proponents of civil society. Rose arrives at a set of similar moves to contemporary theorists of civil society and theorists of the role of subpolitics and social movements in late or postmodernity, but for him the preferred language is of the molecular and of minor politics. While he does not focus on the normative implications of these communities in civil society beyond the state, or idealize them as sites of instructive ethics and deliberation, he nonetheless valorizes them as the privileged site of contemporary politics, struggle, and social innovation.

But neither Hardt and Negri's Deleuzian neo-Marxism nor Rose's post-Foucauldian communitarianism quite succeeds in surpassing the state/civil society problematic. Rather, the key questions related to this problematic return with even greater urgency in light of the claims about the multitude's uncoordinated, transient and revolutionary force and the aestheticized, creative self-creation implied by an ethical life politics, both of which allegedly pave the way for new types of progressive political activism and struggle. In both cases we noticed a marginalization of conventional themes related to formal political organization and the state and a tendentious aestheticizing of nonstate forces, which are ascribed a socially transformative role. We thus detect the emergence of positions that are state phobic in Foucault's sense of the term. At least Hardt and Negri affirm and celebrate the state's dissolution into its ethical, cultural, and economic externality.

Foucault certainly never gave us a "history of the state." Throughout this book we have noted that there is in fact very little *state* in Foucault's analysis, at least if one uses the term to designate the specific juridical-political innovation that arose in Europe after the confessional wars of the seventeenth century. This is because Foucault sought to remove himself "backwards" from institutions, thus performing a "deinstitutionalizing" of our received view of the state. The conventional functionalities and the naturalized objects of institutions were to be deconstructed along with the idea of the state as a centralized locus of power. Foucault wished to develop a framework that did not analyze the state as a given object but instead excavated what he called the "practico-reflexive prism" in which the state appeared (2007b, 276). This term foregrounded the practices and means of calculation through which the state and problems associated with state regulation were made thinkable. This was an approach that he also termed the history of problematizations in which the modern state emerged as an absolutely key concern.

In another book one of us has tried to capture the movement of Foucault's political thought (Dean 2013). In his major studies of the mid-1970s Foucault sought to discover a form of power that displaced what he called the juridical-political theory of sovereignty with its focus on the state. He did this by a kind of bipolar historical narrative in which the newly discovered form of power, whether it be discipline or, soon thereafter, biopolitics, was defined in contrastive terms with sovereignty, and his genealogy was said to reveal a shift from one to another. Elements of this bipolar and contrastive framework of the shift away from state-sovereignty-law are still present in his governmentality lectures, but they undergo a change. Rather than a narrative of the transformation of forms of power consigning the state to a marginal position, there is an endogenous narrative of forms of governmentality, the critical ethos of which leads to a more immanent practice of political sovereignty. In this present book we have concentrated on three related forms of defeating the Leviathan in the lectures of the mid and late 1970s.

In 1976 Foucault performed a decentering of state universality into a multiplicity of political forces by reading historical-political writers from the seventeenth to the nineteenth centuries. In 1978 he broke down notions of the unity of the state into what one might term administrative rationalities, or "reflected practices" of government. And in 1979 he dissolved the state by examining more recent rationalities that aspired to inform the government of the state, namely German *Ordoliberalism* and American neoliberalism. The effect of these moves was that Foucault rendered state power immanent—both on the symbolic level and at the level of law and institutions. The glorious transcendence of the sovereign receded insofar as Foucault emphasized "the entrance of the state in the field of practice and thought" (2007b, 247). Replacing the theories of constitutionalism and law, he descended, as it were, to the plane of immanent practices, to reflexive practices of governing. Opposing the juridico-political framework for analyzing state power, Foucault emphasized the possibility of writing a "history of the state on the basis of men's actual practice, on the basis of what they do and how they think" (358).

In the first move of decentering there was the attempt to make the universalizing claims of the constitutional state but the temporary outcome of a continuous battle, on the model of war. The positive side of this move is that it recognizes the irreducibility of politics as struggle and domination. But while he would ultimately reject this approach, it would also lead to some of Foucault's most strident, state-phobic moments and statements. The Nietzschean component deprived this conflict model of state universality of any possibility of an anchorage in the balance of class or any other social forces, despite whatever other resemblances it might have to the discourse theory of hegemony of Ernesto Laclau and Chantal Mouffe. Subsequently, in the first three lectures in 1978 Foucault would elaborate what is today regarded as his *dispositif* analysis. Here the various dispositifs appear as kinds of technical assemblages, albeit in relation to a domain of virtuality, one emphasized by Deleuze, and sufficiently encompassing materiality to be revisited in today's intellectual context by those influenced by Bruno Latour, Michel Callon, and their colleagues. But these dispositifs of law, security, and discipline simply float along in a Heraclitean river of immanence without explanation or exploration of their sources in social and political relations and conflicts. If the governmentality narrative stressed the becoming immanent of a formerly spectacular, transcendent sovereignty, the dispositifs exist in an eternal flow and flux of practices of administrative and technological immanence.

Finally, we sought to understand Foucault's relationship to civil society that appears in the governmentality lectures as a kind of double optic, at once constructed and natural, through which liberal forms of government can operate. Government becomes innovative—that is, becomes an art—by fabricating something outside itself that it creates in the very act of governing. Civil society and the market become sites of "veridiction" for a constantly self-critical liberal way of governing. This has led us to an understanding of Foucault's narrative of the art of government as containing metaphysical, dialectical, and teleological elements and bearing more than a passing resemblance to aspects of the economic theology it itself skirts.

We have long been tempted to locate a break between the 1976 lectures and the governmentality ones of 1978 and 1979, a break marked by Foucault's sabbatical and his increasing familiarity with American culture and politics. In this respect we have followed Pasquale Pasquino's (1993) advice that Foucault gave up the model of war and battle and replaced its more incendiary language with that of the government of conduct. But whatever discontinuities there might be between these three experimental moments of Foucault's thought, there is also a fundamental continuity. All of them are attempts to deny the state the possibility of laying claim to its defining features. They would challenge the universality it would claim as a constitutional entity, its existence as an innovative and improvised historically specific form of organization with a particular relation to law, and even its own regime of veridiction, that is, its specific forms of truth pertaining to bureaucracy and public service as a set of institutions and practices. Thus, only by interpretive extension can we use Foucault to address the ethos and ethic of office, of national interest or interest of state, or of public service. In all the talk about "demonic" forms of power and combinations of sovereignty and biopolitics in modern states, such as is found in his lectures at Stanford (OS), we hardly detect a murmur on how the invention of impartial and politically neutral public bureaus might be a way of not only facilitating forms of human freedom and limiting capitalism's inequalities but also of containing and preventing the diabolical.

Above all, this narrative of the immanence of governing and forms of power, however arrived at, serves to deprive the state of its defining feature, the claim, which is a normative one, to supremacy within a territorial domain. This is combined with a caricature of sovereignty and a repression of the analysis of law as law. To defeat sovereignty, bringing it down to the great river of immanence by one method or another, Foucault gives us an overblown version of it as a right of death found in Roman *dominium* and the *patria potestas*, the law of the father. Because he seeks to deny the key distinction, which he also relies on, between transcendence and immanence, Foucault cannot see how this image of sovereignty as an omnipotent and omnipresent power captures only its transcendent side, constituted in its glorious liturgies and acclamatory rituals and practices, so brilliantly captured by Agamben (2011). On the other side it would have been possible to analyze sovereignty as a set of practices and competences. We do not claim to make a proper or exhaustive list, but some of the candidates for one might be the right to declare war; the capacity to claim a monopoly of legitimate violence or, under conditions of emergency, to make the final decision; the capacity to maintain public order within a territory; the capacity to levy and collect taxes; and the capacity to shape and form a civilized population by health care, education, and welfare.

Similarly, Foucault's view of law is an impoverished one. We might say that Foucault wanted to view law as anything but law: as a set of commands issued by the sovereign, as an extension of norms, as a technology of government, and as one dispositif among others, grounded in interdiction. As many insights as each of these can garner, there is no analysis of law as a set of practices, as forms of judgment, or as a set of spaces and agents. Nor is there any reflection on the relation of law to the state and the way the constitutional state does not just use the rule of law as a technique but employs law to articulate and organize its own agencies. The constitutional state is not just a law-governed state but a law-regulated and law-organized set of articulated agencies. It is noteworthy, therefore, that throughout his career Foucault refrained from showing any serious interest in the questions of legitimacy or in mechanisms of representation and sovereignty that continue to preoccupy political philosophy and state and democratic theory. Or, to be more precise, he largely addressed such issues on the "second order"—that is, by reading texts that constitute "reflexive prisms" for considering political sovereignty as a governmental practice.

We do not deny that Foucault provides us with a fertile set of concepts that furnish contemporary thought with many local insights into the rationalities and technologies of power that, in part, constitute what we called at the end of Chapter 1 "the regimes of government" of the state. There are exciting and interesting new literatures that continue to draw inspiration from Foucault. And there are potentials that have yet to be fully realized in several areas. We restrict ourselves to listing but a few of the latter. First, contrary to Hardt and Negri's and Rose's commonly optimistic rendering, Foucault's lectures from the 1970s traverse the different modalities of biopolitics, spanning "race war," "medical normalization," and "securitization," which offer analytical frameworks pertinent to contemporary political issues (Villadsen and Wahlberg 2014). There is the question of national identity from the perspective of the genealogy of biopolitics as a mutation in the discourse of "race war," which we examined in Chapter 5. Here, the analysis of biopolitics opens up the study of the formation of statehood around notions of national identity, the people, race, blood, and rightful inheritance. These reflections are clearly helpful in thinking about ethnic nationalism and its worst manifestations, wherever they occur—from the Ukraine to parts of Africa. But it may also prove helpful in questions over refugee resettlement, asylum seekers, and migration in affluent countries from Scandinavia to the United States, the United Kingdom, and Australia, an area in which the work of Didier Bigo is of exceptional importance (2002).

Second, we might look for the points at which political reasoning meets "political eschatology" in Foucault's sense, insofar as it is given to promise a final unification in a perfected social order (see Chapter 8). As is clear in respect to nationalist and populist movements, the paradoxical character of political eschatology portends the dissolution of the state but through the intensification of state violence. Again, this is not simply an atavism of the capitalist peripheries. The relationship between the liberal and neoliberal advocacy of civil society and its values, the market, and statist forms of domination and violence could also be further investigated—whether domestically in the treatment of marginalized groups or internationally as part of humanitarian interventions. The question of how we interrogate poverty—at international or national scales—would again appear central (Ilcan and Lacey 2011; Soss, Fording, and Schram 2011).

Third, it would also be possible to take up Foucault's observations on "medicalization of behavior" and the "subtle mechanisms" of biopolitical security, which, we might add, occupy an indeterminate space between international and domestic concerns (Foucault 2003, 39, 244–45). This combination itself gave rise to the shadowy nature of the enemy against which "society must be defended" and the wide range of rationalities of prevention and precaution with which it does. In Foucault's version this modern, medicalized biopolitics renders threats to the social body predictable and amenable to control or elimination. A range of police, security, and preventive measures could be studied through this prism, including policy initiatives for "deradicalization" of Muslim youth, secret intelligence services' preventive arrests, and the wide range of surveillance and security operations justified by the "war on terror." What is interesting today is that biopolitics gives up the illusion of control and assumes continued uncertainty. Thus risk rationalities shade into logics of catastrophe, and the exhortation of prudential conduct is displaced by a focus on the "resilience" of individuals, communities, and systems (Aradau and van Munster 2011; Walker and Cooper 2011). One could cite a growing and important literature that is following this pathway of governing through and beyond risk and prevention (Amoore 2006; Amoore and de Goede 2008; Best 2014).

A fourth potential concerns the relation of social programs and the redrawing of the conceptual boundaries between state and civil society. Perhaps the titles of recent large-scale reform visions such as the United Kingdom's "Big

Society' and New Zealand's "Future State" are symptomatic in this regard. They seem to rest on a premise about the social order as self-propelling and immanent, without any "outside" in terms of sovereign foundation and intervention. Again, the task is one of recasting the political as the force that disrupts the illusion of the immanence and harmonious self-production of society (Prozorov 2007a, 83). If Timothy Mitchell (1991, 95) is correct in arguing that the definition and redefinition of the state/society division is a key domain of contestation in modern politics, then these and other visions could be placed within a continued examination of how politics is reformulated within contemporary liberal rationalities. While Foucauldian analysis could thus be of considerable help in examining the transformation of the "regime of government" of the state, we should be careful to distinguish between "regime" and the state itself (Du Gay and Scott 2010) and not to identify the "state-effect" with the state itself.

What a Foucauldian position on the welfare state and its current transformation may entail is, however, still up for debate. Certainly, the indications from the Second Left interview we cited in Chapter 10 are not promising. Our position is that to insist on the "demonic" nature of the modern state as a combination of politico-juridical power and a caring, pastoral power exercised over live individuals is overdone. Barry Hindess noted some time ago that Foucault failed to consider the general implications of the coexistence of these two forms of power (Hindess 1997, 266). Thinkers as diverse as Kriegel, Agamben, and, more recently, Sergei Prozorov have addressed the problem of the juridical-institutional structure of sovereignty and the biopolitical management of life. One approach is to try to "reduce all power to its purely formal structure of sovereignty," since the latter is freedom's "rigorous ontopolitical counterpart" (Prozorov 2007a, viii, 147). If it is hard to think about contemporary power relations without a "transcendent" domain of state, sovereignty, and constitutive principle, it is equally hard to understand how freedom can be practiced in modern states, without the biopolitical investment in human capacities and some form of economic management of life (Dumm 1996).

This brings us back to the question of universalism that Foucault analyzed only as a kind of hypocritical claim of the bourgeoisie to represent the entire nation, first articulated by Sieyès. But universalism can also be recovered in a more positive guise in relation to pastoral power. Pastoral power is not simply an "individualizing tactic" if one follows Mika Ojakangas's view that the "'hidden' foundation of bio-politics is love (*agape*) and care (*cura*)" (Ojakangas 2005, 5). Although Foucault was clearly more interested in pastoral power as a technique of subjectivization, he did gesture toward this other side of pastoral power. Perhaps the theological genealogy of pastoral power holds the key to the universalism of the modern state. Contrary to Hardt and Negri's assertion that the nation-state has become an impossibility because of its reliance on transcendent or metaphysical foundations, one could argue that the invention of a transcendent or supreme structure, above confessional conflicts, founded on religious neutrality and toleration of religious difference, is what makes the modern state an inheritor of the universal message of early Christianity.

Notwithstanding these potentials, insights, and local intelligibilities, we doubt that any of this is a substitute for a theoretical-conceptual analysis of the state or a historical sociology of law and sovereignty. We thus conclude that an analysis of government derived from Foucault cannot stand alone. We have suggested that the emphasis on the creative self-fashioning practices of communities, groups, and agents outside of the state needs to consider how the state provides conditions for such practices and facilitates the formation of capacities of such actors. Perhaps a provocative move by contemporary governmentality and post-Foucauldian studies and poststructuralists more broadly would be to combine their deconstructivist analysis with forms of knowledge that, in immediate opposition, claim to speak the truth about society, mapping patterns of inequality and documenting the effects of precarity. This difficult challenge hinges less on an overcoming of the terms of political discourses than on a use of concepts, including state and society, that can move between their changing historical forms and genealogies and the concrete and institutional orders and structures of which they allow us to speak.

We have sought to supplement and challenge the interpretation of Foucault's "decentered analytics of power" as providing a kind of generally applicable guide for studies of political power and the state. There is no doubt today that the central concepts and terms of Foucault's political thought—governmentality, biopolitics, the dispositif, and so forth—have entered the mainstream of many academic disciplines, from international relations to human resource management, critical security studies to ethnography, across the entire world. There is also little doubt that the characteristic rationalities and technologies of contemporary liberal governmentality, such as those of civil society; of public-sector reform; of public-service accountability; of market competition, entrepreneurship, and innovation; and, more broadly, of good governance have become staples of the regimes of government within Western and non-Western states, advanced and emerging economies, and international government and nongovernment organizations. On the one hand, Foucault's time has come for political and social analysis. On the other hand, we must be careful that a decontextualized use of his major concepts does not become seduced by the analytical, theoretical and normative antistatism common to both our own milieu and the one in which he was working.

Perhaps of greatest concern is the extent to which Foucault's political thought has been implicated in the most important and virulent antistatist movement of the last half-century: neoliberalism. This has been not only a matter of François Ewald's immense authority on Foucault's impact on himself and other Maoists and the political choices he has made and the intellectual alliances he has forged. It is also the unfortunate terminus of Foucault's properly political thought in close proximity to the regulatory techniques offered by the American neoliberals. This problematization of Foucault's work is only leavened a little when one realizes that other close associates have forged different directions with more positive approaches to the state. Blandine Kriegel's prostatist and sovereigntist republicanism is the striking example, although we think her position is one that cannot and would not claim to be a legitimate interpretation of Foucault. Elsewhere, we have shown that the work on poverty, the labor market, and the welfare state by those such as Giovanna Procacci, Robert Castel, and Jacques Donzelot can be viewed as reinventing a position that is much more amenable to a social state and perhaps even social democratic tradition (Dean 2010; Villadsen and Dean 2012). Nonetheless, there remains the analytical and normative antistatism of Foucault's work, linked with his critical interrogation of welfare institutions, which makes even this position one of a hard labor of reconstruction.

In his inaugural lecture at the Collège de France Foucault (1971, 28) made a comment about Hegel, which we can now paraphrase with respect to Foucault himself. To detach ourselves from Foucault involves an appreciation of what it costs to do so. We must today be aware of the extent to which, no matter where we turn, Foucault remains close to us and to others with whom we seek to converse. To detach ourselves implies a knowledge that would allow us to think against him, knowledge that could in part be Foucauldian, and knowledge that he would have denied. Yet we have to be prepared for the extent to which our anti-Foucauldianism is a trick he directed toward us, at the end of which we will meet him again as he moves faster than we can to where we wish to go.

BIBLIOGRAPHY

Afary, Janet, and Kevin B. Anderson. 2005. *Foucault and the Iranian Revolution: Gender and the Seductions of Islam*. Chicago: University of Chicago Press.

Agamben, Giorgio. 1998. *Homo Sacer: Sovereign Power and Bare Life*. Translated by Daniel Heller-Roazen. Stanford, CA: Stanford University Press.

———. 2011. *The Kingdom and the Glory: For a Theological Genealogy of Economy and Government*. Translated by Lorenzo Chiesa with Matteo Mandarini. Stanford, CA: Stanford University Press.

Althusser, Louis. 1969. *For Marx*. Translated by Ben Brewster. London: Penguin.

Amoore, Louise. 2006. "Biometric Borders: Governing Mobilities in the War on Terror." *Political Geography* 25 (3): 336–51.

Amoore, Louise, and Marieke de Goede, eds. 2008. *Risk and the War on Terror*. London: Routledge.

Aradau, Claudia, and Rens van Munster. 2011. *Politics of Catastrophe: Genealogies of the Unknown*. London: Routledge.

Aron, Raymond. 1968. *Democracy and Totalitarianism*. Translated by Valence Ionescu. London: Weidenfeld and Nicolson.

Badiou, Alain. 2000. "Of Life as a Name of Being, or, Deleuze's Vitalist Ontology." *Pli: The Warwick Journal of Philosophy* 10:191–99.

———. 2012. *The Adventure of French Philosophy*. Translated by Bruno Bosteels. New York: Verso.

Barret-Kriegel, Blandine. 1992. "Michel Foucault and the Police State." In *Michel Foucault, Philosopher*, edited by Timothy J. Armstrong, 192–97. London: Harvester Wheatsheaf.

Barry, Andrew, Thomas Osborne, and Nikolas Rose, eds. 1996. *Foucault and Political Reason: Liberalism, Neo-liberalism and Rationalities of Government*. London: UCL Press.

Bauman, Zygmunt. 1989. *Modernity and Holocaust*. Ithaca, NY: Cornell University Press.

Beaulieu, Alain. 2010. "Towards a Liberal Utopia: The Connection Between Foucault's Reporting on the Iranian Revolution and the Ethical Turn." *Philosophy and Social Criticism* 36 (7): 801–18.

Beck, Ulrich. 1992. *Risk Society: Towards a New Modernity*. Translated by Mark Ritter. London: Sage.

Beck-Gernsheim, Elisabeth. 1996. "Life as a Planning Project." In *Risk, Environment and Modernity: Towards a New Ecology*, edited by Scott Lash, Bronislaw Szerszynski, and Brian Wynne, 139–52. London: Sage.

Becker, Gary, François Ewald, and Bernard Harcourt. 2012. *Becker on Ewald on Foucault on Becker: American Neoliberalism and Michel Foucault's 1979 "Birth of Biopolitics" Lectures*. Institute for Law and Economics Working Paper no. 614. Chicago: University of Chicago Law School.

———. 2013. *Becker and Foucault on Crime and Punishment*. Coase-Sandor Institute for Law and Economics Working Paper no. 654. Chicago: University of Chicago Law School.

Behrent, Michael C. 2009. "Liberalism Without Humanism: Michel Foucault and the Free-Market Creed, 1976–1979." *Modern Intellectual History* 6 (3): 539–68.

———. 2010. "Accidents Happen: François Ewald, the 'Antirevolutionary Foucault,' and the Intellectual Politics of the French Welfare State." *Journal of Modern History* 82 (3): 585–624.

Best, Jacqueline. 2014. *Governing Failure: Provisional Expertise and the Transformation of Global Development Finance*. Cambridge: Cambridge University Press.

Bevir, Mark. 1999. "Foucault and Critique: Deploying Agency Against Autonomy." *Political Theory* 27 (1): 65–84.

———. 2011. "Political Science After Foucault." *History of the Human Sciences* 24 (4): 81–96.

Bevir, Mark, and Rod A. W. Rhodes. 2010. *The State as Cultural Practice*. Oxford: Oxford University Press.

Bigo, Didier. 2002. "Security and Immigration: Toward a Critique of the Governmentality of Unease." *Alternatives: Global, Local, Political* 27 (1): 63–92.

Blencove, Claire. 2012. *Biopolitical Experience: Foucault, Power and Positive Critique*. London: Palgrave Macmillan.

Blumenberg, Hans. 1985. *The Legitimacy of the Modern Age*. Translated by Robert M. Wallace. Cambridge, MA: MIT Press.

Brenner, Neil, Jamie Peck, and Nik Theodore. 2010. "Variegated Neoliberalization: Geographies, Modalities, Pathways." *Global Networks* 10:182–222.

Burchell, Graham, Colin Gordon, and Peter Miller, eds. 1991. *The Foucault Effect: Studies in Governmentality*. London: Harvester Wheatsheaf.

Bussolini, Jeffrey. 2010. "What Is a Dispositive?" *Foucault Studies* 10 (Nov.): 85–107.

Casarino, Cesare, and Antonio Negri. 2004. "It's a Powerful Life: A Conversation on Contemporary Philosophy." *Cultural Critique* 57:151–83.

Checchi, Marco. 2014. "Spotting the Primacy of Resistance in the Virtual Encounter of Foucault and Deleuze." *Foucault Studies* 18 (Oct.): 197–212.

Clegg, Stewart R. 2001. "Changing Concepts of Power, Changing Concepts of Politics." *Administrative Theory and Praxis* 23 (2): 126–50.

Cohen, Jean, and Andrew Arato. 1992. *Civil Society and Political Theory*. Cambridge, MA: MIT Press.

Cohn, Norman. 1979. *The Pursuit of the Millennium.* Rev. and exp. ed. Oxford: Oxford University Press.

Colas, Dominique. 1997. *Civil Society and Fanaticism: Conjoined Histories.* Translated by Amy Jacobs. Stanford, CA: Stanford University Press.

Collier, Stephen. 2009. "Topologies of Power: Foucault's Analysis of Political Government Beyond 'Governmentality.'" *Theory, Culture and Society* 26 (6): 78–108.

Connolly, William. 1993. "Beyond Good and Evil: The Ethical Sensibility of Michel Foucault." *Political Theory* 21 (3): 365–89.

Cruikshank, Barbara. 1999. *The Will to Empower: Democratic Citizens and Other Subjects.* Ithaca, NY: Cornell University Press.

Dardot, Pierre, and Christian Laval. 2013. *The New Way of the World: On Neoliberal Society.* Translated by Gregory Elliot. London: Verso.

Dean, Mitchell. 1999. *Governmentality: Power and Rule in Modern Society.* London: Sage.

———. 2003. "Empire and Governmentality." *Distinktion* 6:111–22.

———. 2010. "What Is Society? Social Thought and the Arts of Government." *British Journal of Sociology* 61 (4): 677–95.

———. 2013. *The Signature of Power: Sovereignty, Governmentality and Biopolitics.* London: Sage.

———. 2014. "Rethinking Neoliberalism." *Journal of Sociology* 50 (2): 150–63.

Dean, Mitchell, and Barry Hindess, eds. 1998. *Governing Australia: Studies in Contemporary Rationalities of Government.* Cambridge: Cambridge University Press.

Deleuze, Gilles. 1977. "Desire and Pleasure." Translated by Melissa McMahon. *http://eng7007.pbwiki.com/DesireAndPleasure.*

———. 1988. *Foucault.* Translated by Séan Hand. Minneapolis: University of Minnesota Press.

———. 1992a. "Postscript on the Societies of Control." *October* 59:3–7.

———. 1992b. "What Is a Dispositif?" In *Michel Foucault, Philosopher*, edited by Timothy J. Armstrong, 159–66. London: Harvester Wheatsheaf.

———. 1994. *Difference and Repetition.* Translated by Paul Patton. New York: Columbia University Press.

———. 2006. *Foucault.* Translated by Séan Hand. London: Continuum.

Deleuze, Gilles, and Félix Guattari. 1983. *Anti-Oedipus: Capitalism and Schizophrenia.* Translated by Robert Hurley, Mark Seem, and Helen R. Lane. Minneapolis: University of Minnesota Press.

Descombes, Vincent. 1980. *Modern French Philosophy.* Translated by L. Scott-Fox and J. M. Harding. Cambridge: Cambridge University Press.

Dilts, Andrew. 2011. "From 'Entrepreneur of the Self' to 'Care of the Self': Neo-liberal Governmentality and Foucault's Ethics." *Foucault Studies* 12 (Oct.): 130–46.

Donzelot, Jacques, and Colin Gordon. 2008. "Governing Liberal Societies: The Foucault Effect in the English-Speaking World." *Foucault Studies* 5 (Jan.): 48–62.

du Gay, Paul, and Alan Scott. 2010. "State Transformation or Regime Shift? Addressing Some Confusions in the Theory and Sociology of the State." *Sociologica* 2:1–23.

Dumm, Thomas. 1996. *Michel Foucault and the Politics of Freedom*. Thousand Oaks, CA: Sage.

Eribon, Didier. 1991. *Michel Foucault*. Translated by Betsy Wing. Cambridge, MA: Harvard University Press.

Ewald, François. 1999. "Foucault and the Contemporary Scene." *Philosophy and Social Criticism* 25 (3): 81–91.

Ferguson, Adam. 1819. *An Essay on the History of Civil Society*. 8th ed. Philadelphia: A. Finley.

Fine, Robert. 1997. "Civil Society Theory, Enlightenment and Critique." *Democratization* 4 (1): 7–28.

Flyvbjerg, Bent. 1998. "Habermas and Foucault: Thinkers for Civil Society?" *British Journal of Sociology* 49 (2): 208–33.

Foucault, Michel. 1971. "Orders of Discourse." *Social Sciences Information* 10 (2): 7–30.

———. 1972. *The Archaeology of Knowledge*. Translated by Alan Sheridan. London: Tavistock.

———. 1977. *Discipline and Punish: The Birth of the Prison*. Translated by Alan Sheridan. London: Allen Lane.

———. 1979. *History of Sexuality, Volume One: An Introduction*. Translated by Robert Hurley. London: Allen Lane.

———. 1980a. "Georges Canguilhem, Philosopher of Error." *Ideology and Consciousness* 7:51–62.

———. 1980b. "The Confession of the Flesh." In *Power/Knowledge: Selected Interviews and Other Writings*, edited by Colin Gordon, 194–228. Brighton: Harvester.

———. 1983. "Preface." In Deleuze and Guattari 1983, x–xiii.

———. 1988. "Social Security." In *Politics, Philosophy, Culture: Interviews and Other Writings, 1977–84*, edited by Lawrence D. Kritzman, 159–77. New York: Routledge.

———. 1989. *Foucault Live: Interviews, 1966–1984*. Edited by Sylvère Lotringer. Translated by Lysa Hochroth and John Johnston. New York: Semiotext(e).

———. 1991. *Remarks on Marx: Conversations with Duccio Trombadori*. Translated by James Goldstein and James Cascaito. New York: Semiotext(e).

———. 1996. "What Is Critique?" In *What Is Enlightenment? Eighteenth-Century Answers and Twentieth-Century Questions*, edited by James Schmidt, 382–98. Berkeley: University of California Press.

———. 1997. *Ethics: Subjectivity and Truth*. Vol. 1 of *Essential Works of Foucault, 1954–1984*. Edited by Paul Rabinow. New York: New Press.

———. 1998. *Aesthetics, Method, and Epistemology*. Vol. 2 of *Essential Works of Foucault, 1954–1984*. Edited by James D. Faubion. New York: New Press.

———. 2000. *Power*. Vol. 3 of *Essential Works of Foucault, 1954–1984*. Edited by James D. Faubion. New York: New Press.

———. 2003. *"Society Must Be Defended": Lectures at the Collège de France, 1975–76*. Translated by David Macey. New York: Picador.

———. 2004a. *Naissance de la biopolitique: Cours au Collège de France, 1978–1979*. Edited by Michel Sennelart. Paris: Gallimard/Seuil.

———. 2004b. *Sécurité, territoire, population: Cours au Collège de France, 1977–1978*. Edited by Michel Sennelart. Paris: Gallimard/Seuil.

———. 2005. "Faith Against the Shah." In Afary and Anderson 2005, 198–203.

———. 2006. *History of Madness*. Translated by Jonathan Murphy and Jean Khafla. London: Routledge.

———. 2007a. "The Incorporation of the Hospital into Modern Technology." In *Space, Knowledge and Power: Foucault and Geography*, edited by Jeremy W. Crampton and Stuart Elden, 141–52. Aldershot: Ashgate.

———. 2007b. *Security, Territory, Population: Lectures at the Collège de France, 1977–78*. Translated by Graham Burchell. London: Palgrave.

———. 2008. *The Birth of Biopolitics: Lectures at the Collège de France, 1978–1979*. Translated by Graham Burchell. London: Palgrave.

———. 2010. *The Government of Self and Others: Lectures at the Collège de France, 1982–1983*. Translated by Graham Burchell. London: Palgrave.

———. 2011. *The Courage of Truth: The Government of Self and Others II: Lectures at the Collège de France, 1983–1984*. Translated by Graham Burchell. London: Palgrave.

———. 2014. *On the Government of the Living: Lectures at the Collège de France, 1979–1980*. Translated by Graham Burchell. London: Palgrave.

Foucault, Michel, and Gilles Deleuze. 1977. "Intellectuals and Power." In *Language, Counter-Memory, Practice*, edited by D. F. Bouchard, 205–17. Ithaca, NY: Cornell University Press.

Foucault, Michel, Colin Gordon, and Paul Patton. 2012. "Considerations on Marxism, Phenomenology and Power. Interview with Michel Foucault; Recorded on April 3rd, 1978." *Foucault Studies* 14 (Sept.): 98–114.

Giddens, Anthony. 1991. *Modernity and Self-Identity*. Cambridge, UK: Polity.

———. 1998. *The Third Way*. Cambridge, UK: Polity.

Goldschmidt, Niels, and Hermann Rauchenschwandtner. 2007. "The Philosophy of Social Market Economy: Michel Foucault's Analysis of Ordoliberalism." Freiburg Discussion Papers on Constitutional Economics, April. Freiburg: Walter Eucken Institute.

Gordon, Colin. 1986. "Question, Ethos, Event." *Economy and Society* 15 (1): 71–87.

———. 1991. "Introduction." In *The Foucault Effect: Studies in Governmentality*, edited by Graham Burchell, Colin Gordon, and Peter Miller, 1–51. Hemel Hempstead: Harvester Wheatsheaf.

———. 1996. "Foucault in Britain." In Barry, Osborne, and Rose 1996, 253–70.

———. 2013. "A Note on 'Becker on Ewald on Foucault on Becker': American Neoliberalism and Michel Foucault's 1979 Birth of Biopolitics Lectures. A Conversation with Gary Becker, François Ewald, and Bernard Harcourt." *Foucault News*, Feb., 1–14. *http://foucaultnews.files.wordpress.com/2013/02/colin-gordon-2013.pdf*.

Gutting, Gary. 1989. *Michel Foucault's Archaeology of Scientific Reason*. Cambridge: Cambridge University Press.

Habermas, Jürgen. 1996. *Between Facts and Norms: Contributions to a Discourse Theory of Law and Democracy*. Translated by William Rehg. Cambridge, UK: Polity.

Hallward, Peter. 2000. "The Limits of Individuation, or How to Distinguish Deleuze and Foucault." *Angelaki* 5 (2): 93–111.

———. 2006. *Out of This World: Deleuze and the Philosophy of Creation.* London: Verso.

Halperin, David M. 1995. *Saint Foucault: Towards a Gay Hagiography.* New York: Oxford University Press.

Hardt, Michael. 1995. "The Withering of Civil Society." *Social Text* 45 (4): 27–44.

Hardt, Michael, and Antonio Negri. 2000. *Empire.* Cambridge, MA: Harvard University Press.

———. 2002. "Michael Hardt and Antonio Negri Interviewed by Nicholas Brown and Imre Szeman, The Global Coliseum: On *Empire*." *Cultural Studies* 16 (2): 177–92.

———. 2004. *Multitude: War and Democracy in the Age of Empire.* New York: Penguin.

———. 2009. *Commonwealth.* Cambridge, MA: Harvard University Press.

Harrer, Sebastian. 2005. "The Theme of Subjectivity in Foucault's Lecture Series, 'Hermé- neutique du sujet.'" *Foucault Studies* 2 (May): 75–96.

Hayek, Friedrich A. 1967. "The Theory of Complex Phenomena." In *Studies in Philoso- phy, Politics and Economics,* 22–42. London: Routledge and Kegan Paul.

———. 1976. *Law, Legislation and Liberty.* Vol. 2, *The Mirage of Social Justice.* London: Routledge and Kegan Paul.

Hill. Lisa. 1998. "The Invisible Hand of Adam Ferguson." *European Legacy: Toward New Paradigms* 3 (6): 42–64.

———. 2001. "The Hidden Theology of Adam Smith." *European Journal of the History of Economic Thought* 8 (1): 1–29.

———. 2006. *The Passionate Society: The Social, Political and Moral Thought of Adam Ferguson.* Berlin: Springer.

Hindess, Barry. 1997. "Politics and Governmentality." *Economy and Society* 26 (2): 257–72.

———. 1998. "Neo-liberalism and the National Economy." In Dean and Hindess 1998, 210–26.

Hoffman, Marcelo. 2014. *Foucault and Power: The Influence of Political Engagement on Theories of Power.* New York: Bloomsbury.

Hunter, Ian. 1998. "Uncivil Society: Liberal Government and the Deconfessionalisation of Politics." In Dean and Hindess 1998, 242–64.

Ilcan, Suzan, and Anita Lacey. 2011. *Governing the Poor: Exercises of Poverty Reduction, Practices of Global Aid.* Montreal: McGill-Queen's University Press.

Karlsen, Mads Peter, and Kaspar Villadsen. 2014. "Foucault, Maoism, Genealogy: The Influence of Political Militancy in Michel Foucault's Thought." *New Political Science* 37 (1): 91–117.

Keane, John. 1988. "Despotism and Democracy: The Origins and Development of the Distinction Between Civil Society and the State, 1750–1850." In *Civil Society and the State,* edited by John Keane, 35–72. London: Verso.

Kearnes, Matthew. 2006. "Chaos and Control: Nanotechnology and the Politics of Emergence." *Paragraph* 29 (2): 57–80.

Kelly, Mark G. E. 2009. *The Political Philosophy of Michel Foucault.* New York: Routledge.

———. 2004. "Racism, Nationalism and Biopolitics: Foucault's 'Society Must Be Defended.'" *Contretemps* 4 (Sept.): 58–70.

Kornberger, Martin, Stewart R. Clegg, and Chris Carter. 2006. "Rethinking the Polyphonic Organization: Managing as Discursive Practice." *Scandinavian Journal of Management* 22 (1): 3–30.

Kriegel, Brandine. 1995. *The State and the Rule of Law*. Translated by Marc A. LePain and Jeffrey C. Cohen. Princeton, NJ: Princeton University Press.

Laclau, Ernesto. 1996. *Emancipation(s)*. London: Verso.

———. 2000. "Constructing Universality." In *Contingency, Hegemony, Universality*, edited by Judith Butler, Ernesto Laclau, and Slavoj Žižek, 281–308. London: Verso.

Lash, Scott. 2006. "Life (Vitalism)." *Theory, Culture and Society* 23 (2–3): 323–49.

Lazzarato, Maurizio. 2009. "Neoliberalism in Action: Inequality, Insecurity and the Reconstitution of the Social." *Theory, Culture and Society* 29 (6): 109–33.

Lemke, Thomas. 2001. "'The Birth of Bio-politics': Michel Foucault's Lecture at the Collège de France on Neo-liberal Governmentality." *Economy and Society* 30 (2): 190–207.

Lessenich, Stephan. 2011. "Constructing the Socialized Self: Mobilization and Control in the 'Active Society.'" In *Governmentality: Current Issues and Future Challenges*, edited by Ulrich Bröckling, Susanne Krasmann, and Thomas Lemke, 304–19. New York: Routledge.

Levinson, Brett. 2001. "Empire, or the Limit of Our Political Choices." *Rethinking Marxism* 13 (3/4): 209–15.

Löwith, Karl. 1949. *Meaning in History*. Chicago: University of Chicago Press.

Macey, David. 1993. *The Lives of Michel Foucault*. New York: Vintage.

Macfie, Alec. 1971. "The Invisible Hand of Jupiter." *Journal of the History of Ideas* 32 (4): 595–99.

Marks, John. 2000. "Foucault, Franks, Gauls: *Il faut défendre la société*: The 1976 Lectures at the Collège de France." *Theory, Culture and Society* 17 (5): 127–47.

Miller, Peter. 1992. "Accounting and Objectivity: The Invention of Calculating Selves and Calculable Spaces." *Annals of Scholarship* 9 (1/2): 61–86.

Mirowski, Philip. 2009. "Postface." In Mirowski and Plehwe 2009, 417–55.

———. 2013. *Never Let a Serious Crisis Go to Waste: How Neoliberalism Survived the Financial Meltdown*. London: Verso.

Mirowski, Philip, and Dieter Plehwe, eds. 2009. *The Road from Mont Pèlerin: The Making of the Neoliberal Thought Collective*. Cambridge, MA: Harvard University Press.

Mitchell, Timothy. 1991. "The Limits of the State: Beyond Statist Approaches and Their Critics." *American Political Science Review* 85 (1): 77–96.

Müller, Jan-Werner. 2003. *A Dangerous Mind: Carl Schmitt in Post-war European Thought*. New Haven, CT: Yale University Press.

Neal, Andrew. 2004. "Cutting Off the King's Head: Foucault's 'Society Must Be Defended' and the Problem of Sovereignty." *Alternatives* 29 (5): 373–98.

Nealon, Jeffrey T. 2008. *Foucault Beyond Foucault: Power and Its Intensifications Since 1984*. Stanford, CA: Stanford University Press.

Negri, Antonio. 2001. "Interview." *Le Monde*, Oct. 3. libcom.org/library/interview-le
-monde-negri.

Ojakangas, Mika. 2005. "Impossible Dialogue on Bio-power: Agamben and Foucault."
Foucault Studies 2 (May): 5–28.

Ong, Aihwa. 2006. *Neoliberalism as Exception: Mutations in Citizenship and Sovereignty*.
Durham, NC: Duke University Press.

Paras, Eric. 2006. *Foucault 2.0: Beyond Power and Knowledge*. New York: Other Press.

Pasquino, Pasquale. 1993. "Political Theory of War and Peace: Foucault and the History
of Modern Political Theory." *Economy and Society* 22 (1): 77–88.

Peck, Jamie, Nik Theodore, and Neil Brenner. 2009. "Postneoliberalism and Its Malcon-
tents." *Antipode* 41 (1): 94–116.

Poggi, Gianfranco. 1990. *The State: Its Nature, Development and Prospects*. Cambridge,
UK: Polity.

Pottage, Alain. 1998. "Power as an Art of Contingency: Luhmann, Deleuze, Foucault."
Economy and Society 27 (1): 1–27.

Procacci, Giovanna. 1989. "Sociology and Its Poor." *Politics and Society* 17 (2): 163–87.

Prozorov, Sergei. 2007a. *Foucault, Freedom and Sovereignty*. London: Ashgate.

———. 2007b. "The Unrequited Love of Power: Biopolitical Investment and the Refusal
of Care." *Foucault Studies* 4 (Feb.): 53–77.

Rabinow, Paul, and Nikolas Rose. 2003. "Foucault Today." In *The Essential Foucault: Se-
lections from the Essential Works of Foucault, 1954–1984*, edited by Paul Rabinow and
Nikolas Rose, vii–xxxv. New York: New Press.

———. 2006. "Biopower Today." *Biosocieties* 1:195–217.

Raffnsøe, Sverre, Marius Gudmand-Høyer, and Morten S. Thaning. 2014. "Foucault's
Dispositive: The Perspicacity of Dispositive Analytics in Organizational Research."
Organization, Sept., 1–14 (published early online).

Rorty, Richard. 1986. "Foucault and Epistemology." In *Foucault: A Critical Reader*, edited
by David Couzens Hoy, 41–49. Oxford: Blackwell.

Rose, Nikolas. 1993. "Government, Authority and Expertise in Advanced Liberalism."
Economy and Society 22 (3): 283–99.

———. 1996a. "'The Death of the Social'? Re-figuring the Territory of Government."
Economy and Society 25 (3): 327–56.

———. 1996b. "Governing 'Advanced' Liberal Democracies." In Barry, Osborne, and
Rose 1996, 37–64.

———. 1999. *Powers of Freedom: Reframing Political Thought*. Cambridge, UK: Cambridge University Press.

———. 2001. "The Politics of Life Itself." *Theory, Culture and Society* 18 (6): 1–30.

———. 2007. *The Politics of Life Itself: Biomedicine, Power, and Subjectivity in the Twenty-
First Century*. Princeton, NJ: Princeton University Press.

———. 2009. "Normality and Pathology in a Biomedical Age." *Sociological Review* 57:
66–83.

———. 2013. "The Human Sciences in a Biological Age." *Theory, Culture and Society* 30
(3): 3–34.

Rose, Nikolas, and Joelle M. Abi-Rached. 2013. *Neuro: The New Brain Sciences and the Management of the Mind*. Princeton, NJ: Princeton University Press.

Rose, Nikolas, and Peter Miller. 1992. "Political Power Beyond the State: Problematics of Government." *British Journal of Sociology* 43 (2): 173–205.

———. 2008. "Introduction: Governing Economic and Social Life." In *Governing the Present: Administering Economic, Social and Personal Life*, 1–26. Cambridge, UK: Polity.

Rüstow, Alexander. 1942. "Appendix: General Sociological Causes of the Economic Disintegration and Possibilities of Reconstruction." In Wilhelm Röpke, *International Economic Disintegration*, 267–83. London: William Hodge.

Schmitt, Carl. 1986. *Political Romanticism*. Cambridge, MA: MIT Press.

———. 1996. *Roman Catholicism and Political Form*. Westport, CT: Greenwood Press.

———. 2005. *Political Theology: Four Chapters on the Concept of Sovereignty*. Chicago: University of Chicago Press.

———. 2008. *Political Theology II: The Myth of the Closure of Any Political Theology*. Cambridge, UK: Polity.

———. 2010. "The Age of Neutralizations and Depoliticizations." In *The Concept of the Political*. Exp. ed. Chicago: University of Chicago Press.

Scott, Alan. 2011. "Raymond Aron's Political Sociology of Regime and Party." *Journal of Classical Sociology* 11 (2): 155–71.

Sennelart, Michael. 2007. "Course Context." In Foucault 2007b, 369–401.

Simons, Jon. 1995. *Foucault and the Political*. New York: Routledge.

Skinner, Quentin. 1969. "Meaning and Understanding in the History of Ideas." *History and Theory* 8 (1): 3–53.

Smart, Barry. 1983. *Foucault, Marxism and Critique*. London: Routledge and Kegan Paul.

Soss, Joe, Richard C. Fording, and Sandford F. Schram. 2011. *Disciplining the Poor: Neoliberal Paternalism and the Persistent Power of Race*. Chicago: University of Chicago Press.

Stoler, Ann Laura. 1995. *Race and the Education of Desire: Foucault's "History of Sexuality" and the Colonial Order of Things*. Durham, NC: Duke University Press.

Taylor-Gooby, Peter. 1994. "Postmodernism and Social Policy: A Great Leap Backwards?" *Journal of Social Policy* 23 (3): 385–404.

Tepper, Rowan. 2010. *Michel Foucault: Toward a Philosophy and Politics of the Event: Continuity in Discontinuity*. Saarbrücken: Lambert Academic.

Trainor, Brian T. 2003. "Foucault and the Politics of Difference." *Philosophy and Social Criticism* 29 (5): 563–80.

Tribe, Keith. 2009. "The Political Economy of Modernity: Foucault's Collège de France Lectures of 1978 and 1979." *Economy and Society* 38 (4): 679–98.

Tully, James, ed. 1988. *Meaning and Context: Quentin Skinner and His Critics*. Cambridge, UK: Polity.

Villadsen, Kaspar. 2011. "Ambiguous Citizenship: 'Postmodern' Versus 'Modern' Welfare at the Margins." *Distinktion: Scandinavian Journal of Social Theory* 12 (3): 309–29.

———. 2014. "Tecnologia versus ação: Uma falsa oposição atribuída a Foucault nos estudos organizacionais." *Organizacoes & Sociedade* 21 (71): 643–60.

———. 2015. "Michel Foucault and the Forces of Civil Society." *Theory, Culture and Society* (published early online) doi:10.1177/0263276415581895.

Villadsen, Kaspar, and Mitchell Dean. 2012. "State Phobia, Civil Society and a Certain Vitalism." *Constellations: An International Journal of Critical and Democratic Theory* 19 (3): 401–20.

Villadsen, Kaspar, and Ayo Wahlberg. 2014. "The Government of Life: Managing Health, Epidemics, and Scarcity." *Economy and Society* 44 (1): 1–17.

Walker, Jeremy, and Melinda Cooper. 2011. "Genealogies of Resilience: From Systems Ecology to the Political Economy of Crisis Adaptation." *Security Dialogue* 14 (2): 143–60.

Walter, Ryan. 2008. "Reconciling Foucault and Skinner on the State: The Primacy of Politics?" *History of the Human Sciences* 21 (3): 94–114.

Weber, Max. 1978. *Economy and Society: An Outline of Interpretive Sociology*. Edited by Guenther Roth and Claus Wittich. 2 vols. Berkeley: University of California Press.

Weiskopf, Richard, and Iain Munro. 2012. "Management of Human Capital: Discipline, Security and Controlled Circulation in HRM." *Organization* 19 (6): 685–702.

Wolin, Richard. 2010. *The Wind from the East: French Intellectuals, the Cultural Revolution, and the Legacy of the 1960s*. Princeton, NJ: Princeton University Press.

Young, Iris Marion. 1990. *Justice and the Politics of Difference*. Princeton, NJ: Princeton University Press.

Žižek, Slavoj. 1999. "The Specter of Ideology." In *The Žižek Reader*, edited by Edmund Wright and Elizabeth Wright, 53–87. Oxford: Blackwell.

———. 2004. *Organs Without Bodies: On Deleuze and Consequences*. London: Routledge.

———. 2008. *In Defense of Lost Causes*. London: Verso.

INDEX

Governmentality: as analytical tool, 17; and antistatism, 2; genealogy of, 128–44; local and mundane concerns emphasized in, 10–11; neoliberalism as form of, 147–50, 158
Governmentality writers, 2, 10–11, 105–6, 151
Grassroots politics, 48–52
Greece, 115, 168
Gregory of Nazianus, 138, 143
Groupe d'information sur les prisons (GIP), 13, 50, 53, 55
Guattari, Félix, 92–95, 153

Habermas, Jürgen, 9, 26, 59
Hallward, Peter, 118
Halperin, David M., 47–48
Harcourt, Bernard, 153–56, 158
Hardt, Michael, 7, 18, 23–33, 42–45, 87, 169–70, 174, 177
Hayek, Friedrich, 42, 119, 139, 150, 151, 161; *The Road to Serfdom*, 163
Hegel, G.W.F., 26, 143, 178
Hegemony, 77–80
Hill, Lisa, 127–28, 135
Hindess, Barry, 176
Hobbes, Thomas, 69, 71
Holling, C. J., 42
Homo œconomicus, 122–24, 154, 159
Hospitals, 109
Human capital theory, 146, 153, 154, 164
Hume, David, 123
Hunter, Ian, 59–60, 121

Identity politics, 2–3, 48–52
Immanence: creativity and, 118; democracy and, 28; dispositifs and, 103, 108–9; in government, 136, 140–41; power and, 24, 89; resistance and, 24; revolution and, 24, 25; and the state, 87, 171–72; vitalism and, 103
Immanence perspective, 24, 33, 108, 118–19

Immigration, 116
Institutions: critique of, 88–91, 94, 103, 171; diagrams for, 112; dual nature of, 109; failures of, 110
Intellectuals, 49–51, 54–55
International Monetary Fund, 116, 168
Invisible hand, 123, 128, 135, 139
Iranian Revolution, 4, 17, 60, 166

Joachim de Fiore, 130–31, 143
Juridical-political theory of sovereignty, 1–2, 70, 82, 84–86, 171, 176
Juridical subjects, 122–23

Kant, Immanuel, 57, 131; "What Is Enlightenment?," 58
Keane, John, 9
Kelly, Mark, 53
Knowledge, subjugated, 41, 52–56, 67, 73
Knowledge production, 53–56
Kojève, Alexandre, 157
Kornberger, Martin, 117
Koselleck, Reinhardt, 59
Koyré, Alexandre, 144
Kriegel, Blandine, 8, 67, 84–86, 176
Kristeva, Julia, 49

Laclau, Ernesto, 30, 77–78, 172
Lash, Scott, 87–88
Latour, Bruno, 93, 172
Laval, Christian, 147
Law, 96–97, 111, 117–18, 174
Lazzarato, Maurizio, 151, 166
Left, the, 152, 156, 166. *See also* Free Left; Second Left; Ultra-left
Legal psychiatry, 102–3
Lemke, Thomas, 158
Lessing, Gotthold Ephraim, 143
Lettres de cachet, 61–62
Levellers, 71
Levinson, Brett, 30
Liberalism: critical aspects of, 34; economic, 146, 147; eschatology associated